INFORMALITY AND POVERTY
Urban Landscape of India's North-East

INFORMALITY AND POVERTY
Urban Landscape of India's North-East

Editors
B. Datta Ray
Gurudas Das

AKANSHA PUBLISHING HOUSE
NEW DELHI-110002

AKANSHA PUBLISHING HOUSE
4649-B/21, Ansari Road
Darya Ganj, New Delhi - 110 002
Email: ektabooks@yahoo.com
Ph.: 23263193/9811582579

Informality And Poverty : Urban Landscape of India's North-East

First Published 2006
ISBN 81-8370-044-6

PRINTED IN INDIA

Published by M.P. Misra for Akansha Publishing House, New Delhi and Printed at Tarun Offset Press, Delhi

Contents

List of Tables

List of Figures

List of Figures

PREFACE

Broadly speaking, informal sector refers to unorganized urban economic activities that include both self-employed microentrepreneurs in small-scale manufacturing and servicing and the labour force—wage earners as well as the trainees. This sector is often characterized by low skill, low wage, low productivity coupled with high risk, greater insecurity and extremely unfavourable working condition. It is often seen as the inferior segment of the urban labour market from the traditional dualistic point of view. However, an alternative perspective is increasingly gaining ground which, based on country specific studies, views the informal sector as the unregulated, developing country analogue of the voluntary entrepreneurial small firm sector found in advanced countries, rather than a residual.

In fact, the informal sector plays more important role compared to its formal counterparts as far as the livelihood of the urbanites is concerned. It employs between 30 and 70 per cent of the urban labour force in developing countries. Of course, this percentage share will be more in urban spaces located in relatively economically backward areas within the developing countries *a la* north-eastern region of India. This sector, indeed, act as the principal port of entry to paid employment for poorly educated youths. Informal sector enterprises train more apprentices and workers than the formal education system. Moreover, with globalization, informalization of many formal sector jobs is taking place at a rapid space particularly through subcontracting production as well as outsourcing the service activities to unprotected sector as the formal sector players want to get rid of the problems of labour management and reduce labour cost to remain competitive. This trend indicates that the size of the informal sector is going to expand further with every stride of globalization.

Poverty and informality go hand in hand, although the causal relationship between them has not yet been convincingly established. However, the vicious circle of poverty and informality is evidently obvious. A poor man can hardly acquire formal education and training and hence gets into the informal sector which acts as a safety net. As the wage in the informal sector is very low compared to its formal counterparts, he continues to remain poor. However, what is evident for informal labour market that may not explain the case of the microentrepreneurs who are also a part of the informal sector. A microentrepreneur may enter into this sector in order to become master of his own. S/he may opt for the informal option in order to enjoy a greater degree of autonomy and dignity which may not be possible if s/he works as an assembly worker in a formal plant.

Be that as it may, the nexus between informality and poverty needs closer scrutiny. Contributors in this volume, the outcome of a seminar on Informal Sector and Urban Poverty in North-East India, organized by North-East India Council for Social Science Research on June 5, 2004 at Shillong, have made preliminary efforts to understand the various dimensions of trinity—urbanization, informality and poverty in India's north-east.

We thankfully acknowledge the generous support from B.K. Pande and B. Dutta, Director and Joint Director, Department of Urban Affairs, Government of Meghalaya, Shillong, towards the making of this seminar.

B Datta Ray
Gurudas Das

Shillong

Contributors

Banerjee, Amalesh, Netaji Institute of Asian Studies, Kolkata

Barpujari, Indrani : Department of Anthropology, Gauhati University, Guwahati

Barua, Upala : Lecturer, Department of Anthropology, Cotton College, Guwahati

Bhadra, Sujata: Lecturer, Department of Economics, Janata College, Kokrajhar, Assam

Bhattacharyya Thakur, Mini: Reader, Department of Anthropology, Gauhati University, Guwahati

Chakraborty, Gorky: Lecturer, Department of Economics, Doom Dooma College, Assam

Chatterjee, Mahalaya: Reader, Centre for Urban Economic Studies, Department of Economics, Calcutta University, Kolkata

Chatterjee, Shyamalendu: Lecturer, Department of Economics, Maharaja Manindra Chandra College, Kolkata

Das, D.R.: UNDP Fellow, Principal Scientific Officer, Ministry of Non-Conventional Energy Sources, Regional Office, Guwahati

Das Gurudas: Reader, Department of Economics, North Eastern Hill University, Shillong

Das, Rupa: Research Scholar, Department of Anthropology, Gauhati University, Guwahati

Das, Saswati: Economic Research Unit, Indian Statistical Institute, Kolkata

Lyngskor, J. W.: Lecturer, Union Christian College, Barapani, Meghalaya

Mazhari, H.K.: Consultant, Urban Planning, Gurgaon, Hariyana

Passah, P. M.: Former Professor of Economics, North-Eastern Hill University, Shillong

Paul, Ruma: Lecturer, Department of Economics, G.C. College, Silchar, Assam

Paul, Sumana: Lecturer, Department of Education, Women's College, Shillong

Ryngnga, P. K.: Lecturer, Department of Geography, North Eastern Hill University, Shillong

Saikia, Shabeena Yasmin: Research Scholar, Omeo Kumar Das Institute of Social Change and Development, Guwahati

Sarma, Nripendra N.: Faculty, Assam Institute of Management, Guwahati

Sarma, Ujjal Kumar: Research Scholar, Department of Anthropology, University of Delhi, Delhi

Sengupta, Surojit: Lecturer, Department of Sociology, St. Edmund's College, Shillong

Sharma Barua, Chaiti: Economic Research Unit, Indian Statitical Institute, Kolkata

URBANIZATION AND INFORMALITY

1

Urbanisation and Urban Growth in Northeast India

Mahalaya Chatterjee

1. Introduction

Northeastern India is a politico-geographical term covering the states of Assam, Arunachal Pradesh, Manipur, Meghalaya, Mizoram, Nagaland and Tripura. The region stands apart from the rest of India due to its several unique characteristics. It shows diversity in terms of topography and natural resources and in terms of socio-economic and cultural characteristics. According to the 2001 census, the population constitutes about 3.75 per cent of the total population in India. The decadal growth rate of population of this region during 1981-91 was 27.46 per cent and during 1991-2001 was 22.02 per cent. It accounts for about 12 per cent of the country's total tribal population, five states are predominantly tribal with more than 80 per cent of the inhabitants are indigenous tribal.

We can list the special characteristics of the states in the region as follows:

i. All the states of the region have international boundaries

ii. Five states, Arunachal Pradesh, Manipur, Meghalaya, Mizoram and Nagaland, have more than 80 per cent tribal population. Each tribal group maintains a different socio-cultural identity. Consequently, it is difficult for the migrants from among other ethnic groups or from other population groups (within or outside the region) to get assimilated into host population.

iii. Out of seven states, three (Arunachal Pradesh, Mizoram and Nagaland) have Inner Line Permit (ILP) restriction on the movement of the population. The implication of ILP is that any person who is not from these states must have a valid ILP issued by the relevant authority. This provision would clearly limit the inflow of migrants from other states and countries.

iv. All the five states have special status in the Indian Constitution (Schedule VI). The main implication of this provision is that the market for land is completely shielded from outside. Anyone belonging to other community cannot buy and own land in these states.

In view of these restrictions, we can divide the seven states in the three categories:

a. Assam and Tripura, where the social and political restrictions are the least. The socio-demographic characteristics in these two are similar to the other states in India (other than those within northeastern region) and some of the neighboring countries. It is relatively easy for the migrants to be assimilated into the mainstream population.

b. Manipur and Meghalaya without any ILP restrictions; and

c. Arunachal Pradesh, Mizoram and Nagaland, which are tribal states along with the enforcement of the Inner Line Permit.

Based on these characteristics, one would expect variations in the migratory pattern and consequently urbanization and urban growth. The first category states are open for migration from other states in India and also from outside the country. In the second category, migration may take place from other states of the country, whereas in the third category states, migration would be restricted to intra-state movements (Das et.al. 2003).

In this context, this chapter is an attempt to address several issues. After this introductory section, the second section looks into urbanization and urban growth in Northeast India with respect to some traditional indicators like city size distribution, changes in gender ratio and growth rate of towns for the period 1961-2001. This section also tries to assess the level of urban development in terms of household asset holding with the latest available Census data. The third section looks into the functional distribution of towns, i.e., changes in the function of the older towns and the functions of the new, emerging towns, till 1991. For new towns of 2001, we would look into their spatial distribution. The fourth section, with the help of 2001 Census data of household assets, tries to assess the level of underdevelopment and poverty in the northeastern states. In the concluding section, we take up the issues of land availability, changing land-use pattern and sustainable urbanization and suggest some policy options.

2. Urbanisation and Urban Growth in Northeast India (1961-2001)

If we look at the Indian scenario, we would see that historically, the eastern part of India is relatively less urbanised. The presence of the primate city of Kolkata in West Bengal has given a higher level of urbanisation for the state of West Bengal, whereas all the other major states of the region, i.e., Assam, Bihar and Orissa are almost at the lower end of the scale. For Assam, the level of urbanisation has very recently reached the two-digit figure. In the North-east India itself, the two princely states of Tripura and Manipur had their capital cities and only few trading posts boasting as town. During the British period, Shillong and Guwahati were the only two cities, worth-mentioning. Of course, many changes have taken place in the post-independence period. Assam itself got divided into a number of smaller states. As we have noted earlier, now the seven states of the region have varying levels of urbanisation along with varying rates of urban growth. Both of these have impacts on the city-size distribution and changes in gender ratio (two main indicators of urbanisation). In this section, we will look into these changes in each of the states for four decades (i.e. 1961-2001).

Table 1.1

Levels of Urbanisation in North-Eastern States

	1961	1971	1981	1991	2001
Arnchl P.	0.00	3.70	6.56	12.80	20.40
Assam	7.21	8.82	9.88	11.10	12.80
Manipur	8.68	13.19	26.42	27.52	23.90
Meghalaya	15.27	14.55	18.07	18.60	19.60
Mizoram	5.36	11.36	24.67	46.10	49.50
Nagaland	5.19	9.95	15.52	17.21	17.70
Tripura	15.30	10.99	10.43	9.02	17.00

Source: Calculated from Census of India (1961, 1971, 1981, 1991, 2001).

Table 1.1 gives us an idea about the levels of urbanisation in northeast India. As one can see, in 1961, except Meghalaya and Tripura, all the states had a very low level of urbanisation. Arunachal Pradesh was entirely rural. But after fourty years, Mizoram is the most urbanised state of the region where half of the total population lives in the urban areas. But there is a wide gap with all other states. Manipur ranks second and all the other states have levels of urbanisation ranging from 11 to 20 per cent. In the years in between, all these states have definitely benefited (though in different degree) from the planned economic development of the country. On the other hand, all these states have faced different levels of political unrest. This was due to various reasons like conflicts related to ethnicity and language, economic deprivation, external boundary problems, refugee inflow and so on. All these had impacts on the rates of urbanisation in these states, which can be seen from the Table 1.2 below.

Table 1.2

Rates of Urbanisation in North-Eastern States (1961-2001)

	1961-71	1971-81	1981-91	1991-2001
Arnchl P.	- - -	77.31	95.16	59.38
Assam	22.28	12.07	12.35	14.41
Manipur	51.93	100.33	4.16	—13.15
Meghalaya	-4.73	24.19	2.93	5.38
Mizoram	112.00	117.18	86.84	7.38
Nagaland	91.79	55.91	10.95	2.85
Tripura	—28.17	—5.05	—13.55	88.47

Source: Calculated from Census of India (1961, 1971, 1981, 1991, 2001).

As one can see from Table 1.2 in all the four decades, all the states have shown highly varying rates of urbanisation, from as high as 117.18 (for Mizoram in 1971-81) to as low as —28.17 (for Tripura in 1961-71). At present, we do not have the scope to explain each of them separately, but surely we can describe some particular cases. Arunchal Pradesh has shown very high level of urbanisation from the very beginning. One of the reasons is of course mathematical. As it has started from zero level of urbanisation, the percentage change is quite high. But, due to its strategic position, after 1962, the construction of all-weather roads and various defence-related establishments have given a boost to the process of urbanisation in the state. The high rate of urbanisation in Assam in the sixties was mainly due to inflow of migrants from both within and outside the country. But it had slowed due to political agitations for the next two decades, only to gain back its momentum in the last decade (1991-2001). Similarly, Manipur started with a high rate of urbanisation, which even doubled in the seventies. The reason was growth of small trading towns along the international border. But, it has slowed down in the later years and turned negative for political unrests, not only in the state but also in neighbouring countries like Myanmar. Meghalaya has suffered a lot as far as urbanisation is concerned, when the capital of undivided Assam was shifted from Shillong. A large chunk of government employees left for Assam and other states. It recovered somehow, with Meghalaya gaining statehood in 1972 and creation of its own government and secretariat, but after that, the rate of urbanisation has remained slow.

The variation in the rate of growth of urbanisation can be partly explained by the wide variation in the rate of growth of individual towns in the region, in all the states, throughout the period. Table 1.3 gives us an idea about the change in the number of towns and their annual growth rate. We have divided the annual growth rate of towns into four categories, namely below zero (i.e. negative), between zero to five, between five to ten and above ten. For Arunachal Pradesh, the growth rates of all the towns have been positive, throughout the period under our consideration. The majority of the towns showed moderate growth rate till the seventies. From the eighties, the capital of the state, Itanagar, has been growing at a very high rate (i.e. more than 10%).

For the biggest state of the region, Assam, the scene is quite different. For all the decades, there are a number of towns showing negative growth rate. In fact, the number has increased to 10 in the last twenty years. For the other towns, most of them belong to the below five percent category, reflecting the low rate of urbanisation of the state. In the decade of the sixties, twenty-five towns showed more than five per cent growth rate, one could correlate this with the growth of the public sector towns, in the first phase of planned growth of the country. But this impressive growth rate cannot be sustained because of political unrest and slowing down of government investment in the region.

Manipur, again shows a different picture. From 1961, this small state had a higher level of urbanisation in the region and very high rate of urbanisation. This is reflected at the town level also. During the sixties, the existing urban areas showed slow (even negative) growth rate. But after that, due to the emergence of small trading towns and administrative headquarters for newly created districts, the level of urbanisation increased suddenly. The rate of urbanisation crossed 100 per cent. The number of towns in 1971 was 7 and that increased to 24 in 1981. In the following decade, the momentum was not sustained and all the indicators showed downward trend. At the individual level, two towns in the nineties showed more than ten per cent growth rate, but on the whole, the urban process is in the decline in the state, possibly due to insurgency and political unrest.

Table 1.3

Annual Growth Rate of Towns of North-Eastern States

Arunachal Pradesh				
Growth Rate/Decade	**<0**	**0-5**	**5-10**	**>10**
1961-71		2	2	
1971-81		2	2	
1981-91		2	1	1
1991-2001		6	3	1
Assam				
Growth Rate/Decade	**<0**	**0-5**	**5-10**	**>10**
1961-71	2	39	17	8
1971-81	7	49	8	4
1991-2001	10	69	6	5
Manipur				
Growth Rate/Decade	**<0**	**0-5**	**5-10**	**>10**
1961-71	1	2		
1971-81		2	2	3
1981-91	2	17	4	1
1991-2001		2	25	2
Meghalaya				
Growth Rate/Decade	**<0**	**0-5**	**5-10**	**>10**
1961-71		1	2	3
1971-81		5		1
1981-91		6	4	2
1991-2001			8	4
Mizoram				
Growth Rate/Decade	**<0**	**0-5**	**5-10**	**>10**
1961-71			1	1
1981-91			2	4
1991-2001	2	20		
Nagaland				
Growth Rate/Decade	**<0**	**0-5**	**5-10**	**>10**
1971-81		1	1	1
1981-91		2	5	
1991-2001		4	4	1
Tripura				
Growth Rate/Decade	**<0**	**0-5**	**5-10**	**>10**
1961-71			4	1
1971-81	1	5		
1991-2001	2	13	1	

Source: Calculated from Census of India (1961, 1971, 1981, 1991, 2001).

The towns of Meghalaya, like Arunachal Pradesh, showed positive growth rate throughout the period, though there has been wide variation within the towns. The state was the first in the level of urbanisation, due to the presence of Shillong, the capital of undivided Assam. With the shifting of the capital of Assam, there was noticeable decline in the level of urbanisation. But with the creation of the state of Meghalaya in the seventies, the rate of urbanisation increased, but it was not immediately reflected in the number or growth rate of the towns. Only from the eighties, the number of towns doubled, as a number of towns emerged not only within the Shillong agglomeration, but also in the new districts. The growth rates of these towns are also quite high.

Mizoram is the only state in the region, which showed high rate of urban growth both in the state level and town level. At present, it is one of the most urbanised states of the country with almost half the population living in urban areas. Unfortunately, both this high level and rate of urbanisation are not the result of any economic development but political insurgency. The unrest and ethnic problems of the seventies and eighties led to the evacuation of the villages by army operations and settling of the inhabitants in the relatively safe and peaceful towns. With the calming down of the situation during the nineties, the rate of urbanisation has fallen at the state level. In this period, the number of towns has increased from 6 to 22, but the annual rate of growth has been very low. Two of the towns have even showed negative growth rate.

Nagaland, from the sixties, showed a high rate of urbanisation, but for the two consecutive decades, there was no change in the number of towns. During the sixties, all the three towns had an annual rate of growth more than 10 per cent. But for the next decade, it slowed down. From the eighties, the number of towns increased with the creation of new districts and subdivisions, but none of them showed exceptionally high rate of growth in the eighties. The situation remained almost the same in the nineties.

Tripura, on the other hand, showed decrease in the level

of urbanisation from 1961-1991. Agartala was one of the important urban centre in the northeastern region in the post-independence period. For that, Tripura was the most urbanised state of the region, even surpassing Meghalaya. But the refugees from East Pakistan, settled mostly in the rural parts of the state, resulting in gradual decline in the level of urbanisation, which came down to 9 per cent in 1991. The growth of new towns was not remarkable, even some of the well-known urban centres of the erstwhile Princely state were declassified. The situation somehow started to change from the eighties. Four new towns emerged (though with a low rate of growth). This process was intensified during the nineties, when five more new towns came into being. What is noticeable in Tripura is that the positive relation between the change in the level of urbanisation with the political unrest. As the activities of insurgent groups increase, people leave desolate rural settlements for more congested urban areas in search of safety and security.

If we consider the changes in the size class distribution of the urban areas in the north-eastern states, we will get diverse picture for each of the states. To start with Arunachal Pradesh, in 1961, all the four towns belonged to the Class VI category. Of which, the capital town started to grow very fast, so in 1971, it was promoted to Class V category. In the next Census (1981), only one town was left in the smallest category, other two towns were promoted to the Class V category. For Assam in 1961, apart from one city and another town in the Class II category, most of the towns belonged to the Class V category, followed by 18 in Class VI and 10 in both Class III and Class IV categories. But gradually, the towns were promoted to the immediately higher categories. At present, the size distribution of towns in Assam has a good balance of small and medium-sized towns. For a long time, Guwahati was the only Class I city. In 1991, two other towns were promoted to this highest category. According to the last Census (2001), there are four Class I cities in Assam. Interestingly, there is an equal number of towns in the lowest category also. The largest concentration of towns is in the Class V category (51), followed by towns in Class IV (34), III (23) and II (9) respectively.

In Manipur, Imphal was a Class II town in 1961, it became a city in the next Census and the situation remains the same till the last Census (2001). There was a wide gap of this capital town with the other towns in the state from the very beginning. In 1961, the other two towns were too small. As it can be seen from Table 1.4, gradually, the number of towns increased, the distribution of towns within the different size classes also changed over time. But this gap remained. There is no Class II town in the state. Except for the presence of a few towns in the smallest category, other towns have a good pyramid structure of town size. The urban scenario of Megahalaya is dominated by the Shillong agglomeration. Though there are changes in the number of towns within different size classes, in all the Census years, the maximum number of towns belonged to the Class IV category. Unlike other states in the region, from 1991, there are no towns in the state in Class VI category. Considering the extremely slow change in the level of urbanisation in the state, the size class distribution of towns is quite balanced here.

Table 1.4
Size Class of North-Eastern Towns

Arunachal Pradesh						
Size class/Year	**I**	**II**	**III**	**IV**	**V**	**VI**
1971					1	3
1981					3	1
1991				5	5	
2001			3	7	5	2
Assam						
Size class/Year	**I**	**II**	**III**	**IV**	**V**	**VI**
1961	1	1	10	10	26	18
1971	1	4	9	26	20	8
1991	3	5	19	33	20	9
2001	4	9	23	34	51	4
Manipur						
Size class/Year	**I**	**II**	**III**	**IV**	**V**	**VI**
1961		1			1	1

(Contd.)

	I	II	III	IV	V	VI
1971	1			3		2
1981	1		1	4	8	10
1991	1		2	5	16	4
2001	1		4	7	16	5
Meghalaya						
Size class/Year	**I**	**II**	**III**	**IV**	**V**	**VI**
1961		1		3	1	
1971		1		3	1	1
1981	1	3	2	3		3
1991	1	4		4	3	
2001	1	1	5	8	1	
Mizoram						
Sizeclass/Year	**I**	**II**	**III**	**IV**	**V**	**VI**
1961			1			1
1971			1		1	
1981		1	1	4		
1991	1		2	3	5	11
2001	1	1	1	4	7	8
Nagaland						
Size class/Year	**I**	**II**	**III**	**IV**	**V**	**VI**
1971				1	2	
1981			2	2	3	
1991		2	2	3	2	
2001	1	1	4	3		
Tripura						
Size class/Year	**I**	**II**	**III**	**IV**	**V**	**VI**
1961			1	1	3	
1971	1		3		1	1
1981	1		1	4	2	2
1991	1	4	6	3	2	
2001	1	6	8	8		

Source: Calculated from Census of India (1961, 1971, 1981, 1991, 2001).

In Mizoram, like Manipur, there was a wide gap between the largest town Aizwal and the only other town in the state in 1961. The situation remained the same in 1971. After that with explosive urban growth in the state, not only the size of the existing towns increased, but with the emergence of a number of new towns, the size distribution of the towns have undergone change in the last three decades. At present, size distribution of towns in the state has a classic pyramid-like structure, as can be seen in Table 1.4. In 1961, there were three Class V towns in Nagaland, the capital town grew at a faster rate than the other towns. From 1981, a number of new towns emerged with varied growth rates. One can notice that there was no town in the smallest size class ever and at present, there is no town in the Class V category also. Kohima is the only Class I city in the state, the other eight towns are evenly distributed in the other three size classes, i.e., II, III and IV. As in Mizoram, here also, we can say that the state has entered a phase of stable urbanisation, which is reflected in the city size distribution. On the other hand, the urban scenario of Tripura is totally different. Agartala was the largest town in the region but there was not much difference in population size with immediately next town and the other three towns. But after that, contrary to the falling level of urbanisation, there was explosive growth of Agartala. Till 1981, there was no Class II town in the state. The size distribution in the lower end was also unbalanced. With increasing political unrest and insurgency in the countryside, the smaller towns also started to grow and now Tripura can boast of being a state with a city and big and medium-sized towns. For security reasons, people like to live in high-density big towns, and not in desolate smaller towns and countryside.

The increase in population in the urban areas is due to two reasons, either by natural increase or through migration. In general, all towns have a history of high migration in the initial years, low gender ratio indicates the male domination. Gradually, the gender ratio starts to increase with migrants settling down and birth of their new generation. In Table 1.5, we want to look at this phenomenon in all the states of the region. We have divided the gender ratio of the state into four categories, i.e. below 500 (very low), 500-750 (low), moderate (750-1000) and high (above 1000).

The changing gender ratio of the towns in Arunachal Pradesh illustrates this particular aspect of urban change. In 1961, three towns had low gender ratio indicating the high proportion of migrants in the new towns of the state. In 1971, another town was promoted to the moderate gender ratio category. With the settling down of the migrants the gender ratio increased. With the improvement of communication and availability of urban facilities, not only the existing towns but even the new towns of 1981 belonged to the moderate gender ratio category. This went on increasing resulting in all the 17 towns belonging to the high gender ratio category in the latest Census. If we consider the largest state of the region, i.e., Assam, we will find the same phenomenon but, with a different dimension. In 1961, both the very low and high gender ratio categories had two towns each. In the other two categories, other 63 towns were distributed as can be seen from the Table 1.5. This implies that apart from the older urban centres with somewhat settled population, Assam had both in-migrating and out-migrating towns. In 1971, towns in the two extreme categories were no more. There was almost equal number of towns in the two middle categories. Gender ratio went on increasing and in 1991 Census (after decades of political disturbances), we find that the number of towns in the low gender ratio category has fallen down drastically. One town again emerged in the high gender ratio category. This pattern remained the same in 2001, where 122 urban areas out of 125 were clustered in the moderate gender ratio category, indicating family-oriented structure of the Assamese society.

On the contrary, in the three tribal dominated states with history of matriarchal society, we find hardly any urban area with very low or low gender ratio. Most of the towns belonged to the moderate or high gender ratio category throughout the period of our study. In the absence of more information, we can just conclude that urbanisation has not been able to affect the basic pattern of the society in these three states.

Table 1.5

Gender Ratio of Towns of North-Eastern States

Gender Ratio / Year	<500	500-750	750-1000	>1000
Arunachal Pradesh				
1961		3	1	
1971		2	2	
1991		3	10	
2001			17	
Assam				
1961	2	25	38	2
1971		37	31	
1991		8	80	1
2001		1	122	2
Manipur				
1961			2	1
1971			3	4
1981			14	10
1991			20	8
2001			13	20
Meghalaya				
1961			4	1
1971			6	
1981			12	
1991			11	1
2001			11	5
Mizoram				
1961			2	

(Contd.)

1971			2	
1981			4	2
1991			18	4
2001			20	2

Nagaland

Gender Ratio Year	**<500**	**500-750**	**750-1000**	**>1000**
1961		3		
1971	2	1		
1981		7		
1991		3	6	
2001		2	7	

Tripura

Gender Ratio Year	**<500**	**500-750**	**750-1000**	**>1000**
1961			5	
1971			6	
1971			10	
1981			16	
2001		1	21	1

Source: Calculated from census of India (1961, 1971, 1981, 1991, 2001).

Till 1981, most of the towns in Nagaland had low gender ratio, indicating the migrant induced urbanisation of the state. In 1971, two towns had very low gender ratio. With indigenous population settling in the urban areas, the situation improved. In 1991, six towns out of nine were in the moderate gender ratio category and within the next years, all the nine towns became members of this category.

On the contrary, all the towns in Tripura throughout the period of our study, belonged to the moderate gender ratio category reflecting the static nature of the urban population. Only in 2001, we find two new towns, one belonging to the low gender ratio category and the other in the high gender ratio category, indicating inflow and outflow of migrants in the new towns.

In this section, we have discussed in detail, the main characteristics of the urban areas in the northeastern states.

We have seen that even with varied growth rates, the towns in the states have grown substantially in the last four decades. The continuous increase in the gender ratio for most of the towns also indicate the stabilisation of urban population in the region. In the next section, we would like to look into the functions of the towns in the region.

3. Functional Distribution of Towns in Northeast India: Trends and Implications.

An urban area differs from its rural counterpart mainly in terms of occupation of its inhabitants. In fact, one of the criteria, the Census authority uses to identify an urban area (apart from population size and density), is the engagement of more than 75 per cent of the male working population in non-agricultural activities. So, it implies that the main function of the city or town would either be in secondary or tertiary category. The Census authority publishes the occupational distribution of the population down to the town level. Using these data, Ashok Mitra et. al. (1981) did a seminal work on the functional classification of towns of India for 1961 and also extended it to 1971 to find out whether there is any shift in function. Using the same methodology, we have extended the study for 1991 Census. Lack of comparable data has prevented to do the same for 1981 and 1991. The two tables in the Appendix (A1.1 and A1.2) show the functions and their shifts for towns in Assam and other northeastern states.

As we can see from Table A1.1, we have information about functional classification of 50 urban areas of Assam for 1961 and 1971. We find that tertiary activity was the main function of urban areas in Assam. Almost half of the towns had trading as their main function. There were sixteen service towns. Only nine towns had manufacturing as the main activity. But apart from the emerging public sector oil towns, other manufacturing towns were traditional artisan towns producing Assam silk and handicrafts. Within ten years, these traditional artisan towns changed their main function and in 1971, there were only three manufacturing towns left in the state (all of them were oil towns). The number of service towns were reduced by ten whereas, the number of trading towns increased to 41. In 1991, we find 93 urban areas in the state. Of these, sixty were trading towns. The twenty service towns were mainly headquarters of newly created districts. The rest thirteen towns were devoted to manufacturing, apart from the oil towns, there were small manufacturing towns. We do not have comparable data for 2001, but we can certainly say that there cannot be any drastic change in the functional distribution of the state.

For the smaller states of the region, all the towns in both 1961 and 1971 were service towns. The only exception was Imphal, the capital of Manipur. It was a manufacturing town, basically due to the traditional handloom weaving of the state. Even in 1991, the functional distribution of the towns in the six small states has remained almost the same. In Arunachal Pradesh, out of ten towns in 1991, nine were service towns. The sole exception was the manufacturing town of Namsai. The situation was similar in Meghalaya. There were eleven service towns; only the new town Cherapunjee had manufacturing as the dominant activity. All the twenty-two town in Mizoram and nine towns in Nagaland are service towns. Of the eighteen towns of Tripura, only three are trading towns, rest are again service towns. The situation is somehow different in Manipur, where out of 28 towns in 1991, only 19 are service towns. Of the rest, one is a trading town and other are small manufacturing town based on traditional weaving and handicraft. This high proliferation of service towns is due to administrative decision of creating headquarters of the new districts and subdivisions in all the states.

This idea about the functional distribution of the urban area of the north-eastern region leads us to conclude that the urbanisation in the region is not spontaneous, but a result of deliberate administrative decisions. Service sector does not have agglomerative or expansionary potential. As we have seen historically, most of the service towns get transformed to trading towns in course of time. The manufacturing potential is very small in this region. Though, the region has natural resources in terms of forest products and minerals, given the topography and difficult terrain, we cannot think of high level of industrialisation in the area. The present spurt of administrative activities for countering terrorist and insurgent activities will not continue forever.

So as in Assam, trading will be the main force of urbanisation in future for the smaller states also. Whatever be the form of trading activity, the spatial requirement is vital. It is more so given the topography of the area. Two issues become important. As horizontal expansion is not possible how can these trading activities, which subsume allied storage and transportation activities, be accommodated in the future? Secondly: the ethnic issue related to majority of tribal population, community land ownership and matriarchal form of society.

As far as spatial distribution of new towns is concerned, one would find high spatial variation not only in the state level, but also in the district level. According to the 2001 Census, most of the new towns are concentrated in few districts. On the other hand, no new town has emerged in a number of districts. The number of urban agglomerations and towns within it has also increased in the last decade. This type of spatial concentration calls for accommodating a number of urban amenities and facilities within a small space. So, again the land question becomes vital as far as future urbanisation is concerned.

4. An Assessment of the Relative Underdevelopment in the North-eastern Region

There are different ways to assess the underdevelopment and poverty in a particular region. Regional economists, over the years, have tried to compare the supply of natural endowments, factor payments over the regions, the level of infrastructural development, availability of civic and other amenities to compare the levels of development among different regions of the country. We do not have comparable data for all the regions or for a long time period to assess the relative level of underdevelopment of the north-eastern region or even within the states in the north-eastern region. But in 2001 Census, we have the state-wise date on houses and household assets. The Census authority has also given two ranking of the states based on the possession of some household assets and types of houses. We have arranged these data in the following table to have an idea of the situation in the north-eastern states in relation to the country. We have grouped the available data in tables 1.6-1.10

Table 1.6

Access to Permanent Housing and Drinking Water in NE Region vis-a-vis India

Permanent House State	Percentage of Household	All India Rank	Percentage of Hh. in NE	NE Rank
Arunachal Pradesh	20.40	31	00.60	6
Assam	19.70	32	13.64	1
Manipur	8.40	35	00.47	7
Meghalaya	22.22	30	5.90	2
Mizoram	53.00	20	1.19	3
Nagaland	16.3	33	00.75	5
Tripura	9.90	34	00.92	4

Cement Floor State	Percentage of Household	All India Rank	Percentage of Hh. in NE	NE Rank
Arunachal Pradesh	21.00	24	00.62	5
Assam	12.40	31	8.60	1
Manipur	9.50	35	00.52	6
Meghalaya	18.00	25	1.06	2
Mizoram	17.00	27	00.38	7
Nagaland	17.40	26	00.81	4
Tripura	10.00	34	00.93	3

Burnt brick wall State	Percentage of Household	All India Rank	Percentage of Hh. in NE	NE Rank
Arunachal Pradesh	3.70	32	00.11	6
Assam	16.10	25	11.14	1
Manipur	7.40	28	00.41	4
Meghalaya	5.60	30	00.33	5
Mizoram	4.60	31	00.11	7
Nagaland	11.40	26	00.53	2
Tripura	7.50	27	00.69	2

Concrete Roof State	Percentage of Household	All India Rank	Percentage of Hh. in NE	NE Rank
Arunachal Pradesh	1.80	35	00.05	7
Assam	1.90	34	1.35	1
Manipur	2.80	33	00.15	5
Meghalaya	5.90	29	00.34	2
Mizoram	8.40	28	00.19	4
Nagaland	2.90	32	00.14	6
Tripura	3.10	31	00.29	3

(Contd.)

Water Closet

State	Percentage of Household	All India Rank	Percentage of Hh. in NE	NE Rank
Arunachal Pradesh	11.02	26	00.32	7
Assam	15.90	19	11.02	1
Manipur	8.68	33	00.49	4
Meghalaya	12.32	22	00.73	3
Mizoram	19.53	16	00.44	5
Nagaland	8.72	32	00.41	6
Tripura	11.69	24	1.08	2

Drinking water tap

State	Percentage of Household	All India Rank	Percentage of Hh. in NE	NE Rank
Arunachal Pradesh	67.80	9	2.02	4
Assam	9.20	32	6.37	1
Manipur	29.30	23	1.63	6
Meghalaya	34.50	20	2.04	3
Mizoram	31.90	22	00.72	7
Nagaland	42.00	18	1.95	5
Tripura	24.60	26	2.29	2

Source: Census of India 2001 Housing Table downlowed from www.censusindia.net

We start with Table 1.6 which gives us information about the housing condition in the region. The first part is about the possession of permanent house. It is very clear that of the 35 states in India, all the north-eastern states (except Mizoram) are at the lower end of the list. In the six states of the region, only about twenty per cent of the population have a permanent house. Within the region also, there is widespread disparity. Within the region, only 13 per cent of the population living in Assam have a permanent house and it comes down to only 0.47 per cent in Manipur. If we look at the data on cement flooring, the states perform slightly better in all-India ranking, though all of them are in the lower end of the list. Within the region, except Assam and Meghalaya, the percentage is meagre. The same can be said about the possession of houses with burnt-brick walls and concrete roofs. On the whole, we can say that the housing condition in the region is poor compared to all-India level. But one has to remember that the hilly terrain, difficult transportation conditions, regular floods and high rainfall have compelled the people to depend on local materials to make their shelters rather than going for permanent structures with burnt-brick and cement. As far as sanitation (i.e. having a water closet in the house) is concerned, Assam and Mizoram have ranked in the middle-level in all India standards. Within the region, Assam is far ahead of the other states. For the possession of a tap for drinking water, the position is much better in the all-India ranking. Arunachal Pradesh is among the first ten states of the country. Within the region also, the disparity is much less among the states.

Table 1.7

Access to Modern Forms of Energy in NE Region vis-a-vis India

Electricity State	Percentage of Household	All India Rank	Percentage of Hh. in NE	NE Rank
Arunachal Pradesh	54.70	25	1.63	6
Assam	24.90	33	17.26	1
Manipur	60.00	24	3.35	3
Meghalaya	42.70	28	2.52	5
Mizoram	69.60	20	1.57	7
Nagaland	63.60	22	2.97	4
Tripura	41.80	29	3.89	2

LPG State	Percentage of Household	All India Rank	Percentage of Hh. in NE	NE Rank
Arunachal Pradesh	20.20	16	00.60	5
Assam	13.20	25	9.16	1
Manipur	21.80	15	1.22	2
Meghalaya	7.7C	31	00.45	6
Mizoram	37.60	6	00.85	4
Nagaland	9.50	30	00.44	7
Tripura	12.90	26	1.20	3

Source: Census of India 2001 Housing Table downlowed from www.censusindia.net

Table 1.7 gives an idea about the energy use in the states. Though in all-India ranking, most of the states are in the lower end, except Assam, about 50 per cent of the population have electricity connections. But there is widespread disparity in the region. Assam is much ahead of the other states. The possession of LPG (liquefied petroleum gas) as the cooking fuel shows a mixed picture. Assam is rich in mineral oil but other states like Mizoram and Manipur, are much ahead in all-India ranking. Of course, within the region, all the states are far behind Assam in this respect.

Table 1.8

Commercialisation of Space and Access to Banking in NE Region vis-a-vis India

Shop/Office Use State	Percentage of Household	All India Rank	Percentage of Hh. in NE	NE Rank
Arunachal Pradesh	4.8	26	00.18	5
Assam	5.9	21	4.96	1
Manipur	2.5	35	00.17	6
Meghalaya	5.8	22	00.41	3
Mizoram	4.8	25	00.12	7
Nagaland	4.3	29	00.22	4
Tripura	7.7	12	00.91	2
Bank Account **State**	**Percentage of Household**	**All India Rank**	**Percentage of Hh. in NE**	**NE Rank**
Arunachal Pradesh	37.30	16	1.11	4
Assam	20.50	33	14.23	1
Manipur	8.70	35	00.49	7
Meghalaya	20.80	32	1.29	3
Mizoram	31.80	19	00.72	6
Nagaland	15.90	34	00.74	5
Tripura	26.50	27	2.46	2

Source: Census of India 2001 Housing Table downlowed from www.censusindia.net

The two components of Table 1.8 give an idea about the commercialisation of space and penetration of organised banking in the area. All the states have very little space (proportion of buildings) used as commercial space. Except Tripura, they lie at the lower range of the all-India ranking. Within the region, the proportion is very low and again, Assam is well ahead of the other states. As far as possession of bank account is concerned, Manipur is the lowest in all-India ranking. Baring Nagaland, in the other five states, twenty to thirty per cent of the people has at least one bank account.

Table 1.9

Ownership of Vehicles in NE Region vis-a-vis India

Bicycle State	Percentage of Household	All India Rank	Percentage of Hh. in NE	NE Rank
Arunachal Pradesh	17.40	29	00.52	5
Assam	46.40	11	32.15	1
Manipur	38.00	16	2.12	3
Meghalaya	11.00	31	00.65	4
Mizoram	3.10	34	00.07	7
Nagaland	8.10	33	00.38	6
Tripura	30.60	23	2.84	2

Car/Jeep State	Percentage of Household	All India Rank	Percentage of Hh. in NE	NE Rank
Arunachal Pradesh	2.40	21	00.07	7
Assam	2.00	26	1.42	1
Manipur	3.10	14	00.17	2
Meghalaya	2.70	17	00.16	4
Mizoram	3.40	11	00.08	6
Nagaland	3.50	9	00.16	3
Tripura	1.10	33	00.10	5

Other Two wheelers State	Percentage of Household	All India Rank	Percentage of Hh. in NE	NE Rank
Arunachal Pradesh	6.80	27	00.20	4
Assam	5.20	29	3.61	1
Manipur	11.10	18	00.62	2
Meghalaya	2.90	33	00.17	5
Mizoram	6.20	28	00.14	6
Nagaland	2.80	34	00.13	7
Tripura	3.90	31	00.36	3

Source: Census of India 2001 Housing Table downlowed from www.censusindia.net

In Table 1.9 we have data on the possession of vehicles. Of course, the situation is best as far as possession of bicycle is concerned, followed by the other two-wheelers and then four-wheelers. This table indicates the dismal situation of public transportation situation of the region. The people has to arrange for some means of private transportation, though they are not able to spend on housing or better forms of energy.

Table 1.10
Access to Modern Entertainment and Communication in NE Region vis-a-vis India

Radio/Transistor State	Percentage of Household	All India Rank	Percentage of Hh. in NE	NE Rank
Arunachal Pradesh	39.00	19	1.16	6
Assam	30.20	27	20.92	1
Manipur	43.00	13	2.40	3
Meghalaya	32.00	25	1.89	4
Mizoram	42.00	14	00.95	7
Nagaland	32.50	24	1.52	5
Tripura	28.50	29	2.65	2

Telephone State	Percentage of Household	All India Rank	Percentage of Hh. in NE	NE Rank
Arunachal Pradesh	9.20	19	00.27	6
Assam	4.30	31	3.01	1
Manipur	5.30	28	00.30	5
Meghalaya	6.00	26	00.35	3
Mizoram	14.10	12	00.32	4
Nagaland	5.20	29	00.24	7
Tripura	5.20	30	00.49	2

Television State	Percentage of Household	All India Rank	Percentage of Hh. in NE	NE Rank
Arunachal Pradesh	25.70	24	00.76	6
Assam	18.30	31	12.68	1
Manipur	24.30	26	1.35	3
Meghalaya	20.90	29	1.23	4
Mizoram	20.40	30	00.46	7
Nagaland	18.10	32	00.85	5
Tripura	23.70	27	2.20	2

Source: Census of India 2001 Housing Table downlowed from www.censusindia.net

The Table 1.10 shows the modern means of entertainment and communication available in the region. As far as possession of radio/transistor is concerned, even with the presence of inter-state disparity, the situation is quite good. The higher level of literacy provokes the people to know more but, in the absence of electric connection, transistor is the only means for this. The percentage of households possessing television is also quite high compared to the possession of other basic requirements including permanent house. Interestingly, the percentage of households having telephone connection is lowest, compared to these two. Nonetheless, their ranks are low in the all-India standards. For all these three assets, within the region, Assam is well ahead of all the states, distantly followed by Tripura.

This brief discussion about the possession of household amenities and assets leads us to conclude that there is enough scope for marketing of such products in the region. This strengthens our earlier argument that trade and commerce will be the guiding force of urbanisation in the region. Apart from the enhancement of organised trading, in the absence of other employment opportunities, petty and informal trading will increase over time. A study in late eighties found that in the north-eastern region, older and bigger towns in the valley and plains are either growing slowly or stagnating, whereas smaller towns in the hills are growing relatively fast. If the trend remains the same after the 2001 Census, then it will reaffirm our worry about scarcity or urban land in the near future.

5. **Conclusion**

In this chapter, we have shown the trend of urbanisation and urban growth in the seven states of the north-eastern region. Though the region has a low level of urbanisation, the rate of urban growth is highly varied among the states. Going through the functional distribution, we concluded that trade and commerce is the main force behind urbanisation in the region. With the increase in the consumerism, this is going to increase in the future. Along, with the expansion of the formal sector, the informal sector of trade consisting of small and petty traders will also expand. This will enhance the demand for urban land. Excessive vertical growth is neither desirable nor possible in these ecologically fragile hilly states. The issue of preservation of environment and ecological balance is vital here. The demand for residential land will also increase as we have seen the gender ratio for most of the towns in the northeast is on the higher side. The constraint relating to land will also become important. As we have stated in the introductory section, in the five predominantly tribal states, the ownership of land by non-tribals and immigrants is totally prohibited by law. Thus, investment in commerical space or residential space by the trading community (or by any sort of private initiative) is not at all possible.

So, it is high time to think in terms of some perspective plan to tackle the issue of urban land immediately. The state through its urban development department (or urban planning authority) has to take the initiative. One suggestion would be to develop some common facilities for small manufacturers and traders, so that there may not be unnecessary replication and wastage of land. This can be done on a cooperative basis along community ownership. Second alternative would be the government going in for land development and distribution in a large scale. The third alternative would be to go for joint venture with private-public partnership for land and infrastructures development. Of course, in the tribal states, the government has to act in such a manner that the ownership of land by the indigenous people remains intact. On the whole, we can say that if some action is not taken with a long-term perspective, urban growth will result in utter chaos, the recovery from which will become extremely costly.

NOTES

1. The growth rate of towns has been calculated by using the standard formula

   $$\frac{Y_t - Y_t - 1}{Y_t - 1} \times 100,$$

   where Y_t indicated the population of year to in the city/town.

2. The Census authority of India identifies cities/towns based on four criteria. Apart from the criterion of statutory township, the other three are population size (above 5000), population density (500 persons per square kilometer) and the occupation of the male working force (75 per cent in non-agricultural activities). This third criterion is very important in understanding the nature of the town. Dr Ashok Mitra, along with his team, was the first to classify cities and towns based on the occupation of the inhabitants. He took three basic functions of a town as manufacturing, trading and transportation and service. The nine-fold classification of the Census was used to classify the towns. Mitra et al. did not take into account the city/town population engaged in agriculture and allied activities. They calculated the percentage of population under manufacturing (which included mining and quarrying, construction, household and non-household industrial workers), trading and transportation (which included trade and commerce and transport and related activities) and service (other services). The highest of these percentages designated the function of the town. This exercise was first done for the towns of 1961 Census. This was repeated in 1971, to find out whether there was any shift in the functions of the cities/towns. The importance of such an exercise lies in the fact that it points out the main economic force behind the growth and expansion of a town. As manufacturing activities have more linkages than services, a manufacturing town will expand more quickly than a service town. The agglomerating effects of the trade and transport are also more than the service sector. The same exercise was extended to the cities/towns of 1991 Census by Chatterjee & Giri (2001). Till now, as the data on occupation distribution (in nine-fold classification) in the town level, we have not been able to repeat the same exercise for the latest Census (2001).

REFERENCES

1. Chatterjee, Mahalaya and Pabitra Giri (2001): *Functional Classification of Urban Areas in India, 1961, 1971, 1991,* Urban Database Series, No.1, Centre for Urban Economic Studies, University of Calcutta, Kolkata.
2. Das Smita, Amaresh Dubey and Veronica Pala (2003): "Labour Mobility: Evidence from North-Eastern Region of India", *Labour & Development,* Volume 9, No. 2, pp.196-222, V.V. Giri National Labour Institute, Noida.

3. Datta Ray, B. (ed.), (1986): *The Patterns and Problems of Population in North-East India,* Uppal Publishing House, New Delhi.
4. Ganguly, J.B. (ed.), (1995): *Urbanisation and Development in North-East India: Trends and Policy Implication,* Deep & Deep Publications, New Delhi.
5. Mitra, Ashok, Surendra, B.L. Sherry and Brahm Dutt (1981): *Shifts in the Functions of Cities and Towns of India, 1961-71* (An Indian Council of Social Science Research and Jawaharlal Nehru University Study), Abhinav Publications, New Delhi.
6. Office of the Registrar General of India: *Census of India, Primary Census Abstracts* for the years 1961, 1971, 1981, 1991 and 2001. (The last two are in computerized form, available in www.censusindia.net)

APPENDIX

Table A1.1
Functional Classification of Towns in Assam (1961-1991)

DIST NAME	TOWN NAME	Agrpc	Mfgpc	TTpc	Srpc	1991	1971	1961
1	2	3	4	5	6	7	8	9
Dhubri	Golokganj C.T.	10.69	27.08	50.25	22.67	T		
Dhubri	Gauripur T.C.	6	29.45	40.28	30.27	T	T	T
Dhubri	Dhubri M.B.	4.49	29.19	40.06	30.75	T	T	S
Dhubri	Sapatgram T.C.	6.27	38.88	43.56	17.56	T	T	T
Dhubri	Bilasipara T.C.	4.49	33.88	46.18	19.94	T	T	T
Dhubri	Chapar T.C.*	29.16	30.93	41.26	27.81	T		
Dhubri	Mankachar C.T.	21.56	26.26	50.11	23.63	T	T	T
Kokrajhar	Gossaigaon T.C.	13.4	18.9	45.59	35.52	T		
Kokrajhar	Kokrajhar M.B.	7.5	27.3	34.26	38.44	T	T	S
Kokrajhar	Basugaon T.C.	14.64	24.63	53.91	21.47	T		
Bongaigaon	Abhayapuri T.C.	4.12	25.66	34.45	39.9	S	T	T
Bongaigaon	Jogighopa C.T.	27.9	47.53	16.1	36.36	M		
Bongaigaon	Bijni T.C.#	2.5	23.47	51.52	25.01	T		
Bongaigaon	Bongaigaon U.A.	0.94	17.57	64.6	17.83	T		
Bongaigaon	(A) Bongaigaon M.B.	1.15	20.01	59.34	20.66	T	T	T
Bongaigaon	(B) New Bongaigaon Rly. Colony	0.26	9.72	81.54	8.75	T		
Goalpara	Goalpara M.B.	8.22	25.97	35.52	38.51	S	T	S
Goalpara	Lakhipur T.C.#	26.64	27.54	35.06	37.4	S		
Barpeta	Barpeta Road M.B.	3.51	24.63	55.94	19.43	T	T	T
Barpeta	Sorbhog T.C.#	17.78	20.16	56.07	23.77	T		
Barpeta	Barpeta M.B.	1.1	23.47	40.05	36.48	T	T	M
Barpeta	Sarthebari T.C.	10.43	37.78	34.19	28.03	M	M	M
Barpeta	Howli T.C.#	19.02	26.42	50.77	22.8	T		
Barpeta	Bohari C.T.	14.01	29.96	51.57	18.47	T		
Barpeta	Pathsala T.C.**	18.29	26.63	40.69	32.68	T		
Nalbari	Tihu T.C.	6.94	18.51	43.28	38.21	T	T	M
Nalbari	Nalbari M.B.	3.85	24.4	41.73	33.87	T	T	S
Kamrup	Rangia M.B.	6.8	13.08	38.14	48.79	S	T	S
Kamrup	Niz Hajo C.T.**	15.56	35.42	36.39	28.19	T		

(Condt.)

1	2	3	4	5	6	7	8	9
Kamrup	Sualkuchi C.T.	1.08	72.26	11.68	16.06	M		
Kamrup	North Guwahati T.C.	16.83	21.9	28.41	49.69	S	S	M
Kamrup	Amingaon C.T.	6.63	36.64	35.83	27.54	M	T	T
Kamrup	Palasbari M.B.	9.83	30.21	43.61	26.18	T	T	M
Kamrup	Guwahati City (M.Corp.)	2.39	20.65	41.11	38.24	T	T	S
Darrang	Tangla T.C.	4.46	19.26	58.36	22.38	T	T	T
Darrang	Mangoldoi M.B.	7.14	24.2	37.15	38.65	S	S	S
Darrang	Kharupatia T.C.	3.08	20.79	63.53	15.68	T	T	T
Darrang	Udalguri T.C.*	9.96	27.23	39.11	33.66	T		
Sonitpur	Tezpur M.B.	1.6	23.51	41.41	35.09	S	S	S
Sonitpur	Dhekiajuli M.B.	15.41	20.7	48.79	30.5	T	T	T
Sonitpur	Rangapara T.C.**	2.35	16.54	68.43	15.03	T		
Sonitpur	Biswanath Charali T.C.**	6.85	24.75	45.83	29.42	T		
Lakhimpur	Bihpuria T.C.	17.72	18.72	54.33	26.96	T	T	T
Lakhimpur	North Lakhimpur M.B.	10.26	23.38	43.19	33.43	T	T	S
Dhemaji	Dhemaji T.C.	22.29	22.97	35.32	41.71	S		
Marigaon	Marigaon T.C.	31.34	22.8	33.3	43.89	S		
Marigaon	Jagiroad C.T.	12.3	40.82	41.81	17.37	T		
Marigaon	Jagiroad Paper Mill C.T.*	0	92.31	1.55	6.13	M		
Nagaon	Dhing T.C.	21.83	25.75	43.27	30.98	T	T	T
Nagaon	Nagaon M.B.	3.29	27.8	44.65	27.55	T	T	S
Nagaon	Raha C.T.	20.99	16.46	51.15	32.4	T		
Nagaon	Hojai M.B.	6.77	20.29	56.38	23.33	T	T	T
Nagaon	Lanka T.C.	15.85	25.25	52.91	21.84	T		
Nagaon	Lumding U.A.	5.92	10.69	72.03	17.28	T		
Nagaon	Lumding T.C.	19.97	18.41	58.47	23.12	T	T	T
Nagaon	Lumding Rly. Colony C.T.	2.51	9.15	74.74	16.12	T		
Golaghat	Golaghat M.B.	2.17	22.32	45.64	32.04	T	T	S
Golaghat	Bokakhat T.C.	16.03	26.29	41.28	32.43	T		
Golaghat	Dergaon T.C.	3.83	9.65	19.75	70.6	S	S	S
Jorhat	Mariani T.C.	0.27	26.56	58.54	14.9	T	T	T
Jorhat	Jorhat U.A.	3.87	28.99	37.59	33.42	T		
Jorhat	Jorhat M.B.& O.G.	3.75	29.83	38.87	31.3	T		
Jorhat	Jorhat M.B.	0.44	18.43	50.83	30.74	T	T	S

(Condt.)

1	2	3	4	5	6	7	8	9
Jorhat	Kamalabariagaon O.G	19.67	23.35	28.63	48.02	S		
Jorhat	Sarbaibandha O.G.	33.4	25.07	36.59	38.34	S		
Jorhat	Bahotia O.G.	6.47	30.64	36.24	33.11	T		
Jorhat	Sonarigaon O.G.	4.51	23.64	38.73	37.64	T		
Jorhat	Barbheta Chapari O.G.	3.05	22.01	11.64	66.35	S		
Jorhat	Chowdang No.1 O.G.	10.59	38.08	25.25	36.67	M		
Jorhat	Duliagaon O.G.	21.25	48.37	8.6	43.02	M		
Jorhat	Cinnamara Grant O.G.	7.13	89.79	4.52	5.69	M		
Jorhat	Toklai Chah Bagicha O.G.	1.11	28.72	19.59	51.69	S		
Jorhat	Kumar Kaibartta O.G.	2.52	36.47	31.8	31.73	M		
Jorhat	Gohain Tekelagaon O.G.	2.96	35.95	28.54	35.51	M		
Jorhat	Chengeligaon O.G.	9.67	45.54	24.97	29.49	M		
Jorhat	Chekonidhara O.G.	0.99	38.19	22.2	39.61	S		
Jorhat	Kamalabaria N.C. O.G.	2.29	22.74	23.47	53.79	S		
Jorhat	Nakari Bamnngoan O.G.	2.78	26.58	38.45	34.97	T		
Jorhat	Senchoa Gaon C.T.	5.8	14.29	15.27	70.45	S		
Sibsagar	Amguri T.C.#	7.23	23.83	51.99	24.18	T		
Sibsagar	Sibsagar M.B.	1.93	41.37	33.72	24.92	M	M	S
Sibsagar	Nazira T.C.	10.72	38.07	32.21	29.72	M	T	M
Sibsagar	Sonari M.B.**	6.89	28.02	47.43	24.55	T		
Sibsagar	Moranhat T.C.#	3.82	27.89	45.24	26.87	T		
Dibrugarh	Chabua T.C.	1.12	22.65	54.59	22.77	T	T	T
Dibrugarh	Naharkatiya T.C.	6.37	33.93	46.84	19.23	T	T	M
Dibrugarh	Duliajan Oil Town C.T.#	0.25	50.56	12.81	36.63	M		
Dibrugarh	Namrup C.T.**	1.97	60.92	16.31	22.78	M		
Dibrugarh	Dibrugarh U.A	1.43	22.85	44.25	32.91	T		
Dibrugarh	Dibrugarh M.B.	1.26	22.48	45.91	31.61	T	T	T
Dibrugarh	Barbari (AMC Area) C.T.	5.11	31.27	6.13	62.6	S		
Tinsukia	Doom Dooma T.C.	3.13	22.06	56.14	21.81	T	T	T
Tinsukia	Tinsukia M.B.	3.4	26.76	51.2	22.04	T	T	T

(Condt.)

1	2	3	4	5	6	7	8	9
Tinsukia	Makum T.C.#	9.37	47.14	33.67	19.19	M		
Tinsukia	Margherita C.T.**	3.28	44.34	37.58	18.08	M		
Tinsukia	Digboi U.A.	2.73	49.28	26.34	24.38	M		
Tinsukia	Digboi T.C.	4.87	40.42	38.52	21.06	M	T	M
Tinsukia	Digboi Oil Town C.T.	0.4	58.48	13.7	27.81	M	M	M
Karbai Anglong	Diphu T.C.#	8.98	31.93	25.94	42.13	S		
Karbai Anglong	Howraghat T.C.	15.35	15.07	33.3	51.63	S		
Karbai Anglong	Dokmoka T.C.*	54.62	26.39	44.52	29.09	T		
Karbai Anglong	Bokajan T.C.*	17.64	38.07	39.67	22.25	T		
Karbai Anglong	Hamren T.C.*	36.03	34.03	18.53	47.43	S		
Karbai Anglong	Donkamokam T.C.*	75.26	29.87	16.58	53.55	S		
North Cachar Hills	Haflong T.C.	8.93	20.63	20.12	59.25	S	S	S
North Cachar Hills	Mahur T.C.*	8.69	32.8	32.36	34.85	S		
North Cachar Hills	Maibong T.C.*	4.28	31.5	26.66	41.84	S		
Karimganj	Karimganj M.B.	0.97	18.59	42.06	39.34	T	T	T
Karimganj	Badarpur U.A.	1.16	10.84	64.04	25.12	T		
Karimganj	Badarpur T.C.**	2.08	15.32	56.13	28.56	T		
Karimganj	Badarpur Railway Town C.T.	0.11	5.84	72.88	21.28	T	T	T
Hailakandi	Hailakandi M.B.	6.04	19.98	38.03	41.99	S	S	S
Hailakandi	Lala T.C.	24	17.9	45.25	36.85	T	T	T
Cachar	Lakhipur T.C.	11.31	11.62	57.86	30.52	T	T	T
Cachar	Silchar M.B.	1.19	19.56	45.26	35.17	T	T	T

Source : Chatterjee and Giri (2001).

Note : *,* *, # stand for new towns in 1991, 1981 and 1971 respectively.
@, @ @ stand for town declassified in 1971 and 1961 respectively.
M,T,S, stand for town with manufacturing, trade and transport, and service as main function respectively.
Agrpc stands for percentage of agricultural workers to total workers in 1991.
Mfgpc and Srpc stand for percentage of workers in manufacturing and in other services to total non-agricultural workers in 1991 respectively.

Table A 1.2
Functional Classification of Towns in Other North-Eastern States (1961-1991)

STATE AND DIST NAME	TOWN NAME	Agrpc	Mfgpc	Ttpc	Srpc	1991	1971	1961
1	2	3	4	5	6	7	8	9
ARUNACHAL PRADESH								
West Kameng	Bomdila Town#	4.17	21.81	15.26	62.93	S		
Lower Subansiri	Ziro Town*	14.17	17.8	14.51	67.69	S		
Lower Subansiri	Naharlagun Town**	5.16	17.56	21.46	60.97	S		
Lower Subansiri	Itanagar Town**	4.66	24.42	9.26	66.32	S		
West Siang	Along Town#	9.17	14.79	16.97	68.24	S		
East Siang	Pasighat Town#	12.86	24.77	20.07	55.17	S		
Dibang Valley	Roing Town*	6.36	16.43	25.71	57.86	S		
Lohit	Tezu Town#	3.62	20.98	19.07	59.94	S		
Lohit	Namsai Town*	4.39	55.59	16.68	27.73	M		
Tirap	Khonsa Town*	1.36	18.84	14.49	66.67	S		
MANIPUR								
Churachandpur	Churachandpur (C.T.)#	40.9	25.02	18.04	56.94	S		
Chandel	Moreh (NAC)**	31.85	12.08	73.79	14.13	T		
Thoubal	Thoubal (M)#	64.61	41.79	9.15	49.05	S		
Thoubal	Yairipok (NAC)**	67.7	32.23	10.47	57.3	S		
Thoubal	Sikhong Sekmai (NAC)**	68.8	56.48	22.24	21.28	M		
Thoubal	Wangjing (NAC)**	73.9	34.26	24.16	41.58	S		
Thoubal	Heirok (NAC)**	83.46	21.82	20	58.18	S		
Thoubal	Kakching (M)	68.45	41.03	19.17	39.8	M		
Thoubal	Kakching Khunou (NAC)*	77.12	44.2	14.58	41.22	M		
Thoubal	Sugnu (NAC)**	75.8	30.15	29.12	40.72	S		
Thoubal	Samurou (Part) (NAC)**	52.71	50.51	5.32	44.17	M		
Thoubal	Lilong (Thoubal) (Part) (NAC)	58.8	35.5	10.4	54.1	S		
Bishnupur	Oinam (NAC)**	74.75	46.46	9.97	43.57	M		
Bishnupur	Bishnupur (M)#	48.34	37.94	26.66	35.4	M		
Bishnupur	Ningthoukhong (NAC)**	50.27	52.08	13.28	34.64	M		
Bishnupur	Moirang (M) #	55.62	54	17.26	28.74	M		
Bishnupur	Kumbi (NAC)**	76.89	46.67	12.65	40.68	M		
Bishnupur	Kwakta (NAC)*	79.27	38.19	23.9	37.91	M		

(Condt.)

1	2	3	4	5	6	7	8	9
Bishnupur	Nambol (Part) (M)#	58.31	52.94	11.09	35.97	M		
Imphal	Andro (NAC)*	90.94	35.96	11.24	52.81	S		
Imphal	Lamlai (NAC)*	76.88	27.6	22.94	49.46	S		
Imphal	Sekmai Bazar (NAC)**	65.72	21.46	28.34	50.2	S		
Imphal	Lamsang (NAC)**	74.15	37.05	18.53	44.42	S		
Imphal	Lamjaotongba (CT)*	12.55	44.14	23	32.85	M		
Imphal	Lilong (Imphal West) (NAC)	35.41	49.5	12.4	38.09	M		
Imphal	Wangoi (NAC)**	65.3	56.32	11.1	32.58	M		
Imphal	Thonghong Laxmi Bazar	70.54	54.66	10.7	34.64	M		
Imphal	Mayang Imphal (NAC)**	72.49	55.25	14.7	33.05	M		
Imphal	Jiribam (M)**	20.58	28.77	24.9	46.33	S		
Imphal	Samurou (Part) (NAC)**	59.88	28.87	20.91	50.21	S		
Imphal	Nambol (Part) (M)#	72.95	34.06	12.38	53.56	S		
Imphal	Lilong (Thoubal) (Part) (NAC)	76.1	25	7.5	67.5	S		
Imphal	Imphal U.A.	3.1	28.83	25.09	46.08	S		
Imphal	(A) Imphal (M)	3.05	28.59	25.05	46.36	S	M	M
Imphal	(B) Bijoy Govinda	5.06	38.5	26.72	34.79	M		
Imphal	(i) Bijoy Govinda (CT)	1.92	34.12	30.83	35.05	S		
Imphal	(ii) Takyel (OG)	15.02	54.51	11.65	33.83	S	S	S
MEGHALAYA								
Jaintia Hills	Jowai	2	12.11	27.25	60.63	S	S	S
East Khasi Hills	Cherra Punjee**	2.13	46.56	19.54	33.9	M		
East Khasi Hills	Shillong U.A.	3.08	16.86	28.06	55.08	S		
East Khasi Hills	Shillong Municipality	0.51	17.51	29.39	53.1	S	S	S
East Khasi Hills	Shillong Cantonment	0.95	14.59	26.32	59.09	S	S	S
East Khasi Hills	Mawlai	17.48	17.64	26.49	55.87	S	S	S
East Khasi Hills	Nongthymmai	2.19	13.22	22.64	64.14	S	S	S
East Khasi Hills	Pynthor Umkhrah	2.9	16.86	30.14	53	S		
East Khasi Hills	Madanrting	3.77	19.06	26.27	54.67	S		
West Khasi Hills	Nongstoin**	32.49	20.91	20.84	58.24	S		
East Garo Hills	William Nagar**	39.06	20.21	14.11	65.68	S		
West Garo Hills	Tura	10.53	16.96	26.29	56.76	S	S	S
West Garo Hills	Baghmara**	21.61	22.52	29.19	48.29	S		

(Condt.)

1	2	3	4	5	6	7	8	9
MIZORAM								
Aizawl	Zawlnuam	65.62	12.25	23.61	64.14	S		
Aizawl	Mamit*	75.33	17.68	15.04	67.28	S		
Aizawl	Lengpui*	83.14	14.62	22.31	63.08	S		
Aizawl	Sairang*	64.1	27.36	19.52	53.12	S		
Aizawl	Vairengte*	61.25	28.1	13.69	58.21	S		
Aizawl	Bairabi*	81.58	24.08	13.09	62.83	S		
Aizawl	Kolasib**	55.17	18.87	21.93	59.2	S		
Aizawl	North Kawnpui*	77.84	11.38	31.95	56.67	S		
Aizawl	Darlawan*	72.03	13.07	20.26	66.67	S		
Aizawl	Thenzawl*	74.93	36.97	14.37	48.66	S		
Aizawl	Serchhip**	69.84	17.3	17.66	65.04	S		
Aizawl	Saitual*	76.18	19.18	25.34	55.48	S		
Aizawl	Khawzawl*	78.28	11.9	19.05	69.05	S		
Aizawl	Khawhai*90.4		9.47	15.79	74.74	S		
Aizawl	Biate*	80.48	7.65	10	82.35	S		
Aizawl	Champhai**	69.37	12.3	26.01	61.69	S		
Aizawl	North Vanlaiphai*	70.89	7.85	14.2	77.95	S		
Aizawl	Aizawl	13.33	21.59	23.55	54.86	S	S	S
Lunglei	Hnathian	65.45	7.18	19.78	73.04	S		
Lunglei	Lungle#	42.28	12.64	13.27	74.09	S		
Lunglei	Tlabung*	43.89	5	22.1	72.9	S		
Chhimtuipui	Saiha	38.25	11.36	17.09	71.54	S		
NAGALAND								
Kohima	Kohima	6.33	11.6	11.8	76.59	S	S	S
Kohima	Dimapur	7.64	21.62	43.2	35.17	T	T	S
Kohima	Chumukedima*	14.92	11.93	11.32	76.14	S		
Phek	Phek*	17.78	14.52	8.25	77.23	S		
Zunheboto	Zunheboto**	18.6	12.26	22.89	64.85	S		
Wokha	Wokha**	11.52	18.65	15.71	65.64	S		
Mokokchung	Mokokochung	10.8	16.98	25.71	57.31	S	S	S
Tuensang	Tuensang**	19.35	10.29	16.2	73.51	S		
Mon	Mon**	20.29	11.9	7.68	80.42	S		
TRIPURA								
West Tripura	Khowai N.A.	14.98	11.04	32.32	56.64	S	S	S
West Tripura	Teliamura N.A.*	30.28	22.92	38.48	38.6	S		
West Tripura	Jogendranagar C.T.*	7.09	27.92	40.71	31.37	T		
West Tripura	Gandhigram c.T.*	17.98	31.25	19.87	48.88	S		
West Tripura	Singarbil C.T.*	32	14.11	34.08	51.81	S		
West Tripura	Barjala C.T.*	25.64	28.78	22.85	48.37	S		
West Tripura	Pratapgarh C.T	3.36	23.81	42.45	33.74	T		
West Tripura	Badharghat C.T.*	8.94	32.59	26.07	41.34	S		
West Tripura	Sonamura N.A.**	22.33	12.9	34.43	52.67	S		

(Condt.)

1	2	3	4	5	6	7	8	9
West Tripura	Agartala (M)	1.33	12.05	29.07	58.88	S	S	S
North Tripura	Dharmanagar N.A.*	5.28	13.9	43.17	42.94	T	S	S
North Tripura	Kailasahar N.A.	8.41	7.6	28.32	64.08	S		
North Tripura	Kamarghat N.A*	34.29	19.57	30.09	50.34	S		
North Tripura	Kamalpur N.A.**	13.44	6.85	24.11	69.05	S		
South Tripura	Udaipur N.A.	8.99	12.56	30.28	57.16	S		
South Tripura	Amarpur N.A.**	16.41	13.65	28.92	57.43	S		
South Tripura	Belonia N.A.	7.85	10.22	31.93	57.85	S	S	S
South Tripura	Sabroom N.A.**	15.53	7.36	19.16	73.48	S		

Source : Chatterjee and Giri (2001).

Note : as in Table A1.1

2

Urban Labour Market and Informal Sector: A Study on North-East India

Shyamalendu Chatterjee

1. Introduction

This chapter mainly focuses on the urban labour market and informal sector in North-East India. It is a comparative study between the six states in North-East India (We exclude Assam only because Assam needs a separate study). The discussion is divided into four sections. In *Section one,* we discuss the term 'informal sector' used in different economic and social literatures. *Section two* discusses some important features of the urban labour market in North-East India. *Section Three* discusses the type of activities and changing occupational structure that takes place in the informal urban labour market and finally *Section Four* is the concluding section.

Concept of 'Informal Sector'

India is a vast country having a population of billion of which nearly 400 millions are workers. Out of the total workforce, nearly 80 per cent belong to the rural sector and the rest is the urban workforce. According to one estimate, in India, workers in the informal sector accounts for 90 per cent of the total workforce. The term 'informal' *per se,* denotes the informal nature of work in the activity concerned, irrespective of the actual number of workers employed, and irrespective of whether it is within the purview of the requirements for registration. Some studies done in India restrict the informal sector to enterprises employing less than 10 persons. The term informal sector or unorganised sector is broad enough to allow for the following characteristics in its definition (ILO, 1972; Hart, 1973; Emmerji, 1974; Mazumdar, 1976; Merrick, 1976):

a) Ease to entry,
b) Family ownership of enterprises,
c) Small scale of operation,
d) Reliance on indigenous resources,
e) Labour-intensive and adopted technology,
f) Skills acquired outside the formal school system,
g) Unregulated and competitive markets.

In view of the diversity in these characteristics, there is no such thing as a conclusive definition for the informal sector or unorganised sector. Its definition tends to vary from study to study, depending upon data availability. Various terms such as unorganised, traditional, informal or subsistence have been used frequently for analysing this sector. The ILO-UNDP Employment Mission to Kenya (1972) adopted the term 'informal sector' for analysing the employment situation and for working out a strategy in Kenya. In our discussion, we use the term 'informal sector' and 'unorganised sector' in same connotation.

The first National Commission on Labour, under the Chairmanship of justice Gajendragadkar, defined the unorganised sector as that part of the workforce "who have not been able to organise in pursuit of a common objective because of constraints such as (a) casual nature of employment, (b) ignorance and illiteracy, (c) small size of establishments with low capital investment per person employed, (d) scattered nature of establishments, and (e) superior strength of the employer operating singly or in combination."

The National Commission on Self-Employed Women, set up in 1987 under the Chairpersonship of Smt. Ela R. Bhatt, included in their terms of reference, the women workers in the unorganised sector. This report characterised the unorganised sector as one in which women "do arduous work as wage earners, piece-rate workers, casual labour and paid and unpaid family labour." The report also observed that "the unorganised sector is characterised by a high incidence of casual labour mostly doing intermittent jobs at extremely low wages or doing their own account work at very uneconomical returns. There is a total lack of job security and social security benefits."

The 15th International Conference of Labour Statisticians was held in January 1993 at Geneva and the concept and definition of the informal sector adopted in its resolution is presented below in brief:

a) Informal sector may be broadly characterised as consisting of units engaged in the production of goods or services with the primary objective of generating employment and incomes to the persons concerned. These units typically operate at low level organisation, with little or no division between labour and capital as factors of production on a small scale. Labour relations, where they exist, are based mostly on casual employment, kinship, or personal or social relations rather than contractual arrangements with formal guarantees.

b) The production units in informal sector have characteristic features of household enterprises. The owners of these production units have to raise the necessary finance at their own risk and are personally liable, without limit, for any debts or obligation incurred in the production process. Expenditure for production is often indistinguishable for the business and household purpose. The fixed and other assets used do not belong to the production units as such but to their owners.

c) Activities performed by production units of the informal sector are not necessarily performed with the deliberate intention of evading the payment of taxes, social security contributions, infringing labour or other legislation or administrative provisions.

The National Council for Applied Economic Research (NCAER) and Self-Employed Women's Association (SEWA) conducted a joint workshop on the subject of defining the informal sector in March-April 1997. According to them, the informal sector included all workers in informal enterprises, some workers in formal enterprises, self-employed workers, and those doing contract work for informal or formal sector enterprises and contractors.

Salient Features of the Urban Labour Market in North-East India

North-East India comprises of: a) Arunachal Pradesh, b) Assam, c) Manipur, d) Meghalaya, e) Mizoram, f) Nagaland and g) Tripura. This region is mostly hilly (70 per cent) and it is connected with the rest of India only through a narrow corridor in North Bengal. This region is of strategic importance for the country on account of the fact that nearly 90 per cent of its borders form India's international boundaries. The region is marked by uneven spatial distribution of population (Table 2.1) The population density is highest in Assam (340 per sq. km.) and lowest in Arunachal Pradesh (13 per sq. km.). According to 2001 census data, total population in North-East India is 3.85 crores (3.75 per cent of the total population in India) and only 12 per cent of this are urban population.

Table 2.1
Population density in North-East India (per sq. km.)

Sate	Population density
Assam	340
Tripura	304
Nagaland	120
Manipur	107
Meghalaya	103
Mizoram	42
Arunachal Pradesh	13

Source: Census of India, 2001.

Work participation rate (WPR) in the Urban labour market in the six states in North-East India varies widely where Mizoram, Manipur and Tripura show a rising trend; and Nagaland and Meghalaya show a marginal decline but Arunachal Pradesh shows a larger fall over the last decade. It is important to note that WPR in all these six states (except Tripura) is substantially greater than all India average. If we rank the six states in North-East India on the basis of WPR, a change is observed in ranking among the six states during 1991-2001. In 1991, Manipur was ranked 5th among the six states but in 2001 it comes at 2nd position. Meghalaya was in 3rd position in 1991 but in 2001, it comes down to 5th position. Tripura is ranked lowest among these six states but there was a substantial rise in WPR in Tripura during the last decade (Table 2.2)

Table 2.2
Ranking of States by percentage of working population total population/urban

Rank in 2001	State	Work Participation rate 2001	Work Participation rate 1991	Rank in 1991
	India	39.26	37.46	
3	Arunachal Pradesh	43.97	46.24	2
2	Manipur	44.79	42.18	5
5	Meghalaya	41.47	42.67	3
1	Mizoram	52.70	48.91	1
4	Nagaland	42.74	42.68	4
6	Tripura	36.29	31.14	6

Source: Census of India, 2001.

The rate of urbanisation is also widely varied among these six states of North-east India. The rate of urbanisation is comparatively higher in Mizoram and Manipur where percentage of the urban population is much larger than other four states. The share of the urban workforce in total workforce is also unevenly distributed. The share of urban workers in total workers is largest in Mizoram; followed by Manipur. But a higher degree of marginalisation has taken place in the urban labourforce in Manipur and Mizoram (Table 2.3). Majority of the urban working population are engaged in "Other" industrial activities. In Manipur only, household industry plays an important role in providing employment to the urban workers. It is also important to note that in Mizoram and Manipur, urban workers have a strong linkage with agricultural sector. Agriculture provides a substantial amount of employment to the urban workers in Mizoram and Manipur (Table 2.4)

Table 2.3
Distribution of *urban* population, workers and marginal workers in North-East India (%)

State	Share or urban workers in total workers	Share of marginal workers in total urban workers	Share of urban population in total population
Arunachal Pradesh	15.80	7.7	
Manipur	20.85	26.39	24.12
Meghalaya	13.60	12.80	19.63
Mizoram	45.17	23.81	49.50
Nagaland	13.25	9.54	17.74
Tripura	15.16	7.13	17.02

Source: Census of India, 2001.

Table 2.4

Distribution of Urban total workers (main+marginal) in different industrial activities (%)

State	Cultivators			Agricultural Labour			Household Industry Workers			Other Workers		
	P	M	F	P	M	F	P	M	F	P	M	F
Arunachal Pradesh	6.13	3.44	15.44	1.62	1.24	2.93	1.59	1.39	2.26	90.66	93.93	79.37
Manipur	17.87	20.92	13.62	9.62	7.37	12.74	12.90	4.85	24.13	59.61	66.86	49.51
Meghalaya	5.46	4.24	7.91	4.92	3.55	7.70	1.40	1.26	1.69	88.22	90.94	82.70
Mizoram	24.92	21.78	29.42	8.21	6.57	10.58	2.08	1.66	2.68	64.80	69.99	57.34
Nagaland	5.84	3.44	14.93	0.09	0.53	2.31	2.99	1.80	7.52	90.27	94.23	75.24
Tripura	1.58	1.82	0.48	1.97	2.04	1.66	1.77	1.10	4.74	94.68	95.03	93.12

Source: Census of India, 2001.

Findings from National Sample Survey (55th round/July 1999 to June 2000) data also show that work force participation rate (according to the principal status) in urban labour market is comparatively higher in Mizoram (35.1 per cent); followed by Meghalaya (29.6 per cent) and Manipur (29.1 per cent). It is mainly due to the higher participation of women work force in the urban labour market. Women play an important role in the urban labour market of North-East India. Women work force participation rate, particularly in Mizoram (nearly 25 per cent of the urban female population are employed according to principal usual status) and in Meghalaya (nearly 19.6 per cent of the urban female population are employed to principal usual status) is much higher than other four states. It is important to note that male work force participation rate is highest in Tripura among these six states but female work force participation in Tripura is lowest. Table 2.5 shows the distribution of the employed persons in six state according to principal usual status.

Table 2.5

Employed persons per 1000 population according to principal usual status by sex and residence: employed persons per 1000 population [urban]

State	Male	Female	Persons
Arunachal Pradesh	399	100	267
Manipur	436	142	291
Meghalaya	393	196	296
Mizoram	460	246	351
Nagaland	391	158	285
Tripura	490	72	291

Source: NSS Report No. 455 Employment & Unemployment in India, 1999-2000, Key results, p.17.

Note

a) The number of persons/person-days employed per thousand persons/person-day is referred to as the work-force participation rate (WFPR) or the worker-population ratio (WPR).

b) Due to the longer reference period the usual status "Work Force Participation Rates" are expected to be more stable. The usual activity status relates to the activity status of a person during the reference period of 365 days preceding to the date of survey. The activity status on which a person spent relatively longer time (i.e. major time criterion) during the 365 days preceding the date of survey is considered as the principal usual activity status of the person.

Table 2.4 shows in these six states, a high degree of concentration of urban workers in 'others' activities. But till now, 2001 census data do not give further break-up of the 'others' activities. NSS report (Report No. 455) gives us the classification of urban employment in different industrial activities. It is observed that in the urban labour market, tertiary sector rather than secondary sector plays the most important role in employment generation. Manufacturing plays an insignificant role in this regard. Government also (particularly in Nagaland, Meghalaya and Tripura) plays an important supporting role in employment generatin in the urban labour market. But it requires to mention that Government's role in Mizoram and Manipur is comparatively low in employment generation.

Table 2.6 shows share of employment of the urban workers in the tertiary sector. It is normally expected that more employment in urban tertiary sector simply mean a significant presence of *informal activities* in the urban labour market.

Table 2.6
Distribution of urban employment in tertiary sector in the six states: (per '000 distribution)

State	Trade, hotel & restaurant	Transport etc.	Financial business activities etc.	Public administration, education commercial services etc.	Total
Arunachal Pradesh (4)	335	10	9	425	779
Manipur (83)	203	38	13	349	603
Meghalaya (38)	222	48	9	563	842
Mizoram (38)	179	30	21	324	554
Nagaland (48)	110	4	22	695	831
Tripura (37)	242	49	28	574	893

Source: NSS Report No. 455 "Employment & Unemployment in India", 1999-2000, p. A-30.

Note: Figure in parentheses shows the per 1000 distribution of usually working persons in the principal status by broad industry division in manufacturing.

Unemployment and Underemployment in the Urban Labour Market

The unemployment rate is comparatively low in urban population of North-East India rather underemployment that exists to a greater extent among them. The working population are underutilised and seeking more work to supplement their income.

There is a wide variation in the level of urban unemployment in these six states. Among these six states, Arunachal Pradesh has reported lowest level of unemployment (8 per thousand) and Nagaland has reported highest level of unemployment in the urban area (30 per thousand).

Table 2.7 persents the proportion of unemployed (days) per 1000 persons (days) in the urban labour market for these six small states. This table presents the proportion of unemployed based on usual status.

Table 2.7

Number of unemployed per 1000 persons according to usual principal status by sex and residence status during 1999-2000

	No. of unemployed persons		[urban]
State	**Male**	**Female**	**Persons**
Arunachal Pradesh	7	10	8
Manipur	35	16	26
Meghalaya	14	14	14
Mizoram	21	6	14
Nagaland	40	19	30
Tripura	28	7	18

Source: NSS Report No. 455 "Employment & Unemployment in India", 1999-2000, p. 32.

Note: Usual status unemployed consists of persons who have reported unemployment for a relatively longer time during the reference period of one year. However it is possible that some of them had some marginal employment for some short period of time.

The underemployment is comparatively high in Nagaland and low in Meghalaya and Tripura (Table 2.8).

During the year (1999-2000), in the stated age-group (15 years and above), about 5.3 per cent of usually employed urban persons had sought or were available for additional work in Nagaland.

The main reported reason for their seeking or being available for additional work was to supplement their income. The other reason was not enough work.

Table 2.8
Number of usually working (principal) persons (15 years & above), who sought or were available for additional work per 1000 usually working (principal) persons (15 year & above) for each sex during 1999-2000

State	Male	Female	Persons
Arunachal Pradesh	37	5	32
Manipur	44	61	49
Meghalaya	17	12	15
Mizoram	34	45	38
Nagaland	53	53	53
Tripura	15	37	17

Source : NSS Report No. 455 "Employment & Unemployment in India", 1999-2000, p. 41

Note: Underemployment means seeking or available for additional work

Informal Sector and Urban Labour Market

Size of the Urban Informal Labour Market

Informal sector in these six states absorbs a substantial amount of urban workforce. Majority of the workers are engaged in trading and repairing services. The urban informal labour market is characterised by different categories of workers like own account workers, hired labourers and own account enterprises take an important role in employment generation (Table 2.9). The estimated size of the urban informal workforce (non-agricultural workers) in Tripura, Manipur and Meghalaya is relatively larger than Mizoram, Nagaland and Arunachal Pradesh. In Manipur and Tripura, own account workers take important role in running the informal units. Own account enterprise requires low capital and low skill but generate a sustainable income for the household. The annual emolument per hired worker is higher in own account enterprises than establishments in four states (except Meghalaya and Mizoram) [see Table 2.13].

Table 2.9
Total estimated Number of Urban Informal Workers engaged in different type of Enterprises.

State/U.T.	Estimated Number of Urban Workers (in '000)		
	OAE	Establishment	All Enterprises
Arunachal Pradesh	4.33	3.45	7.77
Manipur	39.55	21.05	60.56
Meghalaya	9.83	27.36	37.18
Mizoram	12.29	9.36	21.66
Nagaland	9.85	8.19	18.04
Tripura	38.47	32.98	71.45

Source: NSS 55th Round (July 1999-June 2000).

Note: **Enterprise:** An enterprise is an undertaking which is engaged in the production and/or distribution of some goods and/or services meant mainly for the purpose of sale, whether fully or partly. An enterprise may be owned and operated by a single household or by several households joint, or by an institutional body.

Own account enterprises (OAE): An own account enterprise is an undertaking run by household labour, usually without any hired worker employed on a 'fairly regular basis'. 'Fairly regular basis' means the major part of the period of operation(s) of the enterprise during the last 365 days.

Establishment: Those enterprises, which have got at least one hired worker on a 'fairly regular basis' are called establishments.

Nature and Type of Informal Activities in the Urban Labour Market

The previous discussion in *Section 1 (Table 2.6)* shows greater role and importance of tertiary sector in employment generation in the urban labour market of North-East India. Greater role and importance of tertiary sector in urban employment generation indicates a sizeable portion of the workforce employed in the urban informal sector. Informal activities in the urban labour market in North-East India are concentrated mainly in the trading and repairing services, construction, hotels and restaurants and manufacturing. There are ten important urban informal activities identified by NSS survey where the urban informal workers of these six states are mainly engaged. Table 2.10 listed these ten informal activities with their tabulation category.

Table 2.10
Name of the Informal Activities and their Tabulation Categories

Activity	Tabulation Category
1. Manufacturing	D
2. Construction	F
3. Trading and Repairing Services	G
4. Hotels and Restaurants	H
5. Transport, Storage & Communication	I
6. Financial Intermediation	J
7. Real estate, renting & business activities	K
8. Education	M
9. Health & social work	N
10. Other community, social and personal service acivities	O

Source: NSS 55th Round, 'Informal Sector in India' 1999-2000/salient features; p. 21.

The size of the urban informal sector is comparatively largest in Tripura and Manipur whereas this size is smallest in Arunachal Pradesh. The gender distribution of urban informal workers shows that the share of female urban informal workers in total workers is comparatively large in Manipur and Mizoram. More urban women in these two states are participating in informal activities.

The activities of the urban informal workers in the labour market are unevenly distributed. NSS study has classified ten informal activities (see Table 2.10) but in all these six states informal workers are concentrated in few activities. In construction activity, the size is very small in Arunachal Pradesh and Nagaland. In financial intermediation, the size is negligible in all the six states. But for all these six states it has been observed that the urban informal workers are mainly concentrated in trading and repairing services.

The other important activities that have some role in employment generation in the urban informal labour market are manufacturing (important for Tripura, Manipur, Mizoram), hotels and restaurants (important for Meghalaya), education (important for Tripura) and transport, storage and communication (significant for Tripura only).

The women informal workers are mainly engaged in trading and services. But in Manipur, more than 50 per cent of the informal women workers are engaged in manufacturing activities. In Mizoram also, manufacturing and in Meghalaya and Tripura, hotels and restaurants provide employment to the women informal workers. Table 2.11 shows the size and distribution of male and female urban informal workers in different activities.

Table 2.11
State-wise Distribution of Estimated Number of Urban Workers by Tabulation Category

Tabulation Category	Arunachal Pradesh	Manipur	Meghalaya	Mizoram	Nagaland	Tripura
D (Manufacturing)						
Male	606	8440	3333	3251	2153	8663
Female	008	11676	394	1654	666	818
Persons	614	20290	3727	4905	2819	9481
F (Construction)						
Male	0	5902	4188	326	19	596
Female	0	61	55	6	0	0
Persons	0	5963	4243	332	19	596
G (Trading and repairing services)						
Male	5234	12974	14417	6616	6956	31263
Female	232	7316	3378	5399	2631	642
Persons	5466	20290	17795	12015	9587	31905
H (Hotels and restaurants)						
Male	865	2793	4191	472	1189	3802
Female	80	2218	2319	1201	517	931
Persons	945	5011	6510	1673	1706	4733
I (Transport, storage & communication)						
Male	113	3862	1932	1639	750	7912
Female	5	150	182	86	84	30
Persons	118	4012	2114	1725	834	7942
J (Financial intermediation)						
Male	48	0	0	0	0	197
Female	0	24	0	0	0	0
Persons	48	24	0	0	0	197
K (Real estate, renting & business activities)						
Male	88	1036	209	364	143	3054
Female	0	142	0	0	0	0
Persons	88	1178	209	364	143	3054
M (Education)						
Male	0	1138	1056	65	1203	7395
Female	53	842	820	68	803	188
Persons	53	1980	1876	123	2004	7583
N (Health & social work)						
Male	16	49	204	49	14	1327
Female	0	24	36	37	86	268
Persons	16	73	240	86	100	1595
O (Other community, social and personal activities/excluding domestic services)						
Male	390	1786	303	279	689	3864
Female	32	123	164	145	140	501
Persons	422	1909	467	424	829	4365
Total						
Male	7361	37981	29834	13060	13114	68074
Female	412	22578	7348	8596	4927	3376
Persons	7773	60559	37182	21656	18041	71450

Source: NSS 55th Round: "Informal Sector in India" 1999-2000, pp. A-24, A-25, A-26.

Productivity and Wage of the Workers and Growth of the Enterprises in Informal Sector

The annual value added by the informal urban workers shows their contribution to the economy. The estimated annual value added per worker is comparatively high in Arunachal Pradesh and Mizoram. The value of marginal productivity of the urban informal workers in *Establishments* is much higher in Arunachal Pradesh (estimated annual value added per worker is Rs. 183837 in establishments) and Mizoram (estimated annual value added per worker is Rs. 73075 in establishments). In *Own account enterprises* also, value of marginal productivity per worker in urban area is largest in Mizoram and Arunachal Pradesh (Table 2.12).

Now the question is what type of activities in *Establishments* and in *Own account enterprises* that generate high annual value in Arunachal Pradesh and Mizoram.

In Mizoram, construction activities (F /estimated annual value added per worker is Rs. 115182/-) and in Arunachal Pradesh, the activities in financial intermediation (J / estimated annual value added per worker is Rs.7959867/) add largest annual value per worker in the *establishments* sector.

In *own account enterprises,* the important activities in Mizoram are construction (F / estimated annual value added per worker is Rs. 187838/) and health and social work (N / estimated annual value added per worker is Rs. 117312/) and in Arunachal Pradesh, these are trading and repairing services (G / estimated annual value added per worker is Rs. 65422/) and transport, storage and communication (I / estimated annual value added per worker is Rs. 49147).

But these activities generate low employment in the urban informal labour market of these two states.

In Mizoram, the estimated number of urban informal workers engaged in construction activities are only 1.53 per cent of the total workers engaged in all activities and the number of workers engaged in health and social work is only

0.40 per cent of the total urban informal workers engaged in all activities.

In Arunachal Pradesh, only 0.62 per cent of the total workers are engaged in financial intermediation.

In these two states, the higher annual value added per worker entirely depends on the nature, quality and price of the commodity produced. Construction of high-rise building adds more value in the economy but construction workers are not benefited much. The extent of market is limited within the state for both the activities-construction work and financial intermediation.

Now among these ten activities, trade and repairing services absorb more informal urban workers in these two states. It is observed that in Arunachal Pradesh, 70.32 per cent of the total urban informal workers are engaged in trade and repairing services and in Mizoram 55.48 per cent of the total urban informal workers are engaged in trade and repairing services. But the estimated annual value added per worker is comparatively low in these two activities. This indicates general low productivity of the urban informal workers in the labour market.

Now in these enterprises, the emoluments per hired worker are different for different states. The emolument of the hired workers widely varies between the states. Since the workers are not unionised, the wage rate entirely depends on the owner of the enterprise, market demand of the product and the type and quality of the commodity produced. The state intervention is minimum in wage fixation. It is observed that informal enterprises in Tripura and Manipur employ more hired workers and growth of these enterprises are much higher than other four states. The size of the estimated hired labour force is largest in Manipur and Tripura but estimated annual emoluments in *Establishments* are much lower in Tripura and Manipur (Table 2.13). Although left trade unionism is more pronounced in Tripura, comparatively lower annual emoluments in *Establishments* probably indicates

Table 2.12

Estimated Annual Value Added per worker by Tabulation Category (in rupees)/Urban

State/U.T.	Tabulation Category									
Arunachal Pradesh	D	F	G	H	I	J	K	M	N	O	All
OAE	32724	--	65422	39337	49147	--	--	--	29400	40271	60097
Establishments	73827	--	87014	53917	71767	7959867	25907	3432	--	61307	183837
All enterprises	44500	--	73079	52425	58400	7959867	25907	3432	29400	52464	114973
Manipur	D	F	G	H	I	J	K	M	N	O	All
OAE	13272	83896	30266	20744	35922	55200	22392	18890	75576	25897	24948
Establishments	25311	43771	28165	26482	46650	--	68163	4737	55500	42282	31696
All enterprises	17087	50483	29916	22904	40243	55200	35009	7335	62192	33125	27294
Meghalaya	D	F	G	H	I	J	K	M	N	O	All
OAE	24878	29880	43331	23610	55371	--	--	--	36274	19170	40136
Establishments	25365	35932	35982	29425	53278	--	23669	56983	109153	20788	36172
All enterprises	25275	35906	39117	28554	53629	--	23669	56983	85903	20373	37220
Mizoram	D	F	G	H	I	J	K	M	N	O	All
OAE	49594	187838	74588	45067	80503	--	34170	109800	117312	41280	69335

(Condt.)

	D	F	G	H	I	J	K	M	N	O	All
Establishments	57808	115182	100419	47293	55815	--	88800	42508	83040	35585	73075
All enterprises	54883	138353	82031	46398	65615	--	40082	47013	95041	37837	70952
Nagaland	D	F	G	H	I	J	K	M	N	O	All
OAE	19219	30915	26475	17836	32182	--	15799	15615	49146	26969	25576
Establishments	21149	--	35573	20000	109219	--	44048	44082	42848	23753	34931
All enterprises	20656	30915	28499	19101	68332	--	25229	43631	45849	25052	29822
Sikkim	D	F	G	H	I	J	K	M	N	O	All
OAE	26418	38502	30192	18598	96448	--	59620	43500	138516	26864	30775
Establishments	36587	--	39937	73110	59466	--	33720	23302	25514	26329	53189
All enterprises	33476	38502	34389	63455	74259	--	37148	26056	57801	26605	44204
Tripura	D	F	G	H	I	J	K	M	N	O	All
OAE	21849	86044	37662	14759	21826	14632	26613	17949	40630	15026	30722
Establishments	33984	103163	52041	22215	35389	--	38186	18283	53640	25770	36860
All enterprises	29301	92283	42746	18110	29296	14632	27380	18237	45484	19516	33555

Source: NSS 55th Round, 'Informal sector in India' 1999-2000, pp. A-70, A-73, A-76.

minimum bargaining power of the informal workers in Tripura (Table 2.13). In this state, there is no question of group benefits in own account enterprises and the group benefits in establishments enjoyed by hired workers is comparatively very low. It is also important to note that the estimated annual emoluments per hired worker in establishments is more in Mizoram and Arunachal Pradesh.

Table 2.13
Estimated Annual Emoluments per hired Worker (Rs.) in North-East India

State Estimated annual emoluments per hired worker (combined for all tabulation categories)

Urban	Salary	Group Benefits	Total		Estimated number of workers ('000)
Arunachal Pradesh					
OAE	20211	457	20668		4.33
Establishments	20380	50	20429		3.45
				Total =	7.78
Manipur					
OAE	25770	6814	32584		39.50
Establishments	16283	975	17259		21.05
				Total=	60.55
Meghalaya					
OAE	12320	0	12320		9.83
Establishments	17934	94	18028		27.36
				Total=	37.19
Mizoram					
OAE	18725	0	18725		12.29
Establishments	22026	538	22585		9.36
				Total=	21.65
Nagaland					
OAE	18142	0	18142		9.85
Establishments	18037	22	18059		8.19
				Total=	18.04
Tripura					
OAE	22135	0	22135		38.47
Establishments	11595	53	11648		32.98
				Total=	71.45

Source: NSS 55th round, 'Informal sector in India' 1999-2000 pp: A-115, A-118

Regarding growth and development of the informal enterprises, it is observed that the growth of the small units in the informal sector is stagnant; majority of the own account enterprises in Nagaland, Arunachal Pradesh, Meghalaya and Manipur show no growth. Nearly 62 per cent of the total own account enterprises in Arunachal Pradesh over the last three years (1996-1997 to 1999-2000) show no growth. In Nagaland, it is nearly 70 per cent and in Manipur this figure is 55 per cent and in Meghalaya it is 58 per cent. In Tripura, only 26 per cent of the total own account enterprises are stagnant over the last three years. Comparatively, higher growth is observed in establishments particularly in Tripura, Mizoram and Manipur (Table 2.14).

Conclusion

Work force participation in the urban labour market in North-East India is highly influenced by female participation. Women participation plays a dominant role in the urban labour market in North-East India. The urban workers are mainly engaged in tertiary sector. Manufacturing plays an insignificant role in employment generation. There are no heavy industries. Some large industries generally agro-based, forest-based and mineral-based have developed in these states. Most of the urban informal workers are engaged in trading and repairing services. Trading and repairing services do not add much value in the economy. A low wage, low skilled, low status workforce has developed in the urban labour market. In the urban labour market, own account enterprises and small establishments provide employment to the informal workers. The nature and type of activities in own account enterprises is different in different states and this difference generates a high degree of income differential among the own account workers. The type of ownership in own account enterprises and in establishments in these six states reveals that individual is the sole owner of the enterprise and over the years, most of these enterprises are stagnant. State Government should try to find out the reasons behind the higher rate of stagnancy in these small

Table 2.14

Distribution of Enterprises by Growth Status (From 1996-1997 to 1999-2000)

State/U.T.	Per 1000 distribution of enterprises by growth status/Urban					
	Expanding	Stagnant	Contracting	Operated less than 3 year	Not reported	Total
1	2	3	4	5	6	7
Arunachal Pradesh						
OAE	354	618	11	14	3	1000
Establishments	465	528	7	0	0	1000
Manipur						
OAE	373	553	67	7	0	1000
Establishments	516	375	87	22	0	1000
Meghalaya						
OAE	414	582	0	4	0	1000
Establishments	395	562	5	39	0	1000

(Condt.)

1	2	3	4	5	6	7
Mizoram						
OAE	545	385	45	20	5	1000
Establishments	742	179	39	19	22	1000
Nagaland						
OAE	252	697	36	13	3	1000
Establishments	448	477	52	12	12	1000
Tripura						
OAE	703	259	36	1	1	1000
Establishments	900	89	8	0	3	1000

Source: NSS 55th round, 'Informal sector in India' 1999-2000, pp. A-214, A-217.

Note: The results are based on the data collected during the NSS 55th round, (July-June 2000.

enterprises and provide appropriate training and necessary helps to the owners so that they can run their enterprises properly.

Social security measures for informal workers are absent in the state agenda. Only Tripura Government has introduced Assisted Scheme for Unorganised Workers (Asanghatita Shramik Sahayika Prakalpa) in 2001. This scheme covers all willing wage employed and self-employed workers between the age of 21 and 55 years in the unorganised sector and having an average family income of not more than Rs. 3500- per month. Each subscriber-worker will contribute a sum of Rs. 25/- per month and the State Government shall also contribute an equal matching grant. In the event of attainment of 55 years of age, the total amount along with interest will be paid to the worker. But there are some problems. This scheme assumes a permanent, continuous nature of informal work done by the workers. Normally the activity of an informal worker is not a permanent nature and the worker does not work throughout the whole year. Many informal activities are seasonal in nature. Now during the period of unemployment, who will pay his/her contribution? Again, an informal worker often changes his/her place of work. If an informal worker out-migrate to other states for a seasonal job or for any other kind of informal job then what happens to his/her contribution during the time of his/her absence? All these questions are unanswered. The scheme only says : An account will be under prolonged default if monthly contributions are not paid for six consecutive months. An account under prolonged default will stand revived when making adequate payments in one or more instalment subject to a maximum of six instalments makes the contributions up-to-date". State and Central Government should provide an umbrella during the period of no work. It is very difficult to continue an account for nearly more than thirty-five years by an illiterate, poverty ridden informal worker.

REFERENCES

1. Government of India: National Sample Survey, Report No. 455 'Employment and Unemployment in India, 1999-2000-key results'.
2. Government of India, Register General: Census of India 2001.
3. Government of India, 1969, First National Commission on Labour
4. Government of India, 2002, Second National Labour Commission, Vol.1, Chapter 7A, p. 4.
5. Hart K., 1973, "Informal Income opportunities and the structure of Urban Employment in Ghana", Journal of Modern African Studies, Vol. II, No.1, March, 1973.
6. International Labour Organization, 1972, "Employment, Income and Equality: A Strategy for Increasing Productive Employment in Kenya", ILO, Geneva.
7. Mazumdar, D., 1976, "The Urban Informal Sector", World Bank Working Paper, No. 211, July, 1976a.
8. Merrick, T. W., 1976, "Employment and Earnings in the informal sector in Brazil : The case of Belo Horizonte", Journal of Developing Areas, Vol. 10, No. 3, April, 1976.
9. National Sample Survey, 55th round, 'Informal Sector in India 1999-2000'.

3

Informal Sector In India's Northeast: Migration, Competition and Conflict Situations

Gurudas Das

North-Eastern Region (NER) of India, because of her peripheral location, has remained one of the least developed area in the country in terms of its resource utilisation, productive capacity and production structure[1]. Besides peripheral location, the preponderance of tribal population in four out of seven states that comprises the region[2] and substantial tribal component in the population structure of the other three states (Table -3.1), who are historically lagging behind in terms of their collective socio-economic transformation, has also contributed to the present state of backwardness of the region. Except Assam, Manipur and Tripura, centralised system of governance did not evolve out of internal social dynamics of the societies in Arunachal Pradesh, Meghalaya, Mizoram and Nagaland in the historical past. The superstructure of 'modern state' has been superimposed on them only after the independence of the country in 1947.

Table 3.1
Scheduled Tribe Population as Percentage of Total Population in North-Eastern States, 1991

States	Total	Rural	Urban
India*	8.08	10.08	2.32
Arunachal Pradesh	63.66	68.74	29.04
Assam	12.82	13.94	3.90
Manipur	34.41	43.48	10.53
Meghalaya	85.53	90.82	62.37
Mizoram	94.75	96.32	92.93
Nagaland	87.70	93.19	61.32
Tripura	30.95	35.94	3.34

*Excluding J & K, No Census during 1991.
Source: Census of India, 1991, Series I, Part II-B (iii).

Since then, these states have experienced speedy urbanisation[3]. However, except Assam, the process of urbanisation in the north-eastern states is not rooted in the structural change of their respective economy. It is rather the outcome of the expansion of administrative centres[4]. With the growth of urban pockets particularly centring around the state capitals and district headquarters, the informal sector has come into existence to cater the local demands for goods and services. As a result, the informal sector in north-east is of recent origin.

The term 'informal sector has various connotations. At conceptual level it is generally used to capture the multifarious economic activities that are undertaken outside the realm of 'formal'/'organised' sector. Neither there is a single indicator/or one set of criterion for the determination of its domain, nor there is complete unanimity among the scholars about its conceptual understanding[5]. However, the term is often used to mean the small-scale units engaged in the production and distribution of goods and services. Here, we shall employ the term in this wider sense.

The objective of this article is not to take up any concrete study of the informal sector of the urban areas of NER on the basis of any case study. Rather the idea is to make preliminary attempts, primarily based on impressions, to understand as to how the emerging competition in this sector is giving rise to conflict situations in the region. In fact, no systematic study has yet been done in this area. Although we shall be using some secondary data and make use of a few case studies undertaken for altogether different purposes, we shall basically depend on our impressionistic experiences in articulating the status of the informal sector in NER. As a result, this analysis will have little policy implications without empirical verifications of the trends articulated here.

Place of the Informal Sector in the Economy of NER

Except Assam, none of the north-eastern states has any large-scale industry. Whatever meager number of medium scale industrial units are there, these are mostly public sector units. As a result, organised private sector occupies a little space in the economies of hill states. The manufacturing base, albeit very weak, is almost fully depended on the small-scale units. However, manufacturing activities constitute only a microscopic segment of the informal sector which is characterised by the dominance of trading and service providing activities. Public sectors in these states also exhibit very weak manufacturing base. Mainly the government departments/offices constitute this sector. As a result, beyond government services, self-employment in small-scale enterprises and service providing activities are the only alternative avenues in these economies. In the absence of any significant organised private sector, one can consider the whole private sector as constituting the informal sector of the economy of NER.

The Structure of the Informal Sector

The informal sector in the capital towns of NER, viz., Itanagar (Arunachal Pradesh), Guwahati (Assam), Imphal (Manipur), Shillong (Meghalaya), Aizawl (Mizoram), Kohima (Nagaland) and Agartala (Tripura) is dominated by trading activities. Everywhere retail trading units constitute the principal component. In most cases these units are organised on the basis of single proprietorship and are concentrated in commercial areas of the towns. Next to trading comes service providers and transport operators. As has already been mentioned, the manufacturing activities come, perhaps, at the bottom due to weak linkages between the process of urbanisation and industrialisation which is very pronounced in all the capital towns in NER. The ownership, capital employment and age structures of the informal sector units in these towns and their implications in understanding the resilience and vibrancy of this sector can only be ascertained through detail field investigation.

The Role of Migration

It may be pointed out that state structure in Nagaland, Arunachal Pradesh, Meghalaya and Mizoram was created and the same was expanded in Manipur and Tripura only recently. This has fuelled the process of urbanisation in the respective state capitals which in turn has been catalytic for the growth of the informal sectors in them. The creation of state structure called for manpower acquainted with modalities of running the modern state machinery. Traditional tribal societies of NER were not equipped to supply this manpower. As a result, a large contingent of government employees and professionals from outside had to fill this void. This has resulted into the concentration of non-tribal population in the urban pockets of the tribal states of Arunachal Pradesh, Meghalaya, Mizoram and Nagaland. Migration has played by far the most important role for the urban growth in Tripura. A large-scale migration of the Bengalis from erstwhile East Pakistan into Tripura following the partition of the country has not only changed the population composition of the state in their favour, this has accelerated the process of urbanisation in Tripura in general and Agartala in particular.

Besides the expansion of administration, the initiation of various developmental schemes in the north-eastern states has also subsequently created many opportunities which in turn attracted people from outside as the local population was not ready to respond to them adequately. In fact, during the initial phase of development, while the tribal societies were undergoing social transformation from tradition to modernity, the migrant population has played the key role in every sphere of urban life.

The Census data also corroborate this phenomenon of predominance of migrants in the urban population of NER. For example, in 1971, the proportion of migrants (by place of birth) in the urban population of India was 39.3 per cent, whereas the said proportion was 79.6 per cent in Arunachal Pradesh, 71.7 per cent in Nagaland, 61.0 per cent in Mizoram, 52.8 per cent in Tripura, 50.8 per cent in Assam and 41.8 per cent in Meghalaya (Table 3.2). However, Manipur is the only state where the proportion of migrants in urban population was far lower than the national average[6].

Table 3.2
Percentage of Migrants (by Place of Birth) in Urban Population of the North Eastern States

State	Percentage of Migrants in Urban Population		
	1961	**1971**	**1981**
Arunachal Pradesh	-	79.6	64.6
Assam	55.0	50.8	NA
Manipur	13.1	15.0	10.9
Meghalaya	53.6	41.8	45.9
Mizoram	52.3	61.0	56.8
Nagaland	55.4	71.7	63.5
Tripura	59.7	52.8	41.8
India	44.8	39.3	38.3

Source: S.K. Sinha (1986), *Internal Migration in India*, 1961-81, pp. 37 & 39 as cited in Bhattacharjee (1995).

Data relating to percentage distribution of birth place urban migrants by type of movement reveal the following trends (Table 3.3).

i. Inter-state migration has played a significant role behind the growth of urban centres in Arunachal Pradesh, Meghalaya and Nagaland where the percentage of inter-state migrants far exceed than that of all India percentage.

ii. Migrants coming from outside India have been primarily important for the growth of urban population in Tripura. Their percentage to total birth place urban migrants was 85.5 in 1961, and then came down to 80.9 in 1971 and further declined to 70.3 in 1981. Thus, Tripura provides the sole instance where migrants from outside the country constitute the sizeable section of the urban population. Besides Tripura, cross-country migration also played no insignificant role behind the growth of urban population in Assam and Meghalaya particularly during the early three decades of Independence.

iii. In contrast to the five states of Arunachal Pradesh, Assam, Meghalaya, Nagaland and Tripura, growth of urban population in Manipur and Mizoram was primarily due to the internal migration of people. These two states stand in complete opposition to the general trends elsewhere in the region. Inter-state migration is strikingly very less in case of Mizoram.

Table 3.3
Percentage Distribution of Birth-Place Urban Migrants by Type of Movement in NE States

State	Year	Type of Movement				
		Within District	Inter District	Inter State	From Outside India	Total
Arunachal Pradesh	1961	-	-	-	-	-
	1971	18.0	2.3	56.5	32.2	100
	1981	17.1	6.2	65.5	11.2	100
Assam	1961	21.2	14.2	24.7	39.9	100
	1971	26.6	15.7	26.6	31.0	100
	1981	NA	NA	NA	NA	NA
Manipur	1961	51.4	-	29.7	18.9	100
	1971	60.0	9.2	23.9	6.9	100
	1981	-	-	-	-	-
Meghalaya	1961	26.8	18.9	22.0	32.3	100
	1971	27.6	0.7	45.4	26.3	100
	1981	34.8	8.6	45.5	11.1	100
Mizoram	1961	80.7	7.0	3.3	0.8	100
	1971	92.8	3.5	2.5	3.7	100
	1981	79.6	8.9	10.2	2.3	100
Nagaland	1961	47.2	4.2	32.8	15.8	100
	1971	21.6	6.2	59.5	12.8	100
	1981	25.3	27.2	43.1	4.4	100
Tripura	1961	8.6	-	5.9	85.5	100
	1971	7.7	4.2	7.2	80.9	100
	1981	11.6	8.5	9.6	70.3	100
India	1961	31.4	31.2	24.4	13.0	100
	1971	30.5	33.6	26.0	9.9	100
	1981	31.4	36.7	25.2	6.7	100

Source: S.K. Sinha (1986), *Internal Migration in India*, 1961-81, pp. 37 & 39 as cited in Bhattacharjee (1995).

As analysis of reason of immigration into urban areas from the place of last residence reveals (Table 3.4)

i. Economic motivation has been the prime reason for the immigration of the males from outside the urban areas of NER. More than 70 per cent of the male immigrants in Arunachal Pradesh are motivated by the reason of employment. The same for Tripura is 49 per cent, for Meghalaya, Nagaland and Mizoram it is 37.9, 33.8 and 21.0 per cent respectively.

ii. In contrast to other states of NER, proportion of economic immigrants is small in Manipur and Mizoram where shift of the family, marriage etc. act as prime motivators for migration.

iii. Female immigration, in some of the state, is significantly motivated by economic reason compared to their male counterparts.

Table 3.4
Distribution of Immigrants into Urban Areas of NE States by Reasons, 1981

State	Sex	Reasons				
		Employment	Education	Family Moved	Marriage	Other
Arunachal Pradesh	Male	70.6	4.1	21.9	0.4	3.0
	Female	6.9	0.3	54.8	32.5	5.5
Manipur	Male	25.0	2.6	39.3	1.5	31.6
	Female	1.2	0.8	23.0	58.7	16.3
Meghalaya	Male	37.9	14.1	21.3	2.9	23.8
	Female	8.2	12.8	40.3	19.3	19.4
Mizoram	Male	21.0	6.0	47.7	0.2	25.1
	Female	2.8	4.3	68.2	9.3	15.4
Nagaland	Male	33.8	12.2	15.0	0.3	38.7
	Female	10.1	15.7	45.5	13.1	15.6
Tripura	Male	49.1	6.0	36.0	0.9	8.0
	Female	9.1	1.7	47.0	31.3	10.9

Source: S.K. Sinha (1986), *Internal Migration in India*, 1961-81, pp. 37 & 39 as cited in Bhattacharjee (1995).

Note: In 1981, there was no Census in Assam.

Thus, Census data indicate that inter-state as well as cross-country migration has played an important role in the early phase of urbanisation in NER, save Manipur and Mizoram. As the urban economies of the region are dominated by the informal sector, it may safely be conjectured, in absence of any field survey based data, that migrant labour force is predominantly engaged in this sector. However, it has also been observed that proportion of migrants in the urban population of NER has been declined (Table 3.2) during 1971-81. This trend may be interpreted as an indication of faster pace of internal social change among the indigenous societies which is increasingly enabling them to replace the migrant labour force.

The Informal Manufacturing Sector

Case Study I

A decade back during December 1991 to January 1992, a sample survey of 55 small and tiny industrial units spread over Nahalagun and Itanagar was undertaken by this author in connection with a study to understand the dynamics of growth of entrepreneurs and industrial labour force in Arunachal Pradesh[7]. Out of these 55 units, four were under the public sector. Of the remaining 51 units, seven entrepreneurs were found to run two units each, 23 entrepreneurs were found to run one unit each and in 14 cases, entrepreneurs could not be contacted. Thus for 55 units, the size of the sample of entrepreneurs was reduced to 30.

The Entrepreneurs

Whatever small the sample size might be, this survey revealed the following interesting findings:

(i) Of these 30 entrepreneurs, 13 were tribal and the remaining 17 were non-tribals. While all the 17 non-tribal entrepreneurs were male, there were two females among the tribals. Of the tribal entrepreneurs, 12 belonged to Arunachal tribes and one to Assam tribe. Among the Arunachal tribal entrepreneurs, five belonged to Apa Tains, four to the Adis, two to the Nishis and one came from the Hill Miris. Among the non-tribal entrepreneurs, there were 8 Bengalis; 3 Assamese; 2 Punjabis; 2 Nepalis; 1 Bihari and 1 Marwari.

(ii) Except one Punjabi entrepreneur, none of the non-tribals had trading license of their own. All of them were running their units under the trading license issued to one tribal or another against an agreement of annul payment of a stipulated sum between the license-holder and actual entrepreneur.

(iii) Out of the 12 Arunachalee tribal entrepreneurs, 7 were reported to run their own units independently, in 3 cases partnership with non-tribals had been reported and in 2 cases tribal entrepreneurs were rumoured to have leased out their units to the non-tribals, no concrete evidence for which was, however, available.

(iv) In response to a question as to what did the entrepreneurs do before taking up the present occupation, 47 per cent of the respondents had reported themselves as workers. They used to work in the same line they were practicing at that time. Many of them worked at their respective hometowns and changed their work place for a number of times. They, thus, acquired skill in their respective fields and then moved on to Arunachal in search of higher earning. Even after coming to Arunachal many of them initially worked under private contractors and manufacturing units wherefrom they gradually managed to establish their own units. Twenty per cent of the respondent entrepreneurs revealed contract business as their previous occupation. Another 13 per cent came from other business and from government jobs. Only two entrepreneurs were found without any specific job in the past. It might be noted that all the entrepreneurs came from non-agricultural occupations and none had reported to have worked in agriculture.

(v) It was found that 60 per cent of the entrepreneurs had one or more other business in addition to the surveyed manufacturing units for which they were treated as entrepreneurs. All the Arunachalee tribal entrepreneurs had atleast one more business or other source of income apart from the manufacturing units they own. The remaining 40 per cent who had no other source mostly comprised of those non-tribal entrepreneurs who ran mostly the skill-based tiny industries.

(vi) About 67 per cent of the respondents stated cultivation as the main occupation of their fathers. But none of them claimed to have ever worked as farmer. It indicates that the majority of them were first generation entrepreneurs having no entrepreneurial family background. Thirteen per cent came from families having business background and another 13 per cent from families of the workers. There were only two respondents from the families of government employees. The entrepreneurs having non-agricultural family background were all non-tribals. Except the two female entrepreneurs, none had received any formal entrepreneurial training.

The Enterprise

A type-wise distribution of 55 sample units (Table 3.5) reveals the nascent stage of manufacturing base of the capital town of Arunachal Pradesh. All these units catered to local needs. None of these units reported to have any backward linkages to local economy.

Table 3.5
Type-wise Distribution of Sample Enterprise

Sl.No.	Type	No. of Units	No. of Total Workers	Average Workers per Unit
1.	Fabrication	11	83	7.55
2.	Automobile Servicing	13	51	3.92
3.	Furniture Making	9	85	9.44
4.	Printing	4	95	23.75
5.	Trunk Making	3	10	3.33
6.	Others	15	173	11.53

Source: Das, Gurudas (1995), *op.cit.*, p. 204.
Note: Industrial units engaged in milling, weaving, soap making, manufacturing of electrical accessories, repairing, servicing of electric goods, spun pipe manufacturing, blacksmithy and bakery products are few in the sample and hence clubbed together as "others".

All of them procured raw materials from outside the state particularly from neighbouring towns of Assam. At the time of field survey, the oldest enterprise was reported to be of 17 years old. Majority of the units relied on the government orders.

The Labour Force

In the sample of 55 small and tiny industrial units, a total of 497 workers had been found at the time of survey (Table 3.6). Among them 82 workers were tribals and the remaining 415 were non-tribals. The ratio of tribal workers to their non-tribal counterparts, stood at 1:5. Out of these 55 units, only 9 units reported to have employed tribal workers. Four of these 9 units were under public sector, and the remaining 5 were run by the tribal entrepreneurs. Fifty out of 82 tribal workers, i.e., 61 per cent were employed in the public sector units. The public sector units in the sample employed a total of only 97 workers. Thus out of 400 workers under private sector, there were only 32 tribals. The ratio of tribal workers to that of non-tribals came down to 1:12 in the private sector while it was almost unity in case of public sector.

Why did the percentage of tribal workers in the private sector (informal sector) so low? It was learnt that the entrepreneurs in general prefer non-tribal workers than their tribal counterparts. Many of the entrepreneurs revealed that it is easy to control and get work done from the non-tribals. It may be mentioned that the non-tribal workers do not have any social root in Arunachal. Most of them had entered on the basis of short term Inner Line Permit issued by the government from different entry points[8]. Even though the time for which they might have permitted has expired, most of them did not go for renewal anticipating legal complications. As a result their stay is illegal. Due to this, non-tribal workers do not have the courage to raise their voice against exploitation. For them, staying steadfastly is more important rather than deportation; earning something is more rewarding than sitting idle at home. Due to this helplessness, they readily succumb to any threat or coercion. Thus, the greater scope of exploitation of the non-tribal workers appears to be one of the main causes for which they are preferred over the tribals.

Apart from this, non-availability of sufficient number of tribal workers, greater preference for government jobs on the part of the trained tribal workers, lack of industrial discipline and culture among them and ethnic consideration of the employer in choosing the workers may also explain the low tribal participation in the labour force under private sector.

A sample of 75 workers, out of a total 497 employed in 55 industrial units, i.e., 15 per cent was drawn for detail investigation. The study revealed:

Table 3.6

Sources of Labour in Arunachal Pradesh

State/Area			Number of Workers
Assam			33
	North Lakhimpur	9	
	Tezpur	6	
	Dhemaji	2	
	Nalbari	2	
	Harmoti	2	
	Goalpara	2	
	Mangaldoi	2	
	Other Places	8	
West Bengal			19
	Coochbehar	13	
	Jalpaiguri	3	
	Other Places	3	
Arunachal Pradesh			13
	Zero	4	
	Along	2	
	Other Places	7	
Bihar			6
Uttar Pradesh			1
Andhar Pradesh			1
Nepal			2
	Total		75

Source: Das, Gurudas (1995), *op.cit.*, p. 206.

(i)Of the 75 workers, 33 came from Assam and 19 from West Bengal. These two states jointly contributed almost 70 per cent of the sample labour force. While the majority of the workers from Assam came from adjacent areas of northern bank of the Brahmaputra especially from North Lakhimpur and Tezpur, the workers from West Bengal came mostly from the districts bordering Assam like Coochbehar and Jalpaiguri.

(ii) Out of 33 workers from Assam (Table 3.6), 12 are Assamese and the majority of the rest are Bengalis. For both the ethnic groups—Bengalis and Assamese - the participation of the upper caste Hindus into the labour force is insignificant. The ethnic composition of the workers is shown in Table 3.7.

Table 3.7
Ethnic Composition of Sample Industrial Workers of Arunachal Pradesh

Ethnic Group	Number of Workers
Bengali	35
Assamese	12
Bihari	7
Other Non-Tribals	9
Arunachal Tribes12	
Total	75

Source: Das, Gurudas, 1995, op.cit.

(iii) Among the Arunachal tribes, the Apa Tanis of Zero have comparatively large participation in the labour force followed by the Adis, Nishis and Tagins. In both the townships—Naharlagun and Itanagar-a few Apa Tani inhabited slums have been noticed. These slum dweller Apa Tanis have specialized in the production and sale of Apang, the local rice beer, which is highly demanded by both the local people and workers from outside.

(iv) 67 Per cent of the sample workers have come from rural areas of the country. 43 workers, out of a sample of 75, have reported cultivation being their family occupation, i.e., occupation of their fathers. 32 workers have non-agricultural family background.

(v) It may be pointed out that most of the industrial units in Arunachal Pradesh have come up recently. The oldest unit in the sample was only 17 years old. As a result, like the industrial enterprises, the workers were also found in a state of flux—frequently changing their jobs.

In order to comprehend their unstable features, three related questions were put before the informants: How long are you staying in Arunachal? How long are you working in this unit? What did you do before taking up the present job? Data have been collected from 63 out of 75 workers. Twelve workers being local tribals do not come under the purview of the first question. Twenty-five workers have reported no time lag between their stay and work in the unit where they have been found. Most of the workers in this category were the recent immigrants. Eleven had reported a time lag of 1-2 years. Seventeen workers were found to have a lag of 5-7 years, 4 of 7-9 years and one was found to have a time lag of 11 years. Thus, about 60 per cent of the immigrant non-tribal workers seemed to have started their career in Arunachal with work other than their present job, wherefrom they later moved on to their present job.

An industry-wise position of the earlier occupation of the workers is shown in Table 3.8.

Table 3.8
Earlier Occupation of the Sample Workers before Joining the Industries

Industry	Worked in the same line	Household work including cultivation	Construction Work	Other non-agricultural work	Unemployed	Total
Fabrication	5	1	1	3	2	12
Auto-Servicing	4	-	4	-	1	9
Furniture Making	2	4	7	-	-	13
Printing	5	6	2	1	-	14
Trunk Making	-	-	2	-	-	2
Others	2	3	13	1	6	25
Total	18	14	29	5	9	75

Source: Das, Gurudas, 1995, *op.cit.*, p. 210.

It may be noted that about 39 per cent of the workers in the sample had shifted to manufacturing sector from construction works. Majority of them were brought to Arunachal by the non-tribal contractors and their agents. There were only 18 workers who had practical experience in the line of their present job. Number of workers coming directly from agricultural work is not very significant. Only 14 out of 75 workers reported their partial association with agricultural works. Seventy five percent of the sample workers reported to have received some sort of formal education. Majority of the workers were found to have come from the dropouts of middle school level. In most cases family poverty was reported to be the basic cause of dropouts. The distribution of the sample workers by educational level is shown in Table 3.9. Apart from the two workers having post-higher secondary technical diploma employed in the public sector electronics unit, none of the workers have received any formal training.

Thus, the literacy rate among the industrial workers in Arunachal is higher than that of the state average. This is mainly due to presence of a large number of non-tribal workers in the manufacturing sector of the state.

(viii) All the workers in the sample were of adult age group (15-59). The problem of child labour which is acute elsewhere does not appear to be significant in Arunachal. The age structure of the workers (Table 3.10) reflects the immigrant character of the labour force where workers migrate usually after attaining a reasonable age. While 39 per cent of the male workers is found unmarried, the same for the female is rare. Five of the 14 female workers are widows of either Bengali or Assamese stock. Economic insecurity of the widows and utter neglect on the part of the family members have compelled those widows to migrate and join in the labour force. Most of the married female workers have come from the families of local tribal middle class, and are found working in public sector units only.

Table 3.9
Eductional Level of the Sample Industrial Workers of Arunachal Pradesh

Category	Number of workers in						
	Fabrication	Auto Servicing	Furniture	Printing	Trunk Making	Other	Total
No formal education	1	2	7	-	-	9	19
Primary level (I-IV)	1	-	2	1	1	4	9
Middle school (V-VIII)	5	7	3	6	1	7	29
Under matric (IX-X)	5	-	-	5	-	-	10
Matric	-	-	-	1	-	3	4
Higher Secondary (HS)	-	-	1	1	-	-	2
Post H.S. technical diploma	-	-	-	-	-	2	2
Total	12	9	13	14	2	25	75

Source: Das, Gurudas, 1995, *op.cit.*

Table 3.10
Age, Sex and Marital Status of the Sample Workers of Arunachal Pradesh

Age Group	Male		Female			Total
	Married	Unmarried	Married	Unmarried	Widow	
15-20	1	6	-	-	-	7
20-25	4	9	2	-	1	16
25-30	12	8	4	1	-	25
30-35	8	1	2	-	1	12
35-40	5	-	-	-	2	7
40-45	1	-	-	-	1	2
45-50	4	-	-	-	-	4
50-55	2	-	-	-	-	2
Total	37	24	8	1	5	75

Source: Das, Gurudas, 1995, *op. cit.*

Thus, the Arunachal experience reveals that the non-tribals are playing the dominant role in the informal manufacturing sector. Although tribal entrepreneurship is emerging, their participation in the industrial labour force is conspicuously insignificant. Apart from Arunachal Pradesh, the experience of Meghalaya and Nagaland also suggest a similar trend.

Case Study II: Greater Guwahati

Recently Indian Institute of Entrepreneurship (IIE) Guwahati, has conducted a sample survey of small scale industries operating in Greater Guwahati area. Out of a total of 1750 Small-Scale Industrial (SSI) units, the study[9] surveyed 510 units and found only 247 units functioning while the rest 263 units were found to be closed.

The Entreprise

(i) The study revealed that the Steel Fabrication Units (like gate and grill making, rolling shutters, collapsible gate, etc.) were dominating the existing SSI unit (Table 3.11), followed by Servicing and Repairing units, Printing and Allied units, Wooden Furniture, Steel

Furniture, Food Processing and Engineering units. Most of them only cater to the local needs.

Table 3.11
Type-wise Distribution of Sample Working SSI Units in Greater Guwahati Area

Sl. No.	Category	Working Units	
		Number	**Percentage**
1.	Food Processing	15	6.1
2.	Engineering	12	4.9
3.	Steel Fabrication	64	25.9
4.	Wire netting/Fencing	4	1.6
5.	Steel Furniture	15	6.1
6.	Wooden Furniture	27	10.9
7.	Other Wood based Industries	5	20
8.	Cane and Bamboo	5	2.0
9.	Rubber	3	1.2
10.	Plastic	5	2.0
11.	Metal Product	2	0.8
12.	Chemical	3	1.2
13.	Electrial	4	1.6
14.	Printing Paper and Allied	29	11.7
15.	Bus/Truck Body Building	4	1.6
16.	Tiles/Ceramics	1	0.8
17.	Garments/Textiles	7	2.8
18.	Pharmaceuticals	2	0.8
19.	Service Oriented	35	14.2
20.	Assembling	1	0.4
21	Miscellaneous Units	4	1.6
	Total	247	100.00

Source: Saikia, 2001, *Small Scale Industries in Assam*, p. 27.

(ii) The study shows that majority of the enterprise is of recent origin. In fact, small-scale enterprise started flourishing only in post-Assam Accord period (i.e., after 1985). About 37 per cent of the working SSI units were established between 1987 and 1990 and another 32 per cent between 1991 and 1995 (Table 3.12)

Table 3.12
Smale SSI Units in Greater Guwahati by Year of Establishment

Sl. No.	Period	Number of Units	Percentage
1.	1950-70	16	6.5
2.	1971-75	14	5.7
3.	1976-80	17	6.9
4.	1981-86	28	11.3
5.	1987-90	91	36.8
6.	1991-95	76	30.8
7.	1996-98	5	2.0
8.	1950-98	247	100.0

Source: Saikia, 2001, *op.cit.*, p.31.

(iii) The survey shows that 81.4 per cent of the units were proprietary concern, 11.7 per cent of them were under partnership concern, 6.5 per cent under company and only 0.4 per cent under co-operative form of organization.

The Entrepreneurs

(i) Out of the total of 247 sample entrepreneurs, 75.3 per cent belonged to families with business background, followed by 10.9 per cent service holder families, 7.3 per cent agricultural families and 6.5 per cent industrial families.

(ii) Majority of the entrepreneurs were undergraduate (45.3 per cent), followed by graduates (31.2 per cent) and matriculated (12.9 per cent). Percentage of postgraduates, engineering degree holders, diploma workers, etc., was very small. Together they constituted only 10 per cent.

(iii) Most of the entrepreneurs (51 per cent) fall in the age groups of 40-50 years, followed by 27.1 per cent in 30-40 years, 19.4 per cent in 50-60 years, 4 per cent in 60-70 years and 1.6 per cent were above 70 years. There were only 2.8 per cent of entrepreneurs who were in the age group of 20-30 years.

(iv) The study shows that 42.5 per cent of entrepreneurs were unemployed before starting their respective business ventures. The rest 57.5 per cent were either working in government or private organizations or helping their parent in managing their family business.

(v) Out of the total 247 entrepreneurs, 239, i.e., 96.7 per cent were male and only 8 were female, 95.2 per cent entrepreneurs were married and only 4.8 per cent were unmarried.

(vi) The survey indicates that entrepreneurs belonging to general caste account for 72.9 per cent, followed by other Backward Caste 15.4 per cent, Scheduled Caste 9.3 per cent, Scheduled Tribe 5.6 per cent and More Other Backward Caste 0.8 per cent.

The Labour Force

The study enumerated 1550 workers employed in 247 working SSI units in Greater Guwahati. The average size of employment was, thus, 6 persons per unit. The distribution of units by size of employment is shown in Table 3.13

Table 3.13
Employment Pattern in Sample SSI Units in Greater Guwahati Area

Sl.No.	Category	No. of Units	No. of Employees	Average Employment
1.	Food Processing	15	192	12.8
2.	Engineering	12	70	5.8
3.	Steel Fabrication	64	274	4.3
4.	Wire Netting	4	18	4.5
5.	Steel Furniture	15	68	4.5
6.	Wooden Furniture	27	122	4.5
7.	Other Wood based Industries	5	23	4.6
8.	Cane and Bamboo Furniture	5	22	4.4
9.	Rubber	3	28	9.3
10.	Plastic	5	35	7.0
11.	Metal Product	2	16	8.0
12.	Chemicals	3	43	14.3
13.	Electricals	4	26	6.5
14.	Printing Press and Allied Activiteis	29	209	7.2
15.	Bus/Truck Body Building	4	32	8.0
16.	Tiles/Ceramics	1	7	7.0
17.	Garments/Textiles	7	50	7.2
18.	Pharmaceuticals	2	46	23.0
19.	Repairing and Servicing	35	245	7.0
20.	Assembling	1	6	6.0
21.	Miscellaneous Units	4	18	4.5
	Total	247	1550	6.2

Source: Das, Gurudas (1995), *op. cit.*, p. 205.

The study also revealed that all the SSI units employed adult male persons who constitute 93 per cent of the total work force. None of the units reported to have employed any child labour. However, the study did not look into the socio-cultural background of the workers. As a result no conjecture can be made about the emerging inter-ethnic competition in the informal manufacturing sector in Guwahati.

The Size of the Market

The survey revealed that out of 247 SSI units, 162 units, i.e., 65.59 per cent market their products/services in the city itself. Products like bakery items, wooden furniture, gate and grill, distilled water, chalk crayon, printing job, repairing and servicing of motor vehicles, water pump, TV, radio, watch, etc., are being marketed only in Guwahati city. About 8.9 per cent of SSI units market their products not only in the city itself but also in other neighbouring towns. Items like rolling shutters, fencing, automobile reconditioning, car reconditioning battery, musical instruments, wooden furniture, pickle, jam, jelly, offset printing, screen printing etc. find their market beyond the city limits. SSI units producing items like readymade garments, paints, PVC pipes, transformer, panel board, power tiller, animal feeds, steel furniture, DTP/offset printing, tea packaging, etc., find far more wider market. Forty two units producing these type of products reported to have been marketing all over the state.

Another 25 (10 per cent) units producing items like flooring tiles, canvas products, food processing items like biscuits, squash, chow-chow, steel furniture, bus body, rubber foam, tea blending and packaging market their products in the entire north eastern region.

Only 9 units (3.64 per cent) producing items like cane furniture, tea blending and packaging, wax emulsion, handloom goods, carbon brush, etc., market their products outside the north-eastern region. None of the units exports outside the country.

The Informal Trade Sector

Trading activities constitute the principal component of the informal sector in all the urban settlements in the region in general and state capitals in particular. In Assam, while the wholesale trade has long been monopolized by the Marwaris, the retail trade particularly in commercial hubs is dominated by the Bengalis and other migrant communities. Ethnic Assamese are late entrants in this sector. They occupy only a peripheral space as far as the trading activities are concerned.

Like Assam, trade sector in the hill states of Arunachal Pradesh, Meghalaya and Nagaland is predominantly in the hands of non-tribals—Marwaris controlling the wholesale trade and Bengalis, Punjabis, Biharis and other migrant groups dominating the retail trade. However, unlike Arunachal Pradesh and Nagaland, the local tribals in Meghalaya have made their presence felt in this sector and are fast acquiring competitive business skills.

Manipur, Mizoram and Tripura stand in a different footing. Although the wholesale trade in them is in the hands of the migrant communities like Marwaris and Punjabis local people dominate the retail trade.

Except Arunachal Pradesh and Nagaland, where local tribals still prefer to remain as "sleeping partners" by way of giving away the trade licenses to the non-tribals in lieu of commissions, a process of replacement of the non-locals by the locals is undergoing all over the region. Leading to sharpening the inter-ethnic competition in this sector.

The Informal Transport Sector

Except Itanagar, in all the capital towns of north-eastern states, the public transport system is well developed. For plains towns like Guwahati, Agartala, Naharlagun and Imphal, the public transport system consists of *Pedicabs* (pedal operated rickshaws), motorized tricycles (auto rickshaws) and city buses. For hill towns like Shillong, Kohima and Aizawl, city cabs (taxis), motorized tricycles and city buses provide the public transport services. Majority of the *pedicabs* in Guwahati are run by the Muslim Begnalis/ Assamese mostly coming from lower Assam districts of Dhubri, Barpeta, Nalbari, Bongaigaon, Nawgaon, etc. Many of them are seasonal migrants. During harvesting season they go back to villages to work in fields and then come back to the city during lean season. It is only recently that

Guwahati streets are crowded with autorickshaws. A large section of the autorickshaw operators has come from the educated urban unemployed youths. They are the beneficiaries of government patronage under self-employment schemes. They received financial assistance from the government for the procurement of their vehicles. Ethnic Assamese youths play the dominant role as auto-operators not only in Guwahati city but also in other towns in the Brahmaputra Valley.

In the hill towns of Shillong, Kohima and Aizawl, non-tribals used to work as cab-operators for long. With the growth of local manpower, everywhere tribal cab-operators are replacing them at a faster space. In Aizawl and Imphal, locals are largely engaged in the public transport service activities.

The Informal Service Sector

In all the state capitals in north-east, non-locals are engaged in different personalized service providing activities. Biharis and Bengali Muslims are often found in laundry services, footwear and leather goods repairing services and services of barber. In most cases they run proprietorship business units of their own with or without any permanent place of business. In the hill towns of Shillong, Itanagar, and Kohima, non-tribals are engaged in electrical and electronic goods repair activities and motor-vehicle repair activities. Everywhere Biharis and Nepalis are working as porters. Non-tribal womenfolk work as maids in the homes of urban middle class while their male counterparts act as daily wage labourer in the urban labour market. As these petty jobs are un-remunerative, locals generally shy away from them. The only exception is Mizoram where the local Mizos have learned these skills and themselves supply most of these labour.

Competition, Conflict Situations and Urban Environment

In post-Independent era, political power in Assam came in the hands of the Assamese who were denied state privileges during the colonial period. With the creation of modern state structure, various avenues were opened up. Educated middle class Assamese preferred secured government jobs leaving the entrepreneurial activities to be taken up by others. A similar experience may also be observed in the hill states. With the creation of state structures in Arunachal Pradesh, Meghalaya, Mizoram and Nagaland, the educated local tribals found enough space in the public sector. The general preference of the tribals for government jobs had left the informal sector to grow under the migrant non-tribal initiatives.

But in the absence of any organized private sector, the absorbing capacity of the public sector was exhausted within a short span of time. This has sharpened the inter-ethnic competition for state privileges. With the saturation of the absorbing capacity of the public sector, the growing reserve army among the locals started entering into the informal sector. With the transformation of the urban tribal societies and acquisition of modern skills, they are increasingly eyeing to replace the non-tribals. This inter-ethnic competition for livelihood often aggravates inter-ethnic cleavages. Ethnic identities are often cited in order to legitimise the claims for running business. In many of the tribal communities, socio-political organizations follow a policy of "controlled violence" in order to instill the sense of insecurity among the psyche of the non-tribals. This policy has already yielded good results as far as the interest of the 'sons of the soil' is concerned. This policy has reduced the inflow of migrants on the one hand and accelerated the outflow of early migrants on the other thereby creating some place for the locals to grab.

This inter-ethnic competition for resources/avenues often leads to various forms of culture-conflict[10]. As a result, the socio-political environment particularly in the hill towns often deteriorates. The tribal political elites also often invoke the identity issue in order to mobilise the masses in ethnic lines.

REFERENCES

1. For further elaboration of this point, see, Gurudas Das, 1998, "Liberalisation and Internal Periphery: Understanding the Implications for India's North East", in Gurudas Das and R.K. Purkayastha (eds.), *Liberalization and India's North East*, Commonwealth Publications, New Delhi.

2. NER is comprised of seven states, viz., Arunachal Pradesh, Assam, Manipur, Meghalaya, Mizoram, Nagaland, and Tripura.
3. Debendra Kumar Nayaks, et al., 1995, "Pattern of Urbanisation in the North East", In J. B. Ganguly (ed.), *Urbanisation and Development in North East India: Trends and Policy Implications*, Deep and Deep Publications, New Delhi.
4. Gurudas Das, 1995, "Features of Peripheral Urbanisation: A Study in the Nature and Growth of Urban Settlements in Arunachal Pradesh", in J. B. Ganguly (ed.), *ibid.*
5. For details, see, S. V. Sethuraman (ed.), 1981, *The Urban Informal Sector in Developing Countries: Employment, Poverty and Environment*, International Labour Office, Jeneva.
6. P. R. Bhattacharjee, 1995, "Features of Urbanisation in North East India as reflected in Migration Statistic", in J. B. Ganguały, (ed.), *op. cit.*
7. Gurudad Das, 1995, *Tribes of Arunachal Pradesh in Transition*, Vikas, New Delhi, pp. 197-215.
8. Inner Line Regulation, promulgated during the colonical era, is allowed to continue in Arunachal Pradesh even after Independence. In view of this regulation, outsiders can enter in this state only on the basis of inner line permit issued by the government of Arunachal Pradesh.
9. Sunil Kumar Saikia, 2001, *Small Scale Industries in Assam*, Indian Institute of Entrepreneurship, Guwahati.
10. Gurudas Das, 1998, "Migration, Ethnicity and Competition for State Resources: An Explanation of the Social Tension in the North-East India", in Manis Kumar Raha and Aloke Kumar Ghosh (ed.), *North-East India: The Human Interface*. Gyan Pub. House, New Delhi.

4

Nature of the Urban Informal Sector in Shillong with Special Reference to Roadside Pan-shops

J. W. Lyngskor

Introduction

The importance of the role played by informal sector in the urban economy of the developing countries was realised in the early 60's and 70's when the growth of town and cities in the developing countries was going on very fast. The 'Informal sector' consists of those class of people who are not getting employment in the formal sector but are compelled to work in low income and low productivity areas outside the organized sector and most of them are the migrants from rural areas. The informal sector is characterized by unorganized small-scale operations, labour intensive techniques, low-income levels and sole ownership. This sector is commonly known as the unorganized sector. It is estimated that it employs about 93 per cent of the total workforce in India including agriculture in 1992-93. In India, it was in the Eight Five Year Plan (1992-97), that informal sector was first included in the development policy. Women labour described as 'invisible' goes unacknowledged though it is estimated that about 92 per cent of the total women workers are in the informal sector. Low wages, long hours of work and lack of recognition, but very important for survival of families, mark the lot of women. In urban slums, the number of such women employed as domestic servants, street vendors, and such informal occupations is growing who are in many cases the principal bread winners for the household where the men-folk become drunkards and irresponsible. Keith Hart was the first person to bring out the dichotomy between formal and informal sector in his study of urban Ghana in 1971. Most of the writers agree that 'formal sector' relate to organised large-scale operations, capital-intensive techniques, high-wage rates and salary level. However, John Weeks (1975) introduced a new dimension i.e. state favour to the formal sector and also gave a new term to informal sector as 'un-enumerated' sector in the study of urban imbalance in Africa. Clifford Geertz (1963) used the term 'bazzar economy' in his study of the two towns of Indonesia. Others like Reynolds (1969) had used the term 'modern' and 'traditional sector'. Santos (1979) considered the city consisting of two sub-systems: the 'upper' or 'modern circuit' and the 'lower circuit' where the lower circuit consists of small-scale activities and is almost exclusively for the poor. He assumes dependency of the lower circuit upon the higher circuit. Though earlier it was believed that the informal sector is just a temporary phenomena that is going to be absorbed permanently into the formal sector, yet empirical studies like the one conducted by Kishor C. Samal (1990) in the city of Sambalpur rejected this hypothesis and concluded that informal sector is here to stay permanently and it is growing with the passage of time. Liberalisation policy, unsteady market conditions and growing competitions are pushing people to seek self-employment and remain in the unorganized employment.

While studying the informal sector of Shillong, I choose 'roadside pan-shops', because it fits in well with the definition of informal sector as given by ILO in its mission to Kenya. It defines 'informal sector' as "Informal activities are the way of doing things, characterised by (a) ease of entry, (b) reliance on indigenous resources, (c) family ownership of enterprises, (d) small scale operation, (e) labour intensive and adapted technology, (f) skills acquired outside the formal sector system, and (g) unregulated and competitive markets" (ILO: 1972). Moreover as all know 'pan' or 'kwai' play an important role in the Khasi society in particular as it is a part and parcel of the culture as well as among the people of north-east in general. There is no doubt that this particular sector has played a very important role in giving employment to a very large section of the people especially the women as entry to it is very easy with a minimal capital.

Findings from Earlier Studies

Telher-Waldrof and Waldrof (1983) in their studies in Bangkok found that out of a sample of 79 street vendors their earnings were higher than the earnings of the urban unskilled formal sector workers and that education did not have an impact on earnings. In the same way the migrant status does not have a statistically significant relationship with earnings. House (1984) in his study in Kenya concluded that the informal service sector offered the lowest rewards because of low capital and skill intensity, lower than that in the informal manufacturing sector. A study by Duraiswamy and Narasimhan (1997) on the informal sector in Madras, however, finds that there is significant difference between earnings of migrants and non-migrants but they do not differentiate between the manufacturing and service sectors. Another study by Smith and Metzger (1998) in Mexico conducted on economic aspects of informal services of 1000 street vendors concluded that earnings of street vendors are high relative to formal unskilled wages, and education, experience and capital make significant contributions to earnings in this sector. The Mexico study does not consider the impact of background characteristics such as migrant status on earnings. K.C. Samal (1990), while studying. informal sector in Sambalpur found that there was a strong presence of the rural migrants not only in informal sector but also on formal sector. The 'push' factor is stronger than the 'pull' factor and that there is little actual or potential mobility of workers from the informal sector to formal sector. In a latest study of informal sector of Delhi, Dasgupta (2003) discovered that formal education does not explain differences in earnings but background characteristics do and that earnings of the migrants in the informal service sector are lower than the wages of unskilled workers in the formal sector. For non-migrants, on the other hand, average earnings are higher than that of unskilled factory workers in formal sector.

Objectives and Methodology

In this chapter an attempt is made to understand the nature and characteristics of roadside pan shops, its growth, employment potential and income generation, its problems and prospects, its relationship with the rural immigrants and how it has helped to sustain the family needs and to solve the problem of unemployment in the urban area of Shillong. We have conducted a small sample survey (using a simple random method) through interviewing of the respondents, at least one from each locality, and the total size of the sample is 15 out of a universe of 500 (approx). Of course, I am very much aware about the limitation of this small sample size, nonetheless I can throw some light on this particular informal activity.

The Types, Growth and Size of Roadside Pan Shops in Shillong

Some of the important features of Shillong city are: it has an area of over 26 sq. km including Nongmynsong and its population is 2,67881 according to the 2001 census. It is mainly the headquarter of many Central and State government offices including the military establishments, it does not have manufacturing industries but it is a well-known centre of education in the north-eastern region. Because of its beautiful scenery and good climate, it attracts a large number of tourists. Majority of the people here are in government services. Those who are not in the government jobs are employed either in deficit or in private schools and colleges, which are scattered in every nook and corner of the city. The problem of acute unemployment started within a decade or so as government jobs are already saturated and at the same time the number of educated people have increased by leaps and bound. The types of informal activities found in Shillong are mostly in service sectors like food and tea stalls, casual workers, housemaids, hawkers, pan sellers, paper sellers, salesmen and saleswomen working with private agencies, transport services, petty businesses, coolies, water carriers, flower sellers, private tutors, teer business, rag pickers, barbers, shoe shining, etc. Only a small population is engaged in manufacturing like steel fabrication, furniture, cement block making, sawmills, printing press, body building for trucks and buses, etc. As the government jobs are already saturated, with the increasing number of educated people (both technical and non-technical), the lack of industries and the large population of rural immigrants, more and more people who are less educated are pushed into the informal sector. This can be seen from table 4.1 that the maximum number of people have joined this profession just in recent years and the average number of years of service of these roadside pan sellers worked out to be $7^1/_2$ years.

Table 4.1
Frequency Distribution of Years of Service among Roadside Pan Sellers

	Below 5 years	5-10	10-15	Above 15 years
Frequency	6	4	3	2

Sources : Field Survey

As for the types of pan shops, we can classify them into three types. The first and original one are those shops which were existing for a long time and sell pan along with other consumer goods in a small established shop with proper room and roof and also along with rice and tea stalls. This type is found everywhere in the city including the residential areas. The second type includes those shops which are found in the roadsides without proper room or roof. They just keep a small box of size 2ftx 1ftx 2.5 ft, an umbrella and one plastic sheet and run their business. The origin of this type of shops can be traced back to even 30 years ago but their number had started increasing only for last 10 years. This type is found mainly in bus stations, business centers, near the offices, hospitals, parks, in front of restaurants/tea shops, schools and colleges, cinema halls, and such centrally located places but not common in the residential areas. The third type of shops can be termed as 'mobile shops' that are just started in recent years. These are temporary shops that are run by the small boys or children mostly during winter holidays. They carry pan, bidi, cigarettes and matchboxes in a small basket and sell them while walking in the main roads between Iewduh—Police bazzar and Keating road to the taxi drivers, passengers, etc. They are doing this in order to generate some income to buy their books, copies and uniforms. There are about 20 to 30 children who are engaged in this type of shop. Here I am concentrating on the second type, i.e., the roadside pan shops. The maximum number of this type of shops are concentrated in Barrabazzar, Police Bazzar, and Laitumkhrah, and the rest are distributed in different places across the city. Besides the local people, the Nepalese run the largest number of shops while there are few from other communities also who run these shops, e.g. Bengalees, Biharis, etc. The size of this particular roadside panshop is more than 500 approximately.

Type of Goods Sold, Employment and Income

The type of goods sold in these shops are quite a few, e.g., pan, bidis, cigarettes, matches, sweets, chanas, tamarind, papad, popcorn, tobacco products like khaini, raja, chutki, etc. At times, some of them add some seasonal fruits like sohphie (a local sour fruit), oranges, etc. They cannot add many items because of the lack of space, capital and manpower. Some of them do not have enough capital to invest in other items for sale as it takes some days to finish selling them. This type of petty shops require one person only in each shop. Most of them run it single handedly, while there are others who take help from their relatives in cleaning betel nuts and arranging betel leaves. The sale depends very much on the location of the shop and it fluctuates from time to time depending on many factors. One successful lady can sell up to Rs.1000 per day in certain days but that does not happen everyday. As we see from the table below, majority of them can sell between Rs. 200-250 per day. To be exact the average sale per day is Rs. 321. After deducting the daily

Table 4.2
Frequency Distribution of Amount of Sale Among Roadside Pan Sellers in Shillong (in Rs.)

Amount of Sale/day	Below 200	200-500	above 501
Frequency	4	7	4

Sources : Field Survey

investment (seed money) amount they can earn around Rs. 116 per day on an average. However, for those who are not lucky they earn just Rs. 40-60 per day and for the most successful one can earn between Rs. 200 to Rs. 250 per day during those time when the prices of betel nut and betel leave are low. The average working hours is around 10 hours per day, thus the hourly income works out to be around Rs. 11.60 per hour. Thus, this activity had helped many people to be gainfully employed and to sustain the family needs in whatever little amount it can help especially for old and weak ladies who cannot undertake hard work anymore. The average size of the family is 5.6 per household and all of them live in rented house except one. They pay a monthly average house rent of Rs. 583. The average number of workers per household is 2.13 including the pan seller and the dependency ratio is 1:2.37 per household. With this income they have to support at least one more person excluding herself and in some cases the widows can manage to send their small children to school while the elder one has to earn something to support the family.

Investment

Regarding the source of investments, most of them use their own capital after working as housemaids for some years and one or two get their capital from their parents/husbands.

Table 4.3
Frequency Distribution of Amount of Investment (in Rs.)

	Below 200	200-500	above 501
Initial investment	1 (in 1970's)	5	4
Daily investment	6	8	1

Sources : Field Survey

For any enterprise there are two types of investments: one is initial investment and the other is daily investment. From table 4.3 we know that the maximum number of pan sellers spend between Rs. 200 to Rs. 500 daily for buying their materials. On an average they invest Rs. 205 per day. Regarding the initial investment, of the 10 respondents whose data are available, the maximum number of them invest in the range of Rs. 200 to Rs. 500, and their is only one seller who invested around Rs. 40 in those day of 1970's and the maximum amount of investment needed now is Rs.1000.

Declining Trend in Income

Almost all the roadside pan sellers have complanied that their sales have been declining over the past few years by nearly half, except two of them. These two argue that over the years they have been able to know more friends and customers and their sales have not declined. On the other hand, there are some elements of truth when the majority of them are complaining and the probable reasons for such a decline may be (i) Increase in the number of new entrants into this profession over the past few years due to the pressure of unemployment, ban on timbers and failure of agriculture in rural areas. Naturally, it affects the sale of the existing shops. (ii) The introduction of new products in the market like cold drink, ice-creams, chocolates, potato chips, etc. and the influence of television advertisements may have some effects on the children and youths and thus the sale of sweets, chanas, tamarind, pan etc. by the pan sellers have declined. (iii) The number of items in their stock is too less and they do not upgrade them over time due to lack of capital and space at their disposal.

Relationship between Rural Migrants and this Particular Informal Sector activity

From the survey it is found that more than half of the roadside pan sellers have come from rural areas. Initially when they came to Shillong they started working as housemaids for a few years and some of them spent about 8 years in that profession and after accumulating some capital they started this small business. In some cases, they have come to Shillong through marriage, and after some years when their children have grown up, they started earning through this profession. When we compare the respective income of the migrants and the non-migrants, it is found that the latter have a higher average income per day by more than a hundred rupees. The average age of these pan sellers is 39 years. This confirms that after working for some years as wage workers, they gradually move to become own-account workers or self-employed.

Educational Level of the pan Sellers

Table 4.4
Sex-wise Education-wise Distribution of Pan Sellers

Educational level	Male	Female
Illiterate	1	6
Read up to Class VI	1	5
Class VII and above	Nil	2

Sources : Field Survey

Nearly half of them are illiterate and almost all of this type of shops are run by women. Two of the women have read up to class IX and X but because of lack of other employment opportunities, they join this profession to help supplement their family income. A comparison of the average income of the literate and the illiterate per day shows that the average income of the literates are higher than that of the illiterates and the difference is less than hundred rupees.

Reasons for Joining this Profession

One of the pan sellers, after being dislodged from the Fair Price shop due to the dismantling of the buildinig, has set up his shop for time pass as he is looking for some other better business opportunities. Another old lady carry on this activity just for the sake of it after running it for over 30 years, so as to keep herself busy but does it in a relax manner without caring much for the income. Some have joined this profession because they cannot undertake hard work like housemaids due to old age, so they try their luck here at least to earn some income for their own pocket money but most of them join this profession as there are no other better altenatives for earing their livelihood. The rural migrants move to the city in search of greener pasture due to poverty and failure of agriculture.

Advantage of this Profession Over Others

When we compare this profession with other professions, we find that this type of business has some advantages over others due to the following reasons: (i) the majority of this type of shops do not have to pay rent for fees or licence to the different authorities except in Barrabazzar and Cantonment areas where they pay a very nominal rate, (ii) these shops never sell in credit, (iii) these shops need a very small space say, only 3 sq. ft. which can be set up anywhere by the roadside, (iv) the infrastructure needed for this shop is very less just one wooden box of siz 2ftx 1ftx 2.5 ft, one stool, one umbrella and two pieces of plastics of one meter each, (v) it can be started with a small capital of Rs. 400 to Rs. 600 only, (vi) no special skill is needed for carrying this business and (vii) even if you cannot sell the goods immediately they do not perish easily, they can be kept for a few days, so no wastage unlike vegetables and fruits. Due to these advantages, it attracts many people to enter this profession especially the ladies.

Problems and Prospects

The respondents revealed that none of them have received any government grants or bank loan. The common problem faced by them is the lack of capital to buy their stock of goods, and as a result they have to buy their materials daily, little by little amount at a higher cost. Another common problem is during rainy and windy season, they have to face all kinds of vagaries of weather. Some of them have suffered twice or thrice when the Municipal authorities removed their shops and took it away as they cause obstruction to the pedestrians. Many of them are worried about their future prospects as they find that their sales are decreasing over time. However, one of the prospects of increasing their sale is by selling mitha pan/zarda pan, as there are quite costly and hence give good return.

Conclusion

As the struggle for life gets tougher with the passage of time this kind of self-employment activity proves to be at least better than working as housemaids (which demands more hard work and energy with lower income). One of them have already experienced that this business is better than selling vegetable as it is not of perishable nature. When we compare with the wage rate of the unskilled male casual labourers in the informal sector who earns around Rs. 70/- per day at present, the average income of this small enterprise (mostly women) is better (of course with more working hours than casual workers) and it is higher than the wages of skilled casual labourers in the government sector as well. As it is true with other cities in underdeveloped countries it is very much true here in Shillong also that the informal sector is here to stay permanently and it is growing bigger in course of time especially from now onwards as the system of casualisation of labour is on the increase all over the world. Similarly, my finding that the migrants are more in the informal sector than the native is falling in the same line with other earlier findings in other cities. So far, the informal sector as a whole has not received much attention from the state. Finally, government might think of providing a regulatory framework conducive for the growth of he informal sector.

REFERENCES

1. Govt. of India (2001): *Abstract of Census of India,* Directorate of Census Operations, Delhi.
2. ILO (1972): *Employment, Income and Equality: A Strategy for Increasing Productive Employment in Kenya,* Geneva.
3. Kantor, Paola (1997): *'Informal Sector: Lifting the Shroud': EPW Vol. XXXII No.40, Oct. 4-10.*
4. Dasgupta, Suki (2003): *'Structural and Behavioural Characteristics of Informal Service Employment: Evidence from a Survey in New Delhi' The Journal of Development Studies, Vol.39, No.3, Feb., 2003, pp. 51-80.*
5. Ramanujam, MS & Prasad, Surendra (1993): *'Informal Sector, a Critical Appraisal of the Concept, Issue and Constraints', Manpower Journal,* Vol. XXIV, No.3, Oct-Dec.
6. Samal, Kishor C. (1990): *Urban Informal Sector,* Manak Publications Pvt, Ltd., Delhi.
7. Sarawati S. (2002): *'Protection of Unorganised Labour',* Shillong Times, 31st May.

5

Urbanisation and Service Led Growth

Nripendra N. Sarma

India has accepted the Millennium Development Goals (MDG) which sets, among other things the target of eradicating extreme poverty and hunger and halving the proportion of people in poverty by 2015, achieving universal primary education, improving maternal and child health, etc. But India cannot achieve much on these developmental parameters without mainstreaming backward areas and generating employment. Employment growth was much lower in the nineties as compared to that of the eighties. Migration has increased during the reform period from rural to urban areas. Unlike the pre-reform period; agriculture has failed to absorb unorganised sector workforce. Indeed most unorganised sector job creation has been in sectors like construction and trade. The employment elasticity of growth has dropped in the post-reform period. This signifies that the composition of growth is equally important as the growth itself.

In 1980-81, the services sector (including construction) contributed more than the primary sector (43 per cent at 1993-94 prices as against 40 per cent of the latter). In 2000-2001, the contribution of the services sector had risen to nearly 54 per cent, while that of primary sector had come down to 24 per cent. The secondary sector of mining and manufacturing including electricity and gas had also gone up from around 11 per cent in 1950-51 to 22 per cent in 2000-2001. Over this period, the distribution of workforce among sectors had not kept pace with their respective contributions to GDP.

Though a substantial portion of the rural population has moved to urban areas, the pressure on land has not diminished materially. The loss of employment in the rural and semi-urban industries has not been adequately compensated by increased employment opportunities in the manufacturing or services sector. Broadly, rural agricultural labour and urban casual labour constitute the most vulnerable and economically disadvantaged segments.

Ever since this trend of growth of service sector was set in the nineties, services have gained dominance. Today one can find a large variety of services. Service organisations vary widely in size. At one end of the scale are huge international corporations operating in such industries as airlines, banking, insurance, telecommunications and hotels. At the other end we find a vast array of locally owned and operated small business including restaurants, beauty-parlour and numerous business-to-business services.

Not only in India, the tremendous growth of services sector, mainly due to rise in personal income and increasing complexities of life and products, has resulted in its increased importance to the world economies. As countries develop, the contribution of agriculture to GDP declines and that of services rises. In 1948, 54 per cent of the GDP of the US was generated by services, which has increased to 80 per cent in the year 1999. In 1992, the services sector in the US accounted for 73 per cent of the total employment, up from 55 per cent in 1950. A particular characteristic of the development of service employment over time is that it is less sensitive to business cycle fluctuation than other types of employment. The Economist, May 20, 1995, observed that service output declined less than industrial output in the recession of the early 1990s.

The large and rapidly growing service sector in most nations has resulted in the emergence of a new breed of services, which are mechanised, sophisticated and capital intensive. Globalisation is likely to assist the process of diffusing new service developments across national boundaries and as interest in globalisation intensifies, service firms are making efforts to establish and maintain their international networks and brands.

The bulk of transformation has been in the service sector. The current trend of growth indicates that in future too, India's GDP growth will be continually influenced by the service sector. An India Today-ORG-MARG poll showed that a majority of middle class families want their children to work in the service sector with best job, best incomes and best talents. The service sector is now the showcase of the Indian economy.

Technological advances have made it possible for India to compete on a global basis in areas such as software development and information services.

The total employment in the organised sector in 25 years (1971-1996) has increased by about 57 per cent, the increase in employment in service sector in the corresponding period has been around 70 per cent. The details of some of the fastest growing services in India are given in the following table.

Service Sector (54.1 per cent)			
1) Trade, Hotels, Restaurants, Transport, Storage and Communication 22.3 per cent	2) Financing, Insurance, Real Estate, and Business services 13.2 per cent	3) Community, Social and Personal services 13.3 per cent	4) Construction 5.1 per cent

Source: Service share by sub-sector, 2000-2001. (% of GDP) RBI Annual Report 2000-2001.

With the changing pattern of Indian economy, a shift in employment pattern is bound to happen. The demand for professional services and professionals like bankers, accountants and lawyers will increase.

All the above indicate a trend towards higher standards of living, and in many cases better quality of living. Another indication is that most of the services are sophisticated, where urban consumption is high. There would be a positive correlation between the growth of service sector and urbanisation.

Compared to 50 years ago, the organised industries sector

is bigger, more diversified and technologically more advanced. It has also spread over more states than before providing many new opportunities for ancillary development. A variety of knowledge based as well as export oriented industries have been substantially modernised. Taxation, credit and foreign exchange policies have been modified with a view to encouraging more private investment, with wider facilities for import of foreign technology and equity participation. Another clear trend is towards a progressive reduction in the government's role and enlarging that of the private sector.

India is a large country with several Urban Agglomerations (UAs) and these are comparable to the UAs in many other large countries, for example the US. The US has close to 265 Metropolitan Statistical Areas (MSAs). The number of UAs in India increased from 274 in the 1981 census to 374 in 1991. And according to the 2001 census, the number has increased to 384, much more than the MSAs in the US. But are the public services in our UAs in any way comparable to those in other developing countries, leave alone the US?

According to the Urban Development Ministry, 20 per cent of the country's urban households are denied access to safe drinking water and more than 40 per cent of the garbage generated is left uncollected for want of proper waste management. The growth in the service sector which is urban biased has to be examined in the context of the quality of services also.

With reference to informal sector, Gerry Rodgers of International Labour Organisation (ILO) had developed the concept of 'decent work' as a development objective. The concept of 'decent work' is part of the growing concerns with human development which integrates economic and social objectives. The concept of decent work is not tied to merely providing employment opportunities but extends far beyond that in terms of improving human capabilities, a social voice at the place of work so as to ultimately head to better workers' rights. Since the attainment of decent work necessitates empowerment, training and development should be emphasised. Serious thoughts need to be given for setting up mechanism for promoting informal sector.

Cities and towns are crucial for economic growth and poverty reduction. They constitute a key component of any strategy that aims at enhancing India's competitiveness in the global markets. Nearly 52 per cent of the country's GDP originates in India's 5,500 cities and towns. But the cities and towns are under severe stress and strain when we look at the infrastructure and services. Public investment in city based infrastructure such as water supply, sewerage systems, solid waste disposal, roads and public safety has been stagnating. Current estimates place such investment at 2.25 to 2.5 per cent of the total development budget.

It is possible to attract private investment and management in urban infrastructure if conditions are made conducive for its participation. According to recent projections, India will have approximately 550 million people living in its urban areas by 2020.

Given these trends, significant enlargement of employment opportunities and quality improvement measures have to be sought in the services sector. The problems in these sectors will most likely to be one ensuring that job opportunities in real terms grow sufficiently both to absorb additional labour supply and to improve the quality of life. The challenge is that the service sector has to be the real driver of the real growth.

REFERENCES

1. Debroy, Bibek; Darkness Beneath the Shine: *The Telegraph*, p-8, 28 April 2004.
2. Krishnaswamy K.S.; Growth with Social Justice—Reflections on Employment Question, *Economic and Political Weekly*, March 13, 2004, p. 1129.
3. Lovelock, Christopher and Wirtz Jocjen: *Services Marketing-People, Technology, Strategy*, 5th Edition, Pearson Education, 2004, pp. 3-28.
4. Maiti, Pradip and Chattopadhyay Manabendu; Trends of Living in Urban India; *Economic and Political Weekly*, Nov. 13-20, 1993, pp. 2547-2550.
5. Mathur O. P.; What's the Priority : Urban Misery or Rural Poverty? *Business Standard*, June 7, p. 4, p. 10

6. Ravi Shankar; *Services Marketing*, Excel Books, New Delhi, 2002, pp.18-33.

7. Roy, Sanjay K; State, Ideologies and Urban Poor in Third World. *Economic and Political Weekly*, Dec. 4 1993, pp. 2677-2681.

8. Sridhar, Kala S.; The Complexities of Urban Management; *Business Standard*. p. 5, Kolkata, 22 April, 2004.

9. Syal, Poonam; Employment in Informal Sector. *IJTD Journal*, Jan-June, 2003, pp. 158-183.

6

Urban Informal Sector and Underemployment

P.M. Passah

Many authors on rural-urban migration and urbanization related problems have concluded that migration from rural to urban areas in an underdeveloped or developing country can be expected to be not only substantial but also excessive. It is substantial since agriculture is concentrated in rural areas where a large percentage of the labour force is employed while industry is concentrated in urban areas where much smaller share of labour force is employed. Hence there tends to be a shift of labour force from rural to urban areas leading to an excessive pace of urbanization.

A study by Preston has, however, revealed that while the rate of urbanization has not been, by historical standard, unprecedented in developing countries, the rate of growth of urban population is exceptionally rapid due to the overall rate of growth of population in those countries rather than the rural-urban migration. The only exception might be Africa where the rural-urban migration is a more important factor responsible for the unusually rapid urban growth[1].

Besides overcrowding, the major cities in many less developed countries of the world give an impression of massive underemployment. Generally official unemployment statistics are not a reliable way to measure the extent of underemployment because the underemployed are working. But there is of course a crude way to measure underemployment by labeling all self-employed workers and unpaid family labour as underemployed. The is sometimes used as measure of the size of "the informal sector" in the economy. It is obviously an inaccurate measure since the self-employed may own substantial firms or be highly educated professionals. Nevertheless this measure of underemployment does indicate that underemployment declines sharply across countries as per capita income increases, suggesting that lack of opportunities for wage employment is a major cause of self-employment and unpaid family labour in urban areas[2].

Extent of Underemployment

Gunnar Myrdal's concept of "underutilization of labour" is in full play in underdeveloped regions of the world. According to him, underutilization is the important fact of economic life of these regions and it deserves to be brought to the center of the stage and subjected to detailed analysis.[3] Though underemployment is quite serious in both rural and urban areas, yet there is not much empirical study in North-East India to know its exact size and magnitude.

According to NSS data (19th Round), the Committee on Unemployment in India has estimated that 2.50 million persons in rural areas and 1.20 million persons in urban areas were working less than 14 hours per week. They were so severely underemployed that the Committee preferred to treat them as 'nearly unemployed' and included them in the category of unemployed. Besides this, 23.50 million persons working less than 28 hours per week were severely underemployed in rural areas. Similarly 3.4 million persons (constituting 10.5 per cent of urban labour force) working 15 to 28 hours per week were severely underemployed in urban areas.[4]

That there is severe underemployment in Meghalaya was revealed in the NSS data (27th Round) showing that as much as 58.4 per cent of casual wage labourers in rural and 35.59 per cent of them in urban areas, were underemployed though they remained satisfied with their work and were not seeking or available for better wage paid/salaried employment. As against this, there were as much as 28.75 per cent of the casual wage labourers in rural and 5.08 per cent in urban areas engaged in agriculture activities while 12.81 per cent of them in rural and 59.33 per cent in urban areas engaged in non-agricultural activities are seeking better wage employment.[5]

Theories of Underemployment

There are two leading theories of underemployment in less developed countries. The first is given by W. Arthur Lewis who argues that in less developed countries there is simply not enough demand for wage labour to employ all who want to work at the minimum wage needed for subsistence. The 'surplus' labour survives through a combination of employment in family business (especially farms) and low productivity self-employment. For Lewis there is no conceptual difference between the urban and the rural underemployed; so for a given demand for wage labour, rural-urban migration serves only to shift the location of the underemployed from rural to urban areas. The Lewis theory is consistent with the reduction of self-employment and unpaid family labour as per capita income increases. As capital accumulates in industry, demand for wage labour increases and underemployed labour is absorbed into wage employment by non-family firms.[6]

Michael Todaro describes the second leading theory. He explains that in less developed countries, urban wage employment provides a substantially higher income than rural employment. This wage differential causes migration from the rural areas to the cities and towns where the migrants spend some time underemployed in the "urban traditional sector" until they are lucky enough to obtain wage jobs. It follows therefore that the underemployed in urban areas will shrink only if the urban-rural income differential narrows.[7]

Todaro modified his theory along with John Harris who assume that the source of the urban-rural income differential is a "politically determined minimum urban wage at levels substantially higher than agricultural earnings." This is the key difference between the Lewis and the Harris-Todaro models of underemployment. In the Lewis model, the minimum wage holds in both agriculture and industry whereas in the Harris-Todaro model, the minimum wage is enforced only in industry. One consequence of this difference between the two theories of underemployment is the sharply different predictions regarding the effects of expansion of urban labour demand on agricultural output which must fall in the Harris-Todaro model. Other authors like Gene M. Tidrick also agree that rural-urban migration occurred largely in response to wage differentials and in spite of higher unemployment levels in high-wage areas.[8]

The Concept of Informal Sector

Subsequent to the theories of underemployment propounded by Lewis and Todaro, the concept of "underemployment" has fallen out of favour and has been largely replaced by the concept of the "informal sector". The concept of the informal sector is most commonly defined as firms (including the self-employed) that operate outside the system of government benefits and regulations. The "urban traditional sector" of Todaro may be viewed as the part of the urban economy where the political forces that determine the minimum wage in the Harris-Todaro model do not apply. However according to the International Labour Organization (ILO), "the informal sector" is seen as dominated not by the underemployed but rather by productive small firms that supply essential goods and services. The ILO views urban economies in less developed countries as "dualistic", with a sharp distinction between "informal activities" that are small in scale, labour-intensive, and unregulated, and "formal activities" that are large in scale, capital-intensive, and regulated.[9] Ian Livingstone extends this dualism from the supply to the demand side and states that the informal sector caters to the poor while the formal sector caters to the well-off urban consumers.[10]

Informal Sector Labour Market

The popular view of informal sector activities is that they are primarily those of petty traders, street hawkers, shoeshine boys, and other groups underemployed on the streets of the big towns and cities. Some evidences suggest that the bulk of employment in the informal sector, far from being only marginally productive, is economically efficient, and profit-making, though small in scale and limited by simple technologies, little capital and lack of links with the formal sector. Within the informal sector are employed a variety of workers : carpenters, masons, tailors and other tradesmen, as well as cooks and taxi-drivers offering full range of basic skills needed to provide goods and services for a large though often poor section of the population.

The workers in the informal sector are ordinarily classified as employed although they themselves and the statisticians who are involved in income measurement would be inclined to consider them underemployed. The defining characteristics of the informal sector are the ease of entry and the lack of a stable employer-employee relationship. The urban areas of less developed countries typically have a wide variety of such open entry, casual employment types of jobs.

The existence of earning opportunities in the urban informal sector attracts the labour force from rural agricultural sector. In the typical developing country, most of the formal sector jobs are located in the cities. The urban informal sector workers would therefore be expected to have a better chance of obtaining an urban formal sector job than would an agricultural worker.

The labourers who migrate to the cities ordinarily stay with friends or relatives who give them shelter and feed them while they look for work. A dozen or more people crowded into one room is not uncommon. Squatter settlements and shanty towns house a substantial portion of urban populations. The open unemployment is not very common. Additional household members are expected to contribute to their support. Frequently they assist with the household chores by preparing meals, washing clothes, or caring for children. Simultaneously they search for work and are classified as unemployed.

In a study conducted by A.S. Oberoi and H.K. Manmohan Singh in the Ludhiana city in India, it was found that more than 90 per cent of migrants seeking work found a job within two months of their arrival, which means that migrants are being absorbed fairly quickly into the urban labour market. But much of this is free-entry self-employment. The migrants who take up self-employment on arrival start in the informal sector where they work as street vendors, porters, shoeshine boys and the like. Some of them also work in small family enterprises. All such employment requires little capital or skill. The proportion of migrants who are engaged in the formal sector as own-account workers or employers rises in most cases with length of stay.[11]

The working of the informal sector labour market in most developing economies generally reflect three important characteristics.[12]

1. There is diversity within the informal sector activities. Some are activities with easy-entry and no fixed hours of operation. They may be characterized by self-employment or employment of unpaid family labour or of unskilled labour with non-specific work relations. By contrast, other informal activities exhibit limited entry due to higher costs and/or complicated licensing requirements, irregular hours of operation, and employment of family labour and unskilled labour with semi-specified work relations.
2. People are in informal jobs by choice. Such informal workers feel that they could earn more at the informal sector job they are doing than they could earn in the formal sector or even though they make a little money, they enjoy their work more, because it allows them to choose their own hours, to work in the open air, to talk to friends, etc.
3. While most workers in the easy-entry informal sector felt dissatisfied with their positions and sought better jobs in the formal sector, those in the upper-tier informal sector had typically come from the formal sector and were glad to leave the formal sector behind. There are barriers to entry to many upper-tier informal sector activities e.g. one needs skills and tools to repair shoes or watches. Thus the formal sector was found to provide training for workers to move into upper-tier small-scale employment.

It was Gary Fields who makes a distinction between the "easy-entry" informal sector and the "upper-tier" informal sector.[13] The workers in the easy-entry informal sector resemble the "underemployed" of Lewis and Todaro and who seek better jobs in the formal sector. Certainly, the formal sector has been found to employ preferentially those workers who have acquired trainings and/or experiences in the easy-entry segment of the informal sector.

But Biswajit Banerjee in his study of the role of the informal sector in the migration process in India, contested the "probabilistic migration model" of Todaro. He argues that access to formal jobs is determined largely by one's contact or social network and thus one can line up a formal sector job directly from one's village without engaging in an urban-based job search. Without such contacts one is unlikely to obtain a formal sector job even after migrating to the city and hence one does not migrate readily.[14]

I.L.O. Strategy[15]

It was the ILO which, for the first time in 1972, had drawn attention to the gap that exists between the formal and the informal sectors in the urban economies of the less development and developing countries. In its Mission Report in respect of the Kenyan economy, it recommended various policies which are intended to ensure a dynamic growth of this large segment in an urban economy. The ILO strategy aims at establishing links that are at present lacking between the formal and informal sectors, through redistribution of incomes from the top income groups to the working poor. It has been expected that such transfers of incomes would result in new types of labour-intensive investments in both urban and rural areas. This should not only generate demand for the products of the informal sector but also encourage innovations in labour-intensive techniques in this sector.

The ILO Mission strongly believed that as long as extreme imbalances persists between the relative security and income levels of those with wage-earning jobs in the formal sector and those self-employed in the informal sector, unemployment will also persist. Hence the large differentials will always attract a margin of job seekers to hover in the towns, near the chances of the good jobs, in the hopes of snapping one up.

But the ILO is also aware of the fact that unemployment is not only the result of imbalance in differentials and opportunities. Even with perfect equality, unemployment could arise. The fast rates of population growth, of urbanization and school expansion inevitably make it more difficult to absorb the growing labour force. There would then arise the dynamic imbalances relating to the structure of economic growth in the economy and to the constraints upon it. Rapid growth is needed, but rapid growth can itself generate imbalances which will frustrate its continuation. It was for this reason that the ILO Mission Report is not only concerned with alleviating unemployment, poverty and gross inequality, but also with economic growth on a pattern which can be sustained in the future, and which generates wider and more productive employment opportunities in the process.

Conclusion

There existed a stupendous proportion of poverty in India at the time the ILO Mission Report was made. In tune with the ILO policy recommendations, the Poverty Alleviation Programmes were announced in India in the early 1980's with the *Garibi Hatao* slogan. By the end of the century the poverty ratio in the country was still high of which the urban poverty constituted more than 27 per cent. In the North-Eastern Region, all States, except Mizoram, have higher poverty ratio than the All-India average. Consistent with the poverty eradication programmes, the Government has taken up a number of programmes for the purpose. One such important programme is the Swarna Jayanti Shahari Rozgar Yojana (SJSRY), which was implemented only in December 1997 for the benefit of the urban poor. Another equally important programme is the Development of Women & Children in Urban Area (DWCUA). Both these programmes have to be effectively implemented among the urban poor, and Self-Help Groups (SHG) have to be extensively organized for urban informal sector workers including women and children in every State of the North-Eastern Region.

REFERENCES

1. Preston, Samuel H., "Urban Growth in Developing Countries: A Demographic Reappraisal", Quoted in Meier, G.M., *Leading Issues in Economic Development* (7th Edition-2000) Oxford University Press, pp. 293-94.

2. See, Meier, G.M., *op. cit.*, Exhibi VI. I, pp. 295-96.
3. Myrdal, G., *Asian Drama*, Vol. II (New York, 1968), p. 1020.
4. Datt, R. et. al., *Indian Economy* (31st Edition-1993), S. Chand & Company Ltd., New Delhi.
5. Report of the NSS (27th Round) 1977, NSS Organisation, Department of Statistics, New Delhi.
6. Meier, G.M., *op. cit.*, pp. 290-301.
7. *Ibid.*
8. Tidrick Gene M., Quoted in Meier, G.M., *op. cit.*, pp. 307-11.
9. ILO Mission Report, Geneva, Quoted in Meier, G.M., *op. cit.*, pp. 313-15.
10. Ian Livingstone, Quoted in Meier G.M., *op.cit.*, pp. 316-17.
11. Fields Gary S., "Labour Market Modelling and the Urban Informal Sector: Theory and Evidence", Quoted in Meier, G.M., *op.cit.*, pp. 318-21.
12. *Ibid.*
13. *Ibid.*
14. Biswajit Banerjee, "The Role of the Informal Sector in the Migration Process: A Test of Probabilistic Migration Models and Labour Market Segmentation for India", Quoted in G.M. Meier, *op. cit.*, pp. 323-27.
15. ILO Mission Report, *op. cit.*

7

Urbanisation, Poverty Alleviation and the Role of Informal Sector: The Case of North-Eastern States of India

Amalesh Banerjee

The outstanding experience of our contemporary economic development is that neither huge food stocks at the central level nor the big push strategy of our central planning could eliminate the vicious cycle of poverty altogether. Although there has been significant reduction of poverty both in the rural as well as in the urban areas, not all parts of the country can be equally treated in that respect. In many cases rural urban gap is increasing, urban growth is rapid but rural growth is slow posing serious threat to urban environment. North-Eastern states of the country pose a particular nature of this poverty problem.

Poverty ratio throughout the country in 1999-2000 was 26.10 per cent and the urban and rural poverty ratio were 23.62 and 27.09 per cent respectively. Except Mizoram all north-eastern states have poverty ratio higher than that of national average. In 1999-2000 the urban and rural poverty ratio were 7.47 per cent and 40.04 per cent respectively against 36.92 per cent and 52.62 respectively in 1973-74. Over this period urban poverty has been reduced faster than rural poverty.

The occupation structure of north-eastern states indicate

that in the urban area the tertiary sector is the major contributor in reducing the poverty. Given this situation the urban poverty reducation measures have to be taken carefully.

The first part of this chapter deals with the fundamental of urban development and the slow process of transformation of those centres. In part two, the occupation pattern and the poverty in the urban centres are treated. In part three, we make an evaluation of the government urban development policy as reflected in the five year plans. Part four covers the recommendations for informal and intermediate eco-friendly units for the north-eastern states. Part five is the conclusion.

I. Urban Development

Urbanisation has been slow in north-eastern region of our country. This is particularly due to two reasons. Slow industrialization and the fragmented market structure due to geographical diversification in hills and plains and the poor infrastructure. Feudal and colonial urban centres have their own limitations. Fedual lords of princely states and semi-autonomous hill tribes have developed their own tiny urban centres centering around religious, customs and courts. Tribal urban centres of north-east states fall in this category. While during the colonial rule some communication system and metropolitan trading system had been strengthened, in the otherwise hilly region of the north-eastern states this was completely absent.

If we take the major urban centres of north-eastern states, like Guwahati, Shillong, Imphal, Kohima, Aizwal and Itanagar we can observe that the growth of these urban centres depends on two issues—rapidly growing administrative centres and equally slow progress of the rural economy. The pull factor of urban job attracts the growing youths. The push factor is the slow rural development and the unsustainability of the rural economy to support the growing number. The rapid growth of population in the urban areas of north-eastern states poses a number of problems, human and natural. Human problems are reflected in the per capita income and the poverty intensity and the natural problems are reflected in environment degradation. Urban centres of north-east mentioned above reflect both these types of problems. It requires a mixed approach, intervention by the Government and the market development, to address these problems. We turn to these three areas in turn in next three sections. First, the occupation and poverty aspects of north-eastern urban areas.

II. Occupation and Urban Poverty

In the absence of any large scale industrial plants in most of the north-eastern urban centres, the job attraction is particularly concentrated in government and self-government services. Naturally government sector is unable to absorb the growing army of job seekers. With the extension of education, which is rapid in these states, this sector attracts most of the educated youths. The present occupation pattern of the urban centres may be classified into three categories: the government service sector; the teaching, health and allied service sector; and the informal support activities. The first two categories have limited intake and off take. But these sectors attract the white colour educated job seekers. The third area comprises trading, business and miscellaneous supporting functions. Hence the urban population growing with the time and aggravated by the migration from rural sector results in rise of poverty. Urban poverty in the other parts of the country is also explained by the same terms. The push factor in the rural economy is stronger. The rural sector in the north-eastern states suffers from extremely miserable life conditions in terms of income, health, education and environment. The limited urban white colour jobs are greater attraction to the migrating educated youths from the rural sector.

Hence the only settled ground for urban unemployed population is the informal sector activities. The importance of the informal sector is understood from the table which indicates that the secondary sector employment is almost constant in the north-eastern states over the period from 1987-90 to 1999-2000. Primary sector is also shrinking. Hence the informal occupation activities have to be expanded to strike the balance.

Table 7.1

Employment by Industrial Sectors in North-Eastern States

States	1987-88			1993-94			1999-2000		
	P	S	T	P	S	T	P	S	T
Arunachal Pradesh	56.40	1.00	42.60	79.58	1.91	18.51	67.12	2.47	30.49
Assam	69.30	3.00	27.70	71.64	3.04	25.32	57.90	3.81	38.29
Manipur	60.30	6.40	33.20	55.19	9.11	35.70	63.49	6.33	30.18
Meghalaya	77.63	1.69	20.68	78.80	1.10	20.10	70.34	1.31	28.35
Tripura	40.10	6.20	53.70	41.20	5.50	153.30	38.20	3.87	57.93

Source: Tenth Five Year Plan, Volume III.

P=Primary, S=Secondary and T=Tertiary.

There are wide varieties of informal activities which are extending support to the growing unemployed in the urban sector. Mention may be made of plastic, rubber, grinding, shoe making and repairing, wire, motor parts, wood furnitures, cloth trading, stationary, shops, bag, gangee, grill manufacturing, printing, laundry, hardware, decoration, tea stall, telephone parts, leather goods, fan, taxi driving, lamination, xerox, computer services etc. These varieties of informal activities are present in most of the urban centres of north-east India.

Meghalaya, Manipur, Tripura have some special type of informal sector activities which are quite popular. Knitting, embroidery, woolen and silk weaving have a long tradition in Manipur. Cottage industry products of Assam, Tripura and Arunachal Pradesh have extensive country-wide markets. Games, sports and culture is another sector which has international appeal. Manipur cultural choir is widely acclaimed. However, the quality of those products and services have to be modernized. There are as many as 150 tribes of different ethnic groups and many of whom have distinct cultural products. Those can be efficiently developed and sold in the large Indian market.

However, there are number of hurdles to be met. (a) Road and communication system in the hills have not developed in any integrated fashion. Therefore, each district inhabited by separate ethnic group almost remains an isolated island. The wide vista of open market has almost remain out of range of these secluded land. (b) Therefore, the lack of market infrastructure remains a big obstacle. (c) Electricity and power generation for the development of industry, agriculture and the welfare of the households is yet a far cry in most of the areas. (d) Training and skill formation is another hurdle. To exploit the extended market of the products of artistic quality their upgradation is important. The markets of these products are not only in India but also in the Asian countries. (e) A significant problem is the availability of finance. Banking and cooperative structure is weak in the north-eastern states. Producers are often in the trap of mahajans and money-lenders for obtaining timely credit. The financial institutions are to take up innovative schemes to overcome this gap of credit availability. The present innovative structure of self-help group also has not made much headway in these states. A vigorous drive for formation of self-help groups is surely to support the skill formation as well as to overcome the gender problem and capital scarcity.

III. Government Efforts

Government and NGOs have important roles to play in the development of the informal sector in the urban areas for eradication of poverty and unemployment. Under the Ninth Five Year Plan an integration has been made of different poverty alleviation approaches such as area approach, beneficiary approach and community approache. The Swarna Jayanti Shahari Rozgar Yojana (SJSRY) and Developement of Women and Children in Urban Area (DWCUA) have to be effectively implemented among the poor urban tribal communities. Self-help groups have been extensively organised for the informal sector workers particularly among women.

But different NSS data do not show any encouraging sign of improvement in women employment in urban areas. The 32nd and 55th Round of NSS data reveal decline of self-employed urban women. Women employment, as self-employed casual labour have come down from 47.0 per cent and 33.1 per cent in 1991 to 45.3 per cent and 21.4 per cent of all categories respectively in 1999-2000. Thus the 47th round of NSS data (1991) and 45th round NSS data point to increase in regular employment but decline as casual labor and self-employed women.

Thus, while planning for urban employment is considered, women employment should be given priority because the women are largely employed in the informal sector in the urban area. In the north-eastern states, this is particularly true of urban employment since women are largely educated in traditional artistic skill of crafts which have international demand.

Under the Tenth Five Year Plan large number of programmes are undertaken for improvement of urban slums and environments. Valmiki Ambedkar Awas Yojana, water supply and sanitation schemes cover some of these programmes. Programme for improvement of transport is also another major step.

IV. New Dimension

Urban poverty eradication in the north-eastern states has some speical aspects which have to be carefully examined before undertaking the poverty eradication programme through informal sector development. First is the environment protection problem. Industrial development has to be adopted in tandem with the ecosystem. Labour intensive activities have to be extensively adopted with particular emphasis on absorption of women, as mentioned above.

Under liberalised regime, India is now in the global market where it can buy or sell as much as it can. The opportunity is now for extending India's exports of small manufacturing as China, Indonesai, Bangladesh are doing. These countries are now big exporter of low technology-based labour intensive products like readymade garments, automobiles, pharmaceuticals, hosiery, leather products, shoe manufacturing, pump sets, besides other low technology based urban manufacturing products. Bangladesh and others have low technology based cluster of production units in these prodcuts. There are still hundreds of items under the state control. Public intervention to undertake the cluster approach production programme and to reduce the obstacles are important.

Under the present possibility of extension of India's trade relation with Thailand and other East-Asian countries, export of small manufacturing products from north-eastern states will have advantages.

Many traditional products are already in demand. The urban informal sector in north-east will, thus, have a new phillip.

The modern information technolgy has a vast possibility in Shillong, Aizwal, Kohima and other north-eastern towns. The climate and work environment is of special advantage to develop these knowledge-based services in north-eastern urban centres. Government and the financial institutions should come forward to support the young entrepreneurs in this area.

High literacy rate of Nagaland, Mizoram has an advantage. Women and unemployed youth can be clubbed to form self-help groups to start various types of informal trading, manufacturing and marketing. Dissent voice should be decently organised in the creative channel in urban areas in order to combat despair and to initiate development.

V. Conclusion

North-east has great potential for natural and human resources. Without damaging the environment, the forest, mineral and agricultural resources can be harnessed with the application of medium-type intermediate technology. Urban poverty in this area is not due to industrialisation but rather lack of industrialisation of appropriate type. Urban poverty is low but rural poverty in high which spills over in the urban areas.

The traditional skill and knowledge of artistic production have to be modernised with sufficient training. Hence the informal sector development has to be emphasized.

Service type, knowledge-based and small production units have to be encouraged. This is particularly possible in the modern IT and other knowledge based industries. High literacy rate is an additional advantage.

Open door policy of the government will set a new vista for the north-east. The production of the informal urban sector of this area will find market in East-Asian countries. Just as Chinese and Thai products are flown in the world markets similarly the products of the north-east urban area will flow to the world market.

But obstacles have to be removed. Management training and technology have to be extensively available. Government finance and bank credit should also come sufficiently so as to over come the scarcity of capital. Urban poverty can be erased through the development of urban informal sector.

REFERENCES

1. Banerjee, A.C. (2002), *Decentralized Planning and Development,* Kanishka Publisher, New Delhi.
2. Banerjee, A.C. (2001), *Planning for Development of the North-eastern states,* Kanishka Publisher, New Delhi.
3. D.N. (2004), 'Low Employment Growth', *Economic and Political Weekly,* May 29.
4. Govt. of India, Planning Commission, Tenth Five year Plan.
5. Husain, Zahid and Barik S.K. (2004), *Development and Environment,* Regency Publication, Delhi.

8

Child Labour and Poverty Issues: A Study in Guwahati City

Mini Bhattacharyya Thakur and Rupa Das

Introduction

Child labour can be denominated to all those acts of employment of children of less than a specified legal age. Most of the labour laws in Inida interpret 'child' as any person below 14 years. 'Labour', on the other hand, refers to any work, whether manual or mental, which is also synonymous with 'wage labour' denotes to the workers who do not have any other adequate source of livelihood except the sale of the labour power, i.e., capacity to work either physically or mentally in return of which they get wage/salary.

Child labour is widely prevalent in developing countries like India. The practice of child labour in one form or other is very old in India and is extant since time immemorial. According to 1991 census over 11.28 million children between the ages of 5-14 are engaged as child labour out of about 250 million children in this age group but the World Bank Report of January 2000 has estimated the figure of child labour in India at 80 million. The picture is very pitiful. Children who are working, rarely go to school and are sometimes the family breadwinner. Poverty is a major contributing factor which has given rise to the problem of child labour.

Poverty is a disease that sickens the society. There are various kinds of poverty—economic poverty is the outcome of inadequate finanical resource, geographical poverty refers to a geographical location where people are being deprived of natural resource and other supportive infrastructure. Soical poverty is a product of gender, caste, class. Cultural poverty is created by belief, faith, culture, caste etc. and political poverty is due to the lack of political access and representation.

The World Development Report on Poverty (1990) reports that 1.1. billion people, that is almost one-fifth of the world's population, still live with annual income of less than US $ 370 a year. This is the poverty line defined by the World Bank below which people are deemed unable to buy adequate food and other necessities.

Poverty is a phenomenon of a developing nations. In, India being a developing country, poverty is the most crucial problem. Poverty is not only always with us but every where with us. It is an inter-related condition of deprivations. The trickle down effects of economic growth have not materialized, and millions are now living and working in what is called the informal sector. The situation of poverty is far more worse in a country like India. At the beginning of the new millennium, 260 million people in the country did not have income to access a consumption basket which defines the poverty line. Of these, 75 per cent were in the rural areas. India is a home to 22 per cent of the worlds poor (Five year plan, Vol. II). On an average 30 per cent of Indian population live below the poverty line whose annual household income is Rs. 15,000 or below.

According to the lastest large sample survey data on consumer expenditure made available by National Sample Survey Organisation from its, 55th Round Survey (July 1999-June 2000), the poverty ratio on a 30 day recall basis, is estimated at 27.09 per cent in rural areas, 23.62 per cent in urban areas and 26.10 per cent for the country as a whole. For the states of Madhya Pradesh, Sikkim, Arunachal Pradesh and Assam the combined poverty ratio in 1999-2000 were in the range of 33.47 per cent to 37.43 per cent (Economic Survey 2001-2002). Large number of poor families are forced to involve their children as labourers in order to supplement the family income. According to 1981 census,

Andhra Pradesh had the largest number of child workers, followed by Bihar, Karnataka, Madhya Pradesh, Maharashtra, Rajasthan and Uttar Pradesh which had one million child workers each (Children in Difficult Circumstances 1985-2000). The incidence of child labour is growing at an alarming rate in Assam, particularly in Guwahati city. A recent survey made by Axom Sarba Siksha Abhiyan has revealed that over 4 per cent of the total child population in the state is engaged as child labour numbering over two lakhs (Times of India, 11th August 2003). The issue of child labour is a matter of great concern. In order to remove this malady from the society, alleviation of poverty remains a major challenge before the nation. To eradicate poverty and improve the quality of life of people many anti-poverty programmes are framed and implemented by the government. In Assam a study made by Women's Studies Research Centre on "Social Sector Schemes and Programmes for children and Women in Assam 2002" shows that various programmes are framed for women and children in Assam in order to eradicate poverty and to assure a better life for them. But none of these schemes is specifically targeted the elemination of child labour.

Since 2003 an effort has been made by the Assam government through "Axom Sarba Siksha Abhiyan Mission", to universalite elementary education in Assam. Under this scheme the most challenging group of the deprived children is the Hard to Reach Children which comprises the child labour. This group of children need to impart education to bring them back to the mainstream. Initially the respond was very good but later on the number of students started declining. The evident cause put forward by the students is that education will not bring money nor food. Their main aim is to earn money and support their family to get rid of poverty. They feel very iratic to visit the school even though they are keen to learn but it does not solve their immediate problem of food and financial security.

In this chapter we have made an attempt to study the children employed in various sectors to earn their livelihood at an early age of life. The sample size of our study is 100. The field survey has been done in Guwahati city.

Poverty is one of the important factor that has led to the growth of child labour. Our study shows that 99 per cent children have taken up job at a tender age due to utter poverty. It has been found that the parents whose monthly income ranges from 12,00-18,00 can not feed their children and give them a healthy life and ultimately send their children to the labour market in order to run the family. Poverty is a stratificational reality, once an individual is born in a poor family, there is a tendency to have the same percolate from one generation to another. The "Culture of Poverty" gets perpetuated from one generation to another and poverty tends to become a stratificational reality. Can the stratification system of this kind be reduced to the minimum? We need to have some serious thinking about it. They are the poor whose minimum or basic needs are not satisfied. If their basic needs are fulfilled we can reduce the percentage of child labour. As we know, poverty has a lot to do with child labour therefore Government should seriously implement the various poverty alleviation programmes so that they help in reducing the growing incidence of child labour in our country.

Poverty is very much linked with migration. Rural poverty is carried to urban areas by the people who migrate to the cities in search of a better living. As the expanding employment opportunities for skilled and unskilled workres are found in a growing city in its informal sector, people from a less developed areas migrate to a more developed areas in search of livelihood. It has been found that many farmers and other labourers are compelled to move to urban areas for better opportunities making life miserable in cities. Our study shows that miximum number of child labourers are migrants who came long back from the nearby rural areas with their parents in search of better avenues. In most of the cases, it has been found that the parents of these children belong from agricultural background who have come to the urban areas. They are absorbed in different unorganised sector where they earn subsistance wage. In order to meet their ends they put their children to toil and support their families as a bread winner at an early age. Poverty promotes large families. Parents often perceive children as an important contribution to their family income. A birth of a child is viewed by poor parents as a means of adding to the household labour force. Our study shows that most of the families come from Bengali Muslim, Bihari, Bengali Hindu and Assamese community. Maximum number of child labour comes from Bengali Muslim, i.e. 50, Bihari 30, Bengali Hindu 15 and Assamese 5. The average family size of the Bengali Muslim family is 7-8, Bihari 6-7 and an average of 6 member in Bengali Hindu and Assamese families.

The parents with a very low income and such a family size can not meet the basic needs of their families, therefore, they encourage the children to go out and take up jobs in order to fend their younger siblings and supplement family income. From our study it has been found that the elder siblings get employed at an early age to support and fulfill the needs of the younger one. In some cases we have found that the elder siblings work for long hours in order to give a better life to the younger ones by providng them education and other securities in life. The proportion of children below 14 years is higher among the poors than among the better off. Poor families are consequently handicapped in having relatively a few employable persons within prescribed working age. Thus, there is heavy pressure of young children on poor families, which perpetuates child labour (Kanhere 1993). As long as there is a demand for child labour, it is profitable for the poor to have more children. Many children even start to earn as early as at the age of five. And poor parents are tempted to have supplementary income in the form of wages earned. Most often, for such parents, children are considered as capital. Thus, the human mortal at its tender age is used more as an economic commodity than as human being.

Poverty is very much related to the social institutions such as role of family, peer group, neighbourhood and city environment which has an important role in harbouring and encouraging child labour. The process of socialisation plays a very vital role in determining child's future. Children from a good and enlighten environment usually turn up to be good. Children brought up in an environment where the family members, friends and neighbours are not educated contributes a lot in acquiring many bad habits like gambling, stealing, using of derogatory words and often leads them to addiction and involve them in many anti-social activities. Feeling of disparity and despondency is also equally responsible for acquiring such habits. If not taken care of, it may create in their minds hate and aversion against the society forever and make them rebellious and unreformable (Das and Bhattacharyya 2004).

The incidence of child labour is the result of exploitation of the weak and poorest section of the society. The effect of poverty on the prevelance and perpetuation of child labour is greater than other causes. So far several studies have shwon that poverty causes child labour. So poverty eradication has become a precondition for the removal of child labour.

REFERENCES

1. Chand, Attar. 1987, *Poverty and Underdevelopment: New Challenges—A Gobal Survey,* Gian Publishing House, Delhi.
2. Children in Difficult Circumstances: Summaries of Research, 1985-2000, NIPCCD, New Delhi.
3. Economic Survey 2001-2002, Govt. of India, Ministry of Finance, Economic Division.
4. Five Year Plan, 2002-2007, Sectoral Policies and Programme, Volume-II, Planning Commission, Govt. of India, New Delhi.
5. Mehta, S.K., 1997, *Poverty, Population and Sustainable Development,* Rawat Publishing, Jaipur.
6. Misra, Rabi Narayan, 2003, *Child Labour in Hazardous Sector,* Discovery, Publishing House, New Delhi.
7. Social Sector Schemes and Programmes for Children and Women in Assam, 2002, Womens Studies Research Centre, Gauhati University.
8. Srinivasan Kamla and Veena Gandotra, 1993, *Child Labour: Multi Dimensional Problem,* Ajanta Publishing House, Delhi.

9

Informal Labour Market: A Case Study of Domestic Workers of Kokrajhar Town

Sujata Bhadra

Introduction

This study intends to throw light on the socio-economic background, living conditions, and the working conditions of the domestic workers of Kokrajhar town. It also intends to investigate as to whether they are satisfied with their job and if not, the reason. Attempts have been made to understand the problems that they face in managing these household chores and how they manage it.

Study Area

Kokrajhar town forms a part of North-East region and serves as an important gateway to Assam. It is situated almost in a flat terrain with some low lying areas, and is bounded by the river Gaurang and a tea garden on the western side and river Tarrang on eastern side. Kokrajhar town is well connected to the two National Highways, N.H.—31 C and N.H.—31 on three sides, one towards Karigaon on the north, Bahalpur towards east and Bilasipara towards south which cater bulk of inter-district and inter-state traffic and freight. Kokrajhar is a rapidly growing town with increasing commercial services. It is drawing migrants from rural as well as urban areas owing to its importance as capital centre of Bodoland Territorial Area Districts (BTAD). Most of the people of the town belong to middle and upper-middle class.

Hence, it is a promising area of employment for the poor women both native as well as migrant. In this context, the present study has been conducted.

Methodology and Data Base

The enquiry is in the nature of a survey of a random sample of female domestic workers working in the unorganized sector of Kokrajhar Town. The sample studied in the survey included 52 women; of these all are random selections. The methodology of the study combined a formal interview schedule with a number of informal meetings, talks and participant observation. In this context, the author was primarily concerned with the lives of the poor urban domestic workers of Kokrajhar town.

Analysis:

(1) *The socio-economic background of the domestic servants*

Table 9.1
Distribution of the Respondent's Age

Age of respondent	Frequency	Percentage
16-20	02	03.85
21-25	02	03.85
26-30	10	19.23
31-35	07	13.46
36-40	11	21.15
41-45	06	11.54
46-50	05	09.61
51-55	04	07.69
56-60	01	01.92
61-65	03	05.77
66-70	01	01.92
Total	52	100

Source: Field Survey.

Table 9.1 shows that majority of the domestic workers are concentrated in young and early middle-aged group, i.e.

most of the respondents are within the age of 40 years. The respondents of age 26-40 years of the sample are very prominent and comprises 53.84 per cent, i.e. more than half of the total respondents.

Table 9.2

Distribution of Sample Women by Education and Age-group

Age group	Illiterate	Can only read	Can read and write	Primary education	Frequency
16-20	-	-	-	2	02
21-25	-	1	1	-	02
26-30	5	2	2	1	10
31-35	2	4	1	-	07
36-40	8	2	-	1	11
41-45	6	-	-	-	06
46-50	4	1	-	-	05
51-55	4	-	-	-	04
56-60	1	-	-	-	01
61-65	3	-	-	-	03
66-70	1	-	-	-	01
Total	34 (65.38%)	10 (19.23%)	04 (07.69%)	04(07.69%)	52

Source: Field Survey.

Table. 9.2 reveals that illiteracy may be considered one of the major factors for the wretched livelihood of the domestic workers of Kokrajhar town.

In the study 65.38 per cent workers are illiterate, 19.23 per cent can only read, 7.69 per cent only ready and write and 7.69 per cent have primary education. Here poverty may be considered as a pre-requisite condition for illiteracy.

Table 9.3
Civil Status and Religion of the Respondents

Religon	Married	Unmarried	Divorced/ Deserted	Widowed	Total
Hindu	24	3	4	19	50
Mulsim	1	-	1	-	2
Total	25	3	5	19	52

Source: Field Survey.

The Table 9.3 reveals that 96.15 per cent domestic workers are Hindu, while 3.85 per cent belongs to Muslim community. Also, majority of women i.e. 42 (80.76 per cent) in the sample are Bengali speaking and 5 women are traced (9.61 per cent) from both Hindi and Assamese speaking area.

Table 9.4
Age of Marraige of the Respondents

Age	Frequency	Percentage
16-20	27	55.10
21-25	13	26.53
26-30	07	14.28
31-35	02	04.08
Total	49	100

Source: Field Survey.

It is observed from Table 9.4 that out of 49 respondents, 40 domestic workers are married in age group between 16-25 which comprise 81.63 per cent of the total respondents. From the study it is evident that the people with less economic status tend to marry before they are reaching 26, there is more likelihood that the younger people get married early.

Table 9.5

Family Size of the Respondents

Family size	Frequency	Percentage
One	10	19.23
Two	02	03.85
Three	07	13.46
Four	17	32.69
Five	09	17.30
Six	05	09.61
Seven	02	03.64
Total	52	100

Source: Field Survey.

It can be observed from table 9.5 that 19.23 per cent are single numbered family. Most of them i.e. 63.45 per cent of the respondent have three to six member families. Also this enquiry reveals that though the respondents belong to very low strata of society, they are concerned enough about the size of the family. All the respondents have nuclear type family.

(II) *Living conditions of the domestic workers of Kokrajhar town*

Under this section the living conditions of the domestic workers of Kokrajhar town is elaborated with suitable tables which offer a very frustrating living standard of the respondents.

Table 9.6

Number of children of the respondents

No. of children	Frequency	Percentage
No child	06	12.24
One child	08	16.33
Two child	16	32.65
Three child	09	18.37
Four child	08	16.33
Five child	02	04.08
Total	49	100

Source: Field Survey.

Note: Unmarried women workers are excluded.

From the Table 9.6 it is observed that the respondents are keen to have limited number of children, 50 per cent of them have only 2 to 3 children and more number of children have experienced mostly in case of elderly domestic workers.

Table 9.7
Number of earning members in the family

No. of earning members	Frequency	Percentage
One	16	30.77
Two	24	46.15
Three	11	21.15
Four	1	01.92
Total	52	100

Source: Field Survey.

Table 9.7 reveals that in most cases i.e. 40 cases (76.92 per cent) the number of earning members ranges from 1 to 2, and 3 earning members are observed in 11 cases while only in one case the number of earning members is four. This implies that in most of the families these domestic workers are the sole bread earners of the family. The respondents informed the author that most of the two earning member cases; the small children are also working with meagre amount of money or kind.

Table 9.8
Monthly family income of the Respondents

Family income (in Rupees)	Frequency	Percentage
Below 500	11	21.15
501-1000	25	48.07
1001-1500	14	26.92
1501-2000	02	03.86
Total	52	100

Source: Field Survey.

Regarding the monthly family income of the respondents, the study offers a very gloomy picture where the bulk of the respondents (74.99 per cent) income ranges within Rs. 501 to Rs. 1500 while 21.15 per cent of the sample respondents earn below Rs. 500. It is evident that bulk of family income is within Rs. 1000 though the families having two or more earning members (Table 9.7). These two tables portray the overall standard of living of the domestic workers of the Kokrajhar town.

Table 9.9

Possession of house by the Respondents

Possession of house	Frequency	Percentage
Possessing	11	21.15
Not possessing	41	78.85
Total	52	100

Source: Field Survey.

It has been revealed (table 9.9) that only 11 respondents i.e. 21.15 per cent possess their own house whereas 41 respondents i.e. 78.85 per cent stay in rented house. Moreover, 1 respondent accommodates herself in her friend's veranda and two of them stay with their employer's house. Therefore, rent distribution will be among 38 respondents who live in rented house.

Table 9.10

Amount of monthly rent for house paid by the Respondents

Monthly rent (in Rupees)	Frequency	Percentage
Up to 100	17	44.74
101-200	21	55.26
Total	38	100

Source: Field Survey.

Note: 11 respondents having their own house while 3 of them stay elsewhere free of cost

The condition of the houses both owned or rented are in horrible condition and due to low income they can not afford to repair them. Amongst 38 rented house dwellers, 20 of them pay between Rs. 101-200 as rent while 17 of them i.e. 44.74 per cent pay up to Rs 100. From this rent structure it can be well understood the status and condition of the houses in a district town like Kokrajhar where poor families and their children are living.

Table 9.11
Status of house/electricity/availability of drinking water/toilet/number of rooms

Type	Frequency	Percentage
I. House (all kaccha)		
(a) Thatched roof	13	25.00
(b) Tile roof	29	55.76
(c) Tin roof	10	19.23
II. Electricity	14	26.92
III. Availability of water		
(a) Tube well	21	40.38
(b) Well	31	59.61
IV. Toilet		
(a) Joint kaccha toilet	41	78.85
(b) Own kaccha toilet	10	19.23
(c) Open air	01	
V. Not of rooms		
(a) One	47	90.38
(b) Two	05	09.62

Source: Field Survey.

Table 9.11 illustrates a very unhealthy picture in which the domestic workers are living. All the houses of the respondents are reported to be cow dung layer type floor and of bamboo wall of very bad shape excluding the two workers who have accommodated themselves in brick wall single room without any rent. The respondents reveal that 13 of them i.e. 25 per cent having thatched roof, 27 (55.76 per cent) having tiles (almost terrible) and 10 houses having tin roofing.

Regarding electricity, only 14 households having electric connection and the rest 38 households are bound to sleep almost after sunset as they can not afford the expenditure of high priced kerosene oil.

About availability of drinking water, 21 households of the respondents having tube wells, 31 having kaccha well of their own and 1 well is meant for 4 to 5 households for all purpose use.

Regarding toilet facility, it is the worst, no one is having sanitary latrine, and all are using kaccha toilets. Only the 11 house owners have their own toilet which is also in very bad shape.

In case of the rented accommodations 4 to 5 or more families are sharing one toilet. Furthermore, 47 respondents have one room for dwelling while 5 respondents enjoy only two very small rooms. The case for three room dwelling is not traced during the course of study.

While studying the living conditions of the sample population, frequent indebtedness is reported especially by the respondents' husband and their source of borrowing is mainly money lender and friends.

Table 9.12

Employment of the respondents' husband

Employment of husband	Frequency	Percentage
Employed	45	91.84
Unemployed	04	08.16
Total	49	100

Source: Field Survey.

Regarding employment of respondents' husband, the study reveals 45 (including the husband's of the widows) cases where the husbands of the respondents are employed while in 19 cases they do not have any certain or regular employment. The rest 4 cases it is found that the husbands are unemployed, three of them are very sick and one of them is very old and refuses to work. Furthermore, drinking and gambling habit can not be separated from their normal course of life, only two cases are traced where the respondents' husband do not have any kind of such bad habits and can be considered as an exception.

Table 9.13

Time spent on house work by the Respondents

Time spent (in hrs.)	Frequency	Percentage
Less than 2	04	07.69
2-3	27	51.92
3-4	15	28.85
More than 4	06	11.59
Total	52	100

Source: Field Survey.

Table 9.13 reveals that 80.77 per cent of respondents spend 2-4 hours for their household chore which tells the exhaustive and fearsome story of the poor women of Kokrajhar town. Very few of the respondents are reported to have any severe or chronic illness but the case of fatigue, anaemia, joint pain, malaria, dysentery, etc. are reported as common type of diseases in them.

(III) *Working condition of the domestic workers of Kokrajhar town*

The survey result reflects that the working condition of the domestic workers of Kokrajhar town seems to be exploitative in nature. It is studied that the bulk of women preferred to work as domestic workers in order to fight the poverty. As the earning of these maids are very poor, they often desire to work in more number of houses at a time and they like to choose houses near to each other.

Table 9.14

Number of houses served by the Respondents

No. of houses	Frequency	Percentage
01	18	34.62
2-3	31	59.62
4-5	02	03.84
6-7	01	01.92
Total	52	100

Source: Field Survey.

It is observed from Table 9.14 that the highest number

of respondents (59.62 per cent) serve in 2-3 houses at a time and 18 respondents (34.62) serve in one house. The average working hours in each household has come out with the result of 5-6 hours each day excluding their own household chores.

Table 9.15
Monthly income of the Respondents

Income (in Rs.)	Frequency	Percentage
101-200	13	25.00
201-300	09	17.31
301-400	19	36.54
401-500	03	05.78
501-600	05	09.62
601-700	-	-
701-800	02	03.85
801-900	01	01.92
Total	52	100

Source: Field Survey.

Table 9.15 presents very depressive findings about the monthly income of the respondents. It is observed from the table that more than half of the respondents' (51.94 per cent) monthly income ranges from Rs. 300 to Rs. 600. Only 03.85 per cent respondents' montly earnings ranges from Rs. 701 to Rs. 800 while only 1 respondent earns in between Rs. 801 to Rs. 900 per month. At the most, majority of the domestic workers only get up to Rs. 500 is a very poor monetary reward for their service. This statistics is more than enough to state their poor economic standing in the society.

Now, for the type of work the respondents perform involve mainly washing clothes, scrubbing utensils, sweeping the house, moping the floor, dusting furniture, grinding spices, dressing vegetables, fishes etc. along with some odd jobs like purchasing of milk, watering plants etc. Besides these, occasionlly they also prepare food and assist in other activities without any extra remuneration. In most of the cases they have to look-after the small children or accompany them to school. In general cases, the experience in their work, the respondents reported that the employers treat normally but in case of frequent or long absence, the behaviour of the employers becomes rough. Regarding deduction of wages, only three of the respondents have experienced wage cut 1-2 years back, they left the job and joined new ones. Also, it is reported that if any worker falls sick or has household problems which compels her for frequent or few days' absence then, immediately she is replaced by another maid. This depicts an uncertain working condition of the domestic workers. The study reveals that the job satisfaction is moderate, majority of them have good relation with their employers. Most of the employers treat them sympathetically though few exceptions are noted.

Along with this the respondents expressed their dissatisfaction on the ground of very poor salary, huge work load, rough treatment of the employers while absent, employers' demand for more work along with close supervision of work etc. Further more, festival bonus, medical aid, leave facility are rare or least which compels the workers to work under severe mental pressure. In the course of enquiry, no respondent reported financial assistance from their employers during their sickness or family crisis but some of them get advance from their employers. The respondents reported that the rest or pause in work is a luxury for them; they themselves do not opt for rest because they have to rush to other houses and to own household chores. Also, a majority of respondents experience extreme fatigue in their work.

It has been noticed that none of the respondents has heard about the labour law, trade union for the domestic workers, voluntary organization working for the poor, State Social Welfare Board, Central Social Welfare Board etc.

Conclusion

This case study gives an account of the domestic workers who are largely insecure and unprotected socially and economically and victim of unmitigated hardship. They face challenges in every spheres of their existence and surprisingly, they have learnt to survive in an admirable way by responding to the challenges in an active and creative way. Besides, this section of women workers are forced to live at the margin of survival, they depend for their survival, they depend for their livelihood on manual labour which generates income in cash and kind. Shockingly, the exploitation and miseries of these poor women and children are rarely reported or studied; rather, it is accepted normally as a part of normal life. In this context, it is observed that no such studies have been undertaken to assess the extent of sufferings of these poor women in Kokrajhar town. Women organizations as well as those who fund women studies must think for new avenues in which the routine exploitation of these working women can be dealt with.

REFERENCES

1. Banerjee Nirmala, (1985), *Women Workers in the Unorganized Sector: The Calcutta Experience*, Sangam Books.
2. Joshi, S. Savita, (1995), *Women Workers at the Grass Root Level: A Sociological Study*, Ashish Publishing House, New Delhi.
3. Verma Binita, (1993), *Exploitation of Women Labour in India; Employment Pattern and wage Discrimination*, Deep and Deep Publication.

10

Female Marginalisation in the Informal Labour Market: The Case of Barak Valley of Assam

Ruma Paul

Introduction

Urbanization has been an inevitable process since the onset of the human civilization. Irrespective of how a country defines its urban centers, urban growth is one of the most remarkable processes of spatial organisation that has occurred to human civilization. Urbanization is also an irreversible process (Ramachandraiah, 1997). The spate of urbanization has progressed at a rapid pace also in the developing nations of the world and as per World Bank estimates, about 80 per cent of future economic growth in developing countries will occur in the towns and cities (World resources, 1996).

In India only about 27 per cent of the population is living in urban centers but the magnitude of the urban population (217 million in 1991) is larger than the individual population of many countries of the world. As a result urban infrastructure is burdened with severe strain of population growth with continuous overcrowding and over-flowing of male and female workforce. Now the question that relates to the present discussion is how big is the female workforce in urban India and how are they placed in the urban labour market and whether their involvement in productive work have contributed to enhancement of their productivity in terms of capability and income expansion of their household.

The answer to this would vary with variation of definition of worker. Accepting the NSSO definition and usual status approach, women formed only 14 per cent of the total organised employment and that these organised female employees formed only 4 per cent of all female workers in the country (GOI, 1995). Thus almost 96 per cent of the women workers are employed in the unorganized or the informal sector of the labour market in the country.

The 1980s and 1990s have seen a significant increase in the usage of the term 'informal sector.' This is perhaps due to the attention drawn by feminist writers and critics who have always objected to the way in which women have been incorporated into the existing framework of labour theories, which according to them are thoroughly biased against women. Breman (1996) defines the informal sector as a disparate, irregular and fluid labour system functioning in the lower sector of the economy. In the Indian context, the definition is particularly relevant where most of the women find employment as casual workers (there has been a rise of over 9.70 per cent in urban areas during the period 1972-73 to 1993-94), which signifies that women are slowly being replaced from self-employment and regular employment. In the urban areas with the process of sub-contracting gradually entering the production process, workers are found to move from the organized to the unorganized sectors enlarging the process of marginalisation and casualisation.

The basic purpose of work being recognized and paid, leads to enhancement of income and social status and alleviation of poverty for it is recognized that reduction of poverty is directly proportional to the enhancement of one's capability and well-being.

But the two are always not found to be related. The poor are not necessarily unemployed and all unemployed are not necessarily poor. The relationship depends on the level of productivity and earning that employment generates. Employment contributes to an increase in the household income and positively contributes to the reduction of poverty. Women's employment, their access and control over earning and authority to utilize their income have a greater positive impact on the welfare of the household. On the other hand exclusion of women from earnings or non-recognition and underutilisation of their productive capacity leads to social exclusion and deprivation of their capabilities which are taken to be two of the important qualitative criteria to identify the poor. Thus seen through gender lens, poverty is not merely the impoverished state in which the person actually lives but also in the lack of real opportunity given by social constraints as well as personal circumstances to choose other types of living. Thus though economic poverty encompasses a wider canvas yet examined through gender context lies essentially one capability deprivation and marginalisation of female workers in the employment market leading to poor income and inaccessibility to a decent form of living. This has become more acute considering the growing demands of urbanization and increasing pressures of economic needs compelling women to enter the job market.

The Scenario in India, Assam and Barak Valley: A Comparative Picture

An analysis of various census and NSS reports have revealed that the Female Work Participation Rate (FWPR) in India is much lower than the Male Work Participation Rate (MWPR) and the same trend follows for the state of Assam and Barak Valley (Table 10.1). Comparison of different census data since 1951 to 1991 reveals that whenever there has been a fall in the WPR's of both the sexes, the fall in the FWPR has been more severe. This indicates that whenever there has been a fall in the employment level, the tendency has affected the women much more adversely than their male counterparts. Employment in the unorganized sector reveals that majority of women work in agriculture or is engaged in own farm. In Assam the percentage of women's employment, in the agricultural sector and allied jobs, constitutes 86.4 per cent as against all Barak Valley average of 77.5 per cent. They are engaged either as unpaid family labourers or as agricultural paid labourers as casual workers. This is also true in Barak Valley where the nature of women's work is determined by cropping pattern, crop intensity, farm size and technology used in agricultural sectors. Employment though it exists in the unorganized sector is seasonal in nature. A comparative scenario based on 1991 census for marginal workers indicate that in the rural areas the percentage has varied from 30 per cent in India, 43 per cent in Assam and 34 per cent in Barak Valley and in urban areas the corresponding percentages are 11.35, 10.73 and 9.85 (Table 10.2). This is clear indication of sex typing and segregation, which bring about earning differential and reinforces the fact of significant overcrowding of women workers towards the bottom end of the informal sector.

Table 10.1
Comparison of WPR in Percentage (1991)

	India	Assam	Barak Valley
Total	37.46	36.09	30.08
Female	22.05	21.61	11.38
Male	51.08	49.44	48.98

Source: Statistical profile of Barak Valley 1991 Census.

Table 10.2
Percentage of Marginal Workers

Area	Urban			Rural			Total		
	Male	Female	Total	Male	Female	Total	Male	Female	Total
India	0.72	11.35	2.24	1.37	30.38	10.74	1.21	28.40	8.98
Assam	0.59	10.73	1.72	2.37	43.03	14.80	2.15	41.84	13.58
Barak	0.59	9.85	1.77	1.37	34.11	7.38	1.31	32.69	6.93

Source: Statistical profile of Barak Valley 1991 Census, *Gender and Employment in India*, Papola and Sharma, 1999.

The Case of Barak Valley

Barak Valley comprises of three districts namely Cachar, Karimganj and Hailakandi lying in the southern part of Assam with an area of nearly 6922 square kilometers. Economically the Valley has always been backward since the Mughal rule. The economic picture of Barak Valley greatly changed after the annexation. This has been namely with respect to tea industry, cottage industry and agriculture (Chatterjee, 2000). After the creation of Silchar Town in the year 1834 AD there was a gradual development of urban livelihood. The expansion of tea plantation and growth of tea industry led to creation of employment opportunities of both men and women in the paid sector. Over the year there has been a rapid rise in the total population as well as female population. Sex ratio and literacy are favourably high in the Valley and moreover there has also been a shift of population towards the urban area (Table 10.3). All these however have not changed the relative perception of the women in providing equal opportunities in related fields of agriculture and other services. The increase in the proportion of female workers in agriculture and allied activities from 59.6 per cent in 1961 to 77.5 per cent in 1991 census shows that agriculture still occupies a predominant sector of livelihood. Majority of the workers are engaged as agriculture labourers and few are absorbed as cultivator signifying that majority of them work as casual workers with no independent decision making authority and no control over their land.

Table 10.3
Comparison of Status of Female in India, Assam and Barak Valley (1991)

	India	Assam	Barak Valley
Population Growth*	2.19	2.24	1.93
Sex Ratio	927	923	936
Literacy%	39.3	48.0	46.1
Urban Population%			
1971	19.9	8.8	7.9
1991	25.7	11.1	8.6

Source: Statistical profile of Barak Valley 1991 Census.

An examination and analysis of the data collected reveal that the women of urban Barak Valley are engaged in multifarious activities including weaving, brick making, agriculture, plantation, construction and poultry farming. While many works are done with the male members there are many women who work individually on their own initiative so as to supplement their family income. But most of these works which they perform do not receive their due recognition neither socially nor economically. All these factors expose the vulnerability of these workers and their works, which acts as a cheap source of exploited labour class living under social and economic deprivation, which highlights one major aspect of poverty.

The process of marginalisation is evident from the following empirical facts:

FWPR is much lower than the overall MWPR and this similar trend is observed for all the districts of Cachar, Karimganj and Hailakandi of Barak Valley (Table 10.4).

Table 10.4
Work Participation of Male/Female and Rural/Urban

Area		WPR	Urban	Rural
Barak Valley	Male	57.27	54.15	57.88
	Female	22.45	21.10	22.81
Cachar	Male	58.90	56.00	59.23
	Female	23.52	21.14	23.92
Karimganj	Male	57.58	53.43	58.83
	Female	21.91	20.56	22.83
Hailakandi	Male	52.98	53.33	52.83
	Female	19.64	21.65	18.11

Source: Statistical Profile of Barak Valley (1998)

On the basis of rural urban divide, FWPR does not show any satisfactory trend I though the rural sector in the Valley has been absorbing the largest section of the female labour force in agriculture and cultivation. The picture in the urban sector is again not encouraging as indicated in (Table 10.4).

Unemployment in the Valley is fairly large with 77.55 per cent of the female population have been found to be without any employment. In the urban areas of the Valley almost 78.90 per cent of the female are unemployed. On personal enquiry it has been revealed that a good 50 per cent of the sample unemployed population has voluntarily agreed to remain without any work, which confirms the theoretical underpinnings of the neo-classical home economics, where home can maximize women in household work and males in market produced goods. The unemployment scenario points to a very pertinent fact that a sizeable proportion of educated and capable manpower have not been gainfully employed and it is also evident that factors that determine employment of female workers are different from the factors that govern male employment. Patriarchal dominance and selection of males over females is also existent in spite of growing literacy and satisfactory sex-ratio in the Valley.

Another noticeable aspect is that, the incidence of non-working females is substantially high in urban and rural areas in all the three districts. Among those working, urban proportion of female worker in the unorganzied sector is farily high. This is also substantiated by census data, which show that the total percentage of both the sexes dependant on primary sector is 71 per cent in Barak Valley as against 74 per cent in Assam and 67.3 per cent in India (1991). A large influx on this sector signifies the existence of under-employment and disguised unemployment leaving the woman folk to survive under acute financial crisis.

Possible factors, responsible for this behavioral pattern, which has been identified on the basis of personal interviews, are:

- Preference for male employment is socially more recognized and accepted and hence women are always given the least preference in the socially constructed behavior governing the society.
- Sex discrimination in the labour market inhibits and prevents the entry of women into jobs in spite of

women possessing equal capabilities and efficiency as their male counterparts.

- Absence of employment opportunities in line with the rapid increase in population has led to an increase in the backlog of unemployment and relatively women are the worst victims.

Conclusion and Policy Framework

Despite having huge potentialities, the overall growth and diversification of female work participation in the Valley is not at all encouraging. Existence of casual and marginal female workers highlights the gross underutilization and undervaluation of the productive capabilities of women. Exclusion of women from their economic and monetary rights has led to deprivation and social exclusion, which forms the basis of poverty. With growing urbanization but very slow growth of industrialization the opportunity available has become more stringent. It is thus considered necessary that the female work participation rate should qualitatively improve with more diversion in participation towards secondary and service sector of the economy. Women participation in the urban sector needs to be guarded against wage differential market, unregulated nature of jobs and discriminatory nature of treatment.

It is by now well understood that growth by itself does not guarantee eradication of poverty. Effective interventions are required which must be gender-specific and gender-friendly.

Employment Guarantee Schemes (EGS) often known, as 'women projects' have been highly successful in states like Maharashtra and Kerala. These could be carried out in the Valley as pilot projects to create stable employment through linkages with sectoral programmes.

Work culture, initiating proficiency and efficiency needs to be inculcated among women workers through training and formal teaching so as to survive the advent of the competitive forces of the labour market. With a positive growth of literacy and improved sex ratio this could yield productive results in the economy.

Long term anti-poverty strategy needs to be formulated to embrace sectoral priorities which are not characterized by diminishing returns and building co-operative agencies to benefit the marginalized women workers in the urban informal sectors of Barak Valley.

REFERENCES

1. Breman, J. (1996); *Footloose Labour*, Cambridge University Press, Cambridge.
2. Chatterjee, S. (2000); *A Socio Economic History of South Assam*. Printwell Publishers, Jaipur.
3. GOI (1995); 4th World Conference on Women, 1995. Country Report. Government of India, Department of Women and Child Development, Ministry of Human Resource Development. New Delhi.
4. Mazumdar, A., P. Acharjee and J. Bhattacharjee, (eds), 1998, *Statistical Profile of Barak Valley,* NECAS, Silchar
5. Papola, T.S., and Alakh Sharma, (eds), 1999, *Gender and Employment in India,* Vikas, New Delhi.
6. Ranachandraiah, C. (1997); Weather and Water in Urban Areas. *EPW*, October 25, 1997.
7. World Resource, (1996); Institute of World Resources, 1996-97. New York.

INFORMALITY AND POVERTY

11

Multi-Dimensional Aspects of Poverty in North-East States

Saswati Das
Chaiti Sharma Biswas

Introduction

Until the mid 1960s, the main thrust of development policies all over the world was to accelerate the growth process since the trickle down mechanism was supposed to take care of distributional objectives. Unfortunately, the development experience of many countries during the two decades after second world war raised question about the relevance and efficiency of the 'trickle down' hypothesis since a large fraction of the population of developing countries continued to live in abject poverty. The reduction of poverty became an explicit goal of development and programmes were designed so as to increase income and to create employment opportunities of target group of the population but income was viewed as the only concept of value to individual.

Over recent decades, many economists, including Sen (1985, 1987), have questioned the equivalence of economic growth with upliftment in human well being and the quality of people's lives. Sen defined standard of living in terms of, (i) functioning, which indicates attainment of different attributes, and (ii) capability, which is the ability to attain. The capability approach emphasizes on what a person can do and not what he can purchase as the ultimate metric of well being. Accordingly, a new area of research has been developed during recent decades, which considers human well being as a multi-dimensional concept consisting of both the economic and non-economic dimensions.

Present chapter intends to examine the multi dimensional nature of deprivation of the poor with special reference to the urban poor in the North-Eastern (NE) region. Well being and deprivation are two sides of a coin. So, to say something about the deprivation needs some measure of well being first of all. In the present exercise well being has been analyzed by selecting a list of socio-economic indicators as are permitted by the eixsting database. To put it more simply, the present exercise has considered the three basic needs of human lives, viz., income, education and food. In a socialistic democratic country, where equality and egalitarianism guide the process of development, it is quite natural for the people in the same region having parity in their consumption of resources reflected in the magnitude of these indicators. It is also quite natural for the people in one region to expect their consumption of various resources to be at par with that enjoyed by the people in other regions under the same political territory. Therefore, well being of the poor in the North-Eastern India has been discussed on a comparative basis with other referents. Three referents have been considered. The values of selected indicators for the poor have been compared with their respective values for the state as a whole, for the poor in the country as a whole and for the country as a whole. It is of additional interest to recalculate the number of poor for these states instead of using the poverty line and poverty ratio of Assam for all other states in the region as has been done by the Planning Commission of India (NHDR, 2002).

This chapter extracts the maximum possible information from various reports published by National Sample Survey Organization (NSSO) for the latest quinquennial survey conducted on 1999-2000.

Section I describes the socio-economic-demographic profile of the North-Eastern states giving an overall idea about the region. Section II deals with the problem of poverty estimation in the region. Section III gives the measure and magnitude of selected indicator of well being making comparisons between the poor and their referents. Section IV discusses the concluding observations.

North East Profile

Mainly North-Eastern region consists of eight states namely Arunachal Pradesh, Assam, Manipur, Meghalaya, Mizoram, Nagaland, Sikkim and Tripura located in the North-East corner of India. This region comprises only 8 per cent of the country's total geographical area. Modernization of agriculture and development of heavy industry is considerably hampered in the North-Eastern region as the entire region is mountainous and situated on a seismic zone. Therefore, socio-economic scenario of this region is expected to be quite different from the rest of India. For this typical topograhy both total population and population density are lower relative to other regions of Inida. It comprises only 3.8 per cent of the country's total population with a population density of 149 persons per sq. km, which is significantly less than national population density 32.4. Considering the social aspects it has been observed that Assam is the most (26.64 million) and Sikkim the least (0.54 million) populated state in the North-Eastern region (Cenus 2001). Sex ratio of the North-Eastern region (936 female per 1000 males) is better than that of all India (933) level. Manipur has the highest sex ratio (978) and Sikkim the lowest (875) in this region (Cenus 2001). Literacy scenario is very much impressive in North-Eastern India. Except Arunachal Pradesh, Assam and Meghalaya, literacy rate, in all other North-Eastern States are higher than all India (65.20%) rate.

Tabe 11.1
Socio-Demographic Profile of the North Eastern Region, 2001

States	Population (in millions)			Sex Ratio			% of Literacy		
	Rural	Urban	Combined	Rural	Urban	Combined	Rural	Urban	Combined
Arunachal P.	0.87	0.22	1.09	915	850	901	48.34	78.82	54.74
Assam	23.26	3.38	26.64	940	878	932	60.92	85.76	64.28
Manipur	1.82	0.57	2.39	969	1009	978	65.33	80.04	68.87
Meghalaya	1.86	0.45	2.31	972	985	975	57.00	87.12	63.31
Mizoram	0.45	0.44	0.89	925	951	938	80.46	96.35	88.49
Nagaland	1.64	0.35	1.99	932	809	909	62.99	85.95	67.11
Sikkim	0.48	0.06	0.54	881	828	875	67.67	84.82	69.68
Tripura	2.64	0.55	3.19	948	962	950	70.23	89.51	73.66
India	741.66	285.36	1027.02	946	901	933	59.21	80.06	65.20

Source: Census of India, 2001.

Among the North-Eastern states Mizoram has the highest literacy (88.49%) followed by Tripura (73.66%) as par Census 2001 (Tabel 11.1). Except the above-mentioned states both rural and urban literacy rate of NorthEastern states are higher than all India rate.

Now, concentrating on the economic features of North-Eastern region, it is observed that per capita net state domestic product (PCNSDP) of the North-Eastern states are less than the all India PCNSDP (Rs. 15,626) at current price (Economic Survey, 1999-2000). Among the North-Eastern states Sikkim has the highest PCNSDP (Rs. 14,751) followed by Mizoram (Rs. 14,909) and Assam has the lowest PCNSDP (Rs. 9720). PCNSDP of other North-Eastern States in 1999-2000 ranges between Rs. 12,083 and Rs. 13,352. Except Assam, Sikkim and Tripura, all other North-Eastern state's per capita consumption expenditure (PCCE) is higher than all India (Rs. 590.98) PCCE. Nagaland has the higehst PCCE (Rs. 1005.99) within this region (1999-2000). Both rural and urban PCCE of Nagaland is highest among the North-Eastern states of India. PCCE in rural and urban Assam, and urban Manipur are lower than the respective Indian level PCCE. As a whole in the North-Eastern states except Meghalaya, Mizoram and Nagaland nearly 55 percent of total population belongs to labour force which is less than all India percentage (61.8%). Meghalaya has the highest percentage of labour force (73.6%) within this region. In the North-Eastern region percentage of rural labour force is more than that of urban.

In rural areas percentage of labour force lies between (45.8-79.7) per cent whereas in urban areas it lies between (42.0 to 56.4) per cent. Only notable feature is that in Tripura both rural and urban areas, labour force is very small. In order to know the employment situation of a state or region, labour force is not the only indicator because it does not mean that all of them are gainfully employed, so besides

Table 11.2
Economic Profile of the North-Eastern Region, 1999-2000

States	PC NSDP (current price)	PC consumption Expenditure (Rs.)			% of Persons in Labour force			Incidence of unemployment		
		Rural	Urban	Combined	Rural	Urban	Combined	Rural	Urban	Combined
Arunachal Pradesh	13352	647.9	765.9	672.3	58.1	44.4	55.3	0.5	3.0	0.9
Assam	9720	426.1	814.1	473.4	55.8	50.6	55.2	4.0	9.8	4.6
Manipur	12721	537.8	707.8	596.4	56.3	50.9	54.4	2.0	6.7	3.5
Meghalaya	12083	563.6	971.9	639.1	79.7	47.6	73.6	0.4	4.5	0.9
Mizoram	14909	721.8	1056.6	935.5	76.6	56.4	63.8	0.9	2.9	2.0
Nagaland	12594	941.3	1242.4	1005.9	72.5	50.9	67.6	2.4	9.2	3.5
Sikkim	14751	531.7	905.7	559.9	59.2	55.9	58.8	2.8	8.0	3.4
Tripura	13195	528.4	876.6	589.5	45.8	42.0	45.1	1.2	5.8	1.9
India	15626	486.1	854.9	590.9	66.2	51.1	61.8	1.5	4.8	2.3

Sources: Economic Survey, 2003; NSSO, 2001, Levels and Pattern of Consumption Expenditure in India; NSSO, 2001, Employment and Unemployment Situation in India; NHDR, 2002

labour force it is necessary to know about the rate of employment or the incidence of unemployment. In Assam, Meghalaya, Nagaland and Sikkim the incidence of unemployment is more than that of all India level among which Assam has the highest incidence of unemployment (4.6). For other states the incidence of unemployment is lower than that of all India level. In North-Eastern India rural unemployment rate is lower than that of urban one. Employment situation is relatively better in urban Mizoram and Arunachal Pradesh. Among the rest of the North-Eastern states urban Assam has the highest percentage of unemployment (9.8%) and in other states this percentage ranges between (4.5-9.2) per cent which are mostly higher than all Indian urban (4.8 average) (Table 11.2) With this overall fair background we feel an urge to know the condition of the poor of this region. The following sections will deal with this particular point.

Poverty Estimates: Methods and Results

Normally, poverty is measured in terms of the proportion of a population living below poverty line where poverty line is measured in terms of a given norm. There are widely known inherent and irreducible element of arbitrariness in specifying the poverty line that is expected to capture the minimum living standard separating the poor from the non-poor. The Task Force (1979) defined the poverty line as the per capita expenditure level at which the average per capita, per day calorie intake was 2095 for the urban areas and 2435 calories for rural area. These calorie estimates were rounded off to 2100 for urban areas and 2400 for the rural.

Corresponding to an average daily intake of 2400 calories for rural and 2100 calories for urban area, the average monthly per capita expenditures were worked out to be Rs. 56.64 and Rs. 49.09 at 1973-74 prices for rural and urban respectively. They were taken as poverty lines for the rural and urban areas for 1973-74 and have been used by the Planning Commission for estimating the number of poor for rural and urban India.

To have state specific poverty lines the planning Commission uses state wise consumer price index numbers for industrial workers (CPIIW) for urban area and consumer price index numbers for agricultural labourers (ALCPI) for rural areas. The above estimated poverty lines then need updating over time to take into account the change in the price level.

So, ideally one has to get state specific price indices. But the problem lies with having price data for all states separately. For urban area, center wise CPIIW are constructed by the Labour Bureau. These centers are then grouped according to the states in which they are situated. However, some states have no center from which price data are collected. In such cases, the price index of a neighbouring state is used, on the basis of the similarity in economic and demographic factors.

In case of North-Eastern states, we get separate CPIIW only for Assam and Tripura because there are no urban center in other six states. So we were compelled to assign same CPIIW of Assam to all these six states and estimated the urban poor using the urban poverty line of Assam but population distribution by expenditure classes of the respective states. On the other, we could get separate CPIAL for Assam and Tripura since 1993-94. For Manipur and Meghalaya Labour Bureau gives separate CPIAL since 1995-96. So we estimated poverty lines for 1999-2000 for these two states by inflating poverty line of rural Assam for 1995-96 by CPIAL for these two states. Being adjacent to Manipur and having similar economic and demographic profiles, the rural poverty line of Manipur has been used for rural Nagaland and Mizoram. Similarly, rural poverty line for Meghalaya has been used for rural Sikkim. Matching of state level price data on the basis of physical contiguity and similar socio-economic profiles has also been done by other researchers (Dubey and Gangopadhaya, 1998).

While the construction of poverty lines in this way might not be much satisfactory, it does a fair degree of disaggregation compared to that of using a common poverty line and identical poverty ratio of Assam for the whole region. The official poverty lines (OPL) and re-estimated povery lines (RPL) for 1999-2000 are given in Table 11.3

Table 11.3

Official and Re-Estimated Poverty Lines in the North- Eastern States, 1999-2000.

States	Urban		Rural	
	OPL*	RPL	OPL*	RPL
Arunachal Pradesh	343.99	—	365.43	370.46
Assam	343.99	—	365.43	—
Manipur	343.99	—	365.43	353.17
Meghalaya	343.99	—	365.43	370.46
Mizoram	343.99	—	365.43	353.17
Nagaland	343.99	—	365.43	353.17
Sikkim	343.99	—	365.43	370.46
Tripura	343.99	382.12	365.43	370.46
India	454.11	—	327.56	415.55

Source : National Human Development Report, 2002.

Most commonly used poverty measure is the poverty incidence ratio commonly known as head count ratio (HCR). It measures the proportion of people below the poverty line and is used as an index of poverty . The ratio is defined as: HCR = n/N, where n is the number of people below the poverty line and N is the total population.

Table 11.4
Estimated HCR in the North-Eastern States, 1999-2000.

States	Urban HCR		Rural HCR	
	Planning Commission*	Re-estimated	Planning Commission*	Re-estimated
Arunachal P.	7.47	5.00	40.2	23.07
Assam	7.47	7.47	40.2	40.2
Manipur	7.47	0.50	40.2	11.82
Meghalaya	7.47	—	40.2	6.88
Mizoram	7.47	—	40.2	1.66
Nagaland	7.47	—	40.2	0.23
Sikkim	7.47	4.62	40.2	22.39
Tripura	7.47	6.43	40.2	29.71
India	23.62	23.62	27.09	27.09

Source: National Human Development Report, 2002.

Table 11.4 presents estimated HCR using the poverty lines of Table 11.3. In the second and fourth columns of Table 11.4, we have reproduced urban and rural HCR computed by the Planning Commission for the North-Eastern states for the years 1999-2000 and the third and the fifth columns consist of HCR re-estimated by the present authors. The all-India urban HCR is 23.62 per cent whereas the respective figure for the region is only 7.47 per cent. The scenario is just opposite in the rural area. While all-India rural HCR is 27.09 per cent in 1999-2000, this is as high as 40.2 per cent in the whole region. Thus according to the Planning Commission's estimates we need to seriously worry about poverty levels in the region at least in its rural areas.

According to our estimates, the HCRs of Assam for 1999-2000 are essentially the same as the official ones. But for other states in the region, the estimates diverge from the official estimates. Due to insignificant population proportions in the lower expenditure classes, there is no question of poor estimation in urban areas of Meghalaya, Mizoram and Nagaland. Urban Assam has the highest HCRs (7.47 per cent) followed by Tripura (6.43 per cent) Arunachal Pradesh (5 per cent) and Sikkim (4.62 per cent). Poverty level in urban Manipur is just insignificant (0.50 per cent). Th re-estimated HCRs for rural, furnished in Table 11.4, reveals a good deal of difference in the rates of poverty across the eight states in the region. The first is the noted superior performance of Mizoram and Nagaland, the rural HCRs for these two states are only 1.66 percent and 0.23 percent respectively. The HCRs of Meghalaya (6.88 per cent) and Manipur (11.82 per cent) are also moderately low. But the performance of Sikkim, Arunachal Pradesh and Tripura are not so impressive, the respective HCR for these states are 22.39 per cent, 23.0 per cent and 29.71 per cent. It may be mentioned that the estimated HCRs obtained by the present authors are quite similar to some other eminent independent researchers, outside the Planning Commission. Bhandari and Dubey's work[1] is worth mentioning here. Bhandari and Dubey estimated the HCR using the NSS data for 1999-2000, for the region by their own methodology.

Now the two sets of figures, one is that of Planning Commission and other is of the present authors, in Table 11.4, are remarkable in their deviations, for every state other than Assam. This is because Planning Commission uses poverty ratio of Assam for all other states in the region. Except for Assam they don't even calculate poverty ratios for other North-Eastern states separately, using the population distribution by expenditure classes for the respective states. Assam's poverty figures are being superimposed on the other states.

This is a very misleading effort, as we feel. With this overall low incidence of poverty in the region, except in Assam, let us estimate the magnitude of selected indicators mentioned earlier, for the poor in the region.

Economic Well-being of the Poor

Data on size distribution of income in India are not available on a regular basis and therefore consumer expenditure data are used for studies on poverty and level of living of Indian population. Our present exercise also used the monthly per capita expenditure (MPCE) database provided by NSSO (2001). Average monthly per capita expenditure (AMPCE) for the poor and state as a whole in each urban and rural sector are shown in Table 11.5. It may be observed that the all India AMPCE in the urban sector is Rs. 854.9, the corresponding figure for all India poor is Rs. 354.44. The state level AMPCE in urban areas ranges between Rs. 762.66 (Arunachal Pradesh) and Rs. 1242.39 (Nagaland). The respective figures for the poor in urban sector are Rs. 154.77 (Arunachal Pradesh) and Rs. 333.14 (Tripura). The all India rural AMPCE is Rs. 263.9 for the poor and Rs. 486.16 for the country as a whole. The respective AMPCEs are Rs. 648 (Arunachal Pradesh) and Rs. 941.3 (Nagaland). The AMPCE for the poor in the states of North-Eastern ranges between Rs. 288.405 (Assam) to Rs. 345.53 (Tripura) in rural.

Thus, it is revealed that the state level consumption in urban sector is much higher than the rural sector . But the level of consumption of the poor in urban sector does not differ widely than the poor in the rural. The interstate variation in consumption of the poor is not substantial in both the sectors only with one exception that of Arunachal Pradesh. The AMPCE in urban sector of the state is only Rs. 154.77 compared to more than Rs. 300 in all other states. This is because there is no significant proportion of urban population in the expenditure class of Rs. 300-350 and so urban poor belongs only to the expenditure class of Rs. 0-300. Accordingly, AMPCE of urban poor in this state is far low compared to the corresponding state level as well as all India level for the poor. As mentioned in the previous section that the question of estimating poor does not arise in urban areas of three states, viz., Meghalaya, Mizoram and Nagaland. However, among the remaining five states urban Manipur shows minimum disparity in AMPCE of the poor against the state level and all India level. All the North-Eastern states have AMPCE for the rural poor higher than that of poor at all India rural. Reversibly, all India urban AMPCE for the poor is higher than the respective figures for all the states in the region.

The share of the poor in aggregate per capita expenditure

(APCE), i.e. considering State Level per capita expenditure, is a good indicator to assess the deprivation of the poor, compared to other referents. It is evident from Table 11.5 that the percentage share of the poor in APCE is very little in urban areas.

Table. 11.5

HCR, AMPCE and Expenditure Share of the Poor in the North-Eastern States, 1999-2000

States	Re-estimated HCR	APMCE poor	State Level	Share of poor (%)
		Urban		
Arunachal Pradesh	5.0	154.77	762.66	1.01
Assam	7.47	311.55	814.12	2.55
Manipur	0.50	329.59	707.77	0.23
Meghalaya	—	—	972.18	—
Mizoram	—	—	1056.63	—
Nagaland	—	—	1242.39	—
Skikkim	4.62	315.36	905.69	1.49
Tripura	6.43	333.14	876.6	2.6
India	23.62	354.44	854.9	9.9
		Rural		
Arunachal Pradesh	23.07	303.83	648	10.87
Assam	40.2	288.4	426.13	27.38
Manipur	11.82	306.06	537.8	5.85
Meghalaya	6.88	336.51	563.45	4.17
Mizoram	1.66	319.69	721.84	0.77
Nagaland	0.23	315.25	941.31	0.08
Sikkim	22.39	315.18	531.77	13.34
Tripura	29.71	345.53	528.41	19.48
India	27.09	263.9	486.16	14.82

Source : Level and tauern of Consumer Expenditure in India 1999-2000, NSSO, 55th round.

The share is least in Arunachal Pradesh, 5 per cent poor in the urban sharing only 1.01 per cent of APCE. Having largest percentage of urban poor in Assam (7.4 per cent) only 2.55 per cent of AMPCE is enjoyed by the poor in the state. Performance of Manipur is superior to other states in the region, 0.5 per cent poor sharing 0.23 per cent of APCE which is about half of what they should share. At all-India 9.9 per cent of APCE goes to 23.6 per cent urban poor. So performance of Manipur and Tripura is representative to that of all-India level while Arunachal Pradesh, Assam and Sikkim are left behind.

The deprivation of the poor in terms of share in APCE has slightly different dimension in rural sector of the region. Having top most level of poverty in rural Assam the poor shares 27.38 per cent of APCE which is about 68 per cent of what they deserve. In Mizoram, percentage of rural poor is least but deprivation is high, about 2 per cent rural poor enjoy less than 1 per cent of APCE. Deprivation of rural poor, in terms of share in APCE is least in Assam, followed by Tripura. On the other, deprivation is highest in Nagaland, 2.3 per cent rural poor enjoying 0.08 per cent of APCE. Rural poor in four states, viz., Arunachal Pradesh, Manipur, Mizoram and Nagaland have lower shares in APCE compared to the share of rural poor at all-India.

Educational Attainment of the Poor

As par NSS definition 1999-2000, a person who can both read and write a simple message with understanding in at least one language is considered as literate (NSS, 2001). Literacy is defined as the ratio of literate persons to all persons aged 7 years and above.

In urban areas literacy rates among the poor for all the states are satisfactorily high. Arunachal Pradesh has the highest literacy rate of 90.5 per cent for persons followed by Manipur (87 per cent). It may be noticed that percentage of literates among poor in urban sector of Arunachal Pradesh is marginally higher compared to the state level percentage of literates, far and far above compared to the rate for all India poor and moderately higher compared to the all India rate. Male literacy among poor in urban Arunachal Pradesh is as high as 95.5 per cent which is also quite higher than the figure for state level (91.8 per cent). Difference between poor and state level is highest in Sikkim (44.9 per cent and 87.1 per cent). So both in rural and urban India the literacy rates among poor are found to be much lower than the rates in the North- Eastern states except Assam. Assam shows the highest difference between state level poor and the poor at all India in urban. Among the North-Eastern states, Meghalaya showed the highest rural literacy rate among the poor (70.62 per cent) which is moderately higher than the rates for all India rural poor (41.56 per cent), and the country as a whole (56.0 per cent), but quite lower than the rate for the state level (75.5 per cent). In terms of literacy rate Mizoram showed the highest difference between poor and state level. While literacy rate is just 49.38 per cent among the poor persons, the figure for state level is as high as 90.5 per cent. Performance of Manipur is worst, only 40.9 per cent rural poor being literate in the state. In a developing country, it is normally observed that literacy rates for males are higher than those for females. It is observed from Table. 11.6 that the literacy rate in each North-Eastern state is

Table 11.6: Level of Education Among the Poor in the North Eastern States, 1999-2000

State	Category	M/F/P	Percentage distribution of population by educational level				
			Literate	primary	primary	middle	secondary & above
1	2	3	4	5	6	7	8
				Urban			
Arunachal Pradesh	Poor	male	95.50	7.50	17.60	20.0	50.40
		female	84.80	13.20	29.10	16.70	25.90
		persons	90.50	10.20	23.00	18.40	38.80
	State level	male	91.80	14.20	12.70	17.80	47.20
		female	85.30	17.10	26.10	14.00	28.10
		persons	89.00	15.40	18.60	16.10	38.80
Assam	Poor	male	67.48	40.74	15.58	9.55	1.66
		female	38.88	20.62	14.89	3.12	0.20
		persons	54.27	31.44	15.35	6.57	0.97

(*Condt.*)

1	2	3	4	5	6	7	8
	Statel level	male	90.60	13.30	17.80	20.20	53.30
		female	80.80	15.00	16.80	19.10	29.90
		persons	86.10	14.10	17.30	19.70	35.00
Manipur	Poor*	persons	87.00	30.20	16.60	30.20	10.10
	Statel level	persons	87.20	13.00	11.30	17.40	45.50
Sikkim	Poor*	persons	44.90	21.40	4.80	12.70	6.00
	Statel level	persons	87.10	23.50	16.00	15.90	32.70
Tripura	Poor	male	75.80	38.80	9.60	19.70	7.60
		female	43.56	20.08	11.84	9.98	1.66
		persons	58.90	29.10	13.15	12.40	4.16
	State level	male	91.70	28.50	13.80	26.30	31.10
		female	78.20	21.00	14.10	19.30	23.90
		persons	85.20	20.70	13.90	22.90	27.60
All India	Poor	male	69.28	24.05	16.95	15.57	12.62
		female	50.42	19.72	13.31	10.59	6.71
		persons	60.02	21.92	15.17	13.16	9.83
	State level	male	86.50	16.40	14.90	17.70	37.50
		female	72.30	15.70	14.30	15.30	27.00
		persons	79.80	16.10	14.70	16.50	32.50
			Rural				
Arunachal Pradesh	Poor	male	52.23	23.09	17.51	8.70	3.43
		female	45.91	20.42	10.53	8.86	3.34
		persons	49.27	21.56	15.44	8.78	3.32
	State level	male	57.30	14.10	18.10	12.40	12.80
		female	44.80	14.10	14.50	8.60	7.40
		persons	51.40	14.20	16.40	10.60	10.20
Assam	Poor	male	66.06	28.22	19.21	13.09	5.53
		female	49.02	22.13	14.37	9.49	2.76
		persons	57.96	25.32	16.92	11.38	4.38
	State levels	male	76.20	22.90	19.60	19.70	14.10
		female	60.60	21.90	15.60	14.50	8.60
		persons	69.00	22.40	17.70	17.30	11.50
Manipur	poor	male	53.62	6.20	13.85	17.52	16.00
		female	45.09	12.04	18.90	5.88	8.24
		persons	40.90	7.80	14.10	9.36	4.84
	State level	male	74.90	12.80	16.30	19.30	26.40
		female	61.90	14.40	14.80	15.70	21.80
		persons	68.60	13.60	15.60	17.60	16.90

(*Condt.*)

1	2	3	4	5	6	7	8
Meghalay	Poor	male	70.36	44.48	17.26	8.52	0.00
		female	59.14	32.10	21.40	5.64	0.00
		persons	70.62	46.42	21.90	5.64	0.00
	State level	male	78.70	34.00	27.90	11.70	5.10
		female	72.30	30.20	24.60	12.40	5.20
		persons	75.50	32.10	26.30	12.00	5.20
Mizoram	Poor*	persons	49.38	13.00	20.13	16.25	0.00
	State level	persons	90.50	21.40	28.20	30.10	10.80
Sikkim	Poor	male	73.44	43.53	15.84	9.48	4.59
		female	57.90	35.73	13.56	7.40	1.07
		persons	65.23	39.26	14.70	8.40	2.27
	State levels	male	81.10	35.10	16.80	13.90	15.30
		female	65.80	28.90	14.50	12.00	10.20
		persons	74.00	32.30	15.80	13.00	13.00
Tripura	Poor	male	73.09	31.27	25.49	14.41	1.87
		female	57.53	32.63	18.69	5.39	8.50
		persons	67.78	32.82	23.08	10.30	1.52
	State level	male	84.00	28.80	24.60	20.20	10.30
		female	69.50	30.50	21.40	12.90	4.70
		persons	77.20	29.60	23.10	16.80	7.60
All India	Poor	male	53.42	24.27	13.12	10.00	6.03
		female	29.64	15.73	7.88	4.33	1.64
		persons	41.56	20.02	10.54	7.19	3.81
	State level	male	67.80	22.10	15.40	15.30	15.10
		female	43.40	16.50	11.40	9.00	6.40
		persons	56.00	19.40	13.50	12.30	10.90

Source: Literacy and Levels of Education in India 1999-2000, NSSO, 2001.

*Male-female distributions by level of education for lower expenditure classes are not provided by NSSO.

much higher for male than that of the female. Similarly, rates for rural sector are normally lower than the corresponding rates for urban sector. Table 1 1.6 also reveals that the gap between literacy rates for poor persons and the state as a whole do not vary largely across the states and this is true for both rural and urban sectors. With very few exceptions, rates for poor persons are generally lower than the corresponding state level figures.

The situation is not so encouraging at the primary, middle and secondary and above level of education among the poor in the region. The interstate variation in this regard is very wide between 4.8 per cent (Sikkim) to 23 per cent (Arunachal Pradesh) in urban. Similarly, middle secondary and above level of education in urban ranges between 6.57 per cent (Assam) to 30.2 per cent (Manipur) and 0.97 per cent (Assam) to 38.8 per cent (Arunachal Pradesh) respectively. The performance of the poor against the state or all India poor or the country as a whole is mixed, i.e. in some cases performance of the poor are better compared to their referents and in some cases worse. The rural picture is quite different. Though the overall low rate of primary, middle, secondary and above education are observed but in all cases the rates for the poor are consistently lower than those for the state figures. Some states have performed better compared to all India poor or country as a whole in respect of the above said level of eudcation.

Thus, one may conclude that in terms of literacy rates among the poor, the North-Eastern states are not going behind compared to all India rates. In terms of higher level of education the picture is quite different. So it is seen to be a paradox in the region, with a moderately high level of literacy with very low level of higher education among the poor.

Nutritional Scenario of the Poor

In urban areas, except Assam and Tripura, all other North-Eastern states have very negligible number of poor population, so food related data for these states were not provided by NSSO. To assess the nutritional scenario household size plays an important role as nutrition statement always relating it with per household or per capita. So first we concentrate on the average household size. Both rural and urban average household size of poor is larger than that of state level. Urban Assam has the largest average household size (5.72) for poor followed by Tripura (5.31) which are smaller than average household size (table 11.7) of India (5.88). Average size of poor household in rural areas in (table 11.7) larger than that of all India level (5.83). Average size of rural household for poor and state level in Assam (6.28 and 5.48) is largest among the North Eastern States.

Whatever may be the component of nutrients, the poor people of the North-Eastern states generally consume two square meals a day. Average number of meal consumed both by urban and rural poor households per month is more than the state level average. Average number of meal consumed by urban poor household per month in Tripura (443) is higher

Table 11.7

Average No. of Meals Consumed by Poor Households Per Months in the North Eastern States, 1999-2000

State	Category	Avg.	Avg. No. of meal consumed per hhd	Percentage of persons reporting "0" meals
		Urban		
Assam	Poor	5.72	394	0.0
	State level	4.09	273	0.8
Tripura	Poor	5.31	443	0.40
	State level	4.17	344	0.20
India	Poor	5.88	425	1.42
	State level	4.53	320	1.00
		Rural		
Arunachal	Poor	6.18	428	0.75
Pradesh	State level	4.98	357	1.10
Assam	Poor	6.28	447	0.79
	State level	5.48	400	0.70
Manipur	Poor	5.73	366	1.41
	State level	5.21	339	1.60
Meghalaya	Poor	6.20	403	1.09
	State Level	5.07	314	0.60
Sikkim	Poor	5.87	425	0.08
	State Level	4.63	323	0.50
Tripura	Poor	5.05	424	0.28
	State Level	4.63	393	0.40
India	Poor	5.83	429	0.06
	State Level	5.04	372	0.10

Source: Nutritional Intake in India 1999-2000, NSSO, 2001.

Note: We omitted those North-Eastern states in the table for which data for poor class is not available.

than all India urban average (425). But urban poor in Assam (394) consume less than all India (Table 11.7) urban poor. State level urban average number of meals consumed per household per month in the North-Eastern states (except Tripura and Manipur) are less than all India average (320). Besides, none of the North-Eastern states reporting about zero meal a month in urban areas for poor. In Tripura 0.40 per cent urban poor having zero meal per month which is less than state level zero meal. At state level among the North-Eastern States. Arunachal Pradesh have the highest percentage of urban people with zero meal per month. Otherwise North Eastern percentage of person with zero meal at state level are less than all India percentage (1.42).

In the North-Eastern states it is seen that number of average meal consumed by rural poor is more than the state level average number of meal. Among the North-Eastern states average number of meal consumed by rural poor of Manipur is lowest (366) followed by Meghalaya (403) which are less than all India average meal (429) consumed. For rest of the North-Eastern states average number of meal consumed by rural poor is more than all India average. At state level, lowest number of meal is consumed by rural Meghalaya (314) followed by Sikkim (323). Except Assam (400) and Tripura (393), average number of meal consumed per rural household per month at home are less than all India average (372). In Sikkim the difference in average number of meal intake between poor and state level is maximum. In the rural areas of North-Eastern states, percentage of poor people having no meal per month is more than all Indian percentage (0.06). At state level percentage of people having zero meal in a month is less than that of rural India (0.10). But compared to state level, percentage of rural poor with zero meal per month is always less except Assam and Meghalaya.

Nutrient provides energy, which comes from calorie, protein and fat to a person. So a standard measuring rod is needed to compare the nutritional status of both urban and rural poor of North-Eastern states. As par ICMR re-commendation, standard per capita per day (PCPD) intake of calorie for rural areas are 2400 Kcal and that for urban areas are 2100 Kcal. As there are no such rural and urban recommendation given separately for protein and fat intake, so we have considered the overall recommendation of ICMR about protein (50 gm) and fat (40 gm) intake PCPD as standard and analyzed the data compared to this standard. It is observed that PCPD calorie intake at state level is always more than that of poor. And it is applicable for both rural and urban areas of North-Eastern states and India as a whole. Here both in urban Assam and Tripura PCPD calorie consumption of poor is less than that of state level and it is much less than the standard 2100 Kcal (Table 11.8). PCPD protein and fat intake of poor in urban areas are far less than the state level in every North-Eastern states. It is also true for urban India. A similiar picture is revealed for per consumer unit per day (PCUPD) urban intake of calorie, protein and fat in North-Eastern states where consumer unit is the rate of equivalence of a normal person determined on the basis of age-sex composition of a person. Consumer unit of a normal male person doing sedentary work and belonging to the age group 20-39 is taken as one unit and the other coefficients are worked out on the basis of calorie requirements (NSSO definiton). In the Northe-Eastern region it is seen that both in Assam (poor: 1891 Kcal and State level: 2630 Kcal) and Tripura (poor: 2086 Kcal and state level: 2761 Kcal) a large gap exists in PCUPD calorie intake between poor and the state level. For North-Eastern states and India there exists a large gap in protein and fat intake between poor and State level in urban areas. Again in urban area PCUPD intake of protein and fat of poor in North-Eastern India is less than all India urban intake.

Except Assam and Meghalaya, all other North-Eastern state's rural PCPD calorie intake of poor is nearer to that of standard 2400 Kcal (Table 11.8). Where all India PCPD intake of calorie for the rural poor is only 1671 Kcal. Except Tripura PCPD intake of calorie for rural poor is less than the state level among rest of the North-Eastern states. State level rural PCPD calorie intake in Mizoram (4481 Kcal) and Arunachal

Pradesh (4473 Kcal) exceeds the standard calorie intake. Except Arunachal Pradesh (61.42 gm), all other North-Eastern state's and India's PCPD protein intake of rural poor are less than the standard intake of protein. PCPD protein intake of rural poor in Assam and Meghalaya is much less than the standard intake. But the state level rural PCPD protein intake is more than the required rate and it is also more than that of poor in the North-Eastern region. At state level rural Manipur (114.90 gm) has the highest protein intake among the North-Eastern states. In Assam (14.26), Meghalaya (13.64) and all India (19.62), PCPD fat intake of rural poor is far below from the standard intake. Fat intake is highest in Tripura (79.08 gm) followed by Manipur (61.36 gm), among rural poor. Rest of the North-Eastern state's PCPD fat intake of poor is slightly higher than the standard intake. At state level, rural people of Arunachal Pradesh (157.60 gm), Manipur (453.80 gm) and Mizoram (167.20 gm) consume huge amount of fat. At state level, except Tripura (49.0 gm), rest of the rural North-Eastern state's and India's fat intake are less than the required rate. There exist a sizeable gap between PCPD calorie intake of poor and state level, both in rural North-Eastern region and India. And this gap is maximum in rural Arunachal Pradesh. Both for protein and fat there is a large gap between PCUPD intake of rural poor and state level.

So far we have discussed about the nutrients which are the main source of daily energy to a person and come through various foods namely cereals, pulses, vegetables etc. to the body. So it is important to know the composition of a food basket. In the North-Eastern states a common feature is that cereals comprise the lion share of the food basket and other food are consumed less. But we will now see the difference of the composition of food basket between the poor and state level. Percentage of total calorie intake from cereal in urban Assam and Tripura is more than 80 per cent which is higher than that of all India (69.25 per cent) level (Table 11.9). Compared to state level it can be said that for poor, percentage of calorie intake from cereal is more than that

Tabel 11.8
Per Day, Per Capita and Per Consumer Unit Nutrients Intake of the Poor in the North-Eastern States, 1999-2000

State	Category	Per Capita per Day intake of			Per Consumer Unit per Day intake of		
		Calorie (Kcal)	Protein (gm)	Fat (gm)	Calorie (Kcal)	Protein (gm)	Fat (gm)
		Urban					
Assam	Poor	1478	35.9	14.5	1891	45.9	18.5
	State level	2174	56.5	38.7	2630	68.3	46.8
Tripura	Poor	1763	41.9	13.7	2086	49.6	16.3
	State level	2281	58.4	39.9	2761	70.7	48.3
India	Poor	1660	45.78	25.93	2058	56.77	32.14
	State level	2156	58.5	49.6	2637	71.5	6.70
		Rural					
Arunachal Pradesh	Poor	2248	61.42	56.92	2773	75.76	70.22
	State level	4473	93.90	157.60	5463	114.70	192.40
Assam	Poor	1580	38.98	14.26	1955	48.23	17.64
	State level	1915	47.70	22.3	2342	58.30	27.20
Manipur	Poor	2361	45.51	61.36	2908	55.92	76.42
	State level	8349	114.90	453.80	10246	141.00	556.90
Meghalaya	Poor	1503	36.42	13.64	1879	45.54	17.02
	State level	1858	47.8	22.9	2287	58.39	28.2
Sikkim	Poor	2023	43.93	55.37	2482	53.97	67.77
	State level	2024	52.60	39	2456	63.80	47.30
Tripura	Poor	2307	44.11	79.08	2789	53.24	95.87
	State level	2293	53.30	49.50	2753	64.00	59.40
India	Poor	1671	45.01	19.62	2097	56.48	24.63
	State level	2149	59.10	36.10	2668	73.40	44.90

Source: Nutritional Intake in India 1999-2000, NSSO, 2001.

of state level which are around 64-66 per cent. In general among the North-Eatern states at urban state level, percentage of calorie intake from cereal in Nagaland is highest followed by Tripura which are more than that at all India (55.14 per cent) level. In urban Manipur (10.80 per cent) lowest per cent of calorie comes from cereal relative to other North-Eastern states. It is seen that like rural areas maximum percent of protein in urban areas also comes from cereal both for poor and state level. At state level in urban areas it is observed that in comparison to rural areas percentage of protein intake from cereals are less, but percentage of protein intake from other sources are more than that of rural areas both in North-Eastern states and all India. But for the poor protein intake from cereals are maximum in urban Assam (76.09 per cent) which is even higher than that of rural Assam (73.59 per cent). Also this percentage of calorie intake from cereal for poor is higher than that of state level. Similar picture is also found in all India, besides cereal there are also other sources of protein like pulses, milk, egg, fish and meat. Percentage of protein intake from pulses both in Assam and Tripura for urban poor are less than that of state level. This percentage of protein intake from pulses for those two said states are less than all India percentage. Relative to all India (6.04 per cent), percentage of protein intake from milk and milk produts in Assam (3.22 per cent) and Tripura (1.80 per cent) are far less for urban poor. And this percentage for poor is significantly less than that of state level. But the picture reverses when we come to the percentage of protein intake from egg, fish and meat. Here, this percentage in urban areas of Assam (5.80 per cent) and Tripura (7.37 per cent) are much higher than all India (4.34 per cent). Again percentage of protein intake from egg, fish and meat for poor are less than state level percentage in urban areas.

Table 11.9

Distribution of Nutrients from Different Food Groups for the Poor in the North-Eastern States, 1999-2000

State	Category	% intake of Calorie from Cereals	Cereal substitute	Total cereals	%intake of Protein from Cereals	Pulses	Milk & Milk products	Egg, fish & meat
Urban								
Assam	Poor	80.43	---	80.43	76.09	8.90	3.22	5.80
	State Level	64.59	0.00	64.59	57.15	10.95	10.43	11.29
Tripura	Poor	80.95	0.00	80.95	74.43	7.39	1.80	7.37
	State Level	66.45	0.03	66.48	58.08	8.91	9.27	13.23
India	Poor	69.19	0.06	69.25	70.44	10.62	6.04	4.34
	State Level	55.05	0.09	55.14	57.03	13.10	12.43	5.98
Rural								
Arunachal Pradesh	Poor	25.55	2.61	28.16	49.99	5.50	11.82	24.47
	State Level	39.38	0.34	39.72	44.01	12.63	9.89	17.82
Assam	Poor	80.7	0.012	70.71	73.59	7.12	1.73	8.95
	State Level	75.91	0.01	75.92	68.24	8.94	3.90	9.22
Manipur	Poor	72.04	0.024	72.06	78.91	6.24	1.13	5.68
	State Level	22.15	0.01	22.16	35.08	37.39	10.56	6.06
Meghalaya	Poor	75.94	2.84	78.78	68.08	4.74	1.99	12.15
	State Level	71.79	1.50	73.29	61.15	4.51	3.16	16.84
Sikkim	Poor	69.17	0.00	69.17	72.13	5.70	10.92	5.43
	State Level	67.96	0.00	67.96	60.98	7.53	13.57	9.12
Tripura	Poor	66.24	0.132	66.37	68.14	5.42	6.63	9.76
	State Level	65.69	0.09	65.78	62.31	7.34	7.69	10.80
India	Poor	77.66	0.112	77.77	77.30	9.44	3.04	2.76
	State Level	67.55	0.16	67.71	67.43	10.91	9.19	4.04

Source: Nutrition intake in India 1999-2000, NSSO, 2001.

Except Arunachal Pradesh and Meghalaya there are very little cereals substitutes in rural areas of North-Eastern states. Percentage of cereal consumption of rural poor is more than the state level in the rural areas of most of the North-Eastern states and India. Only in Arunachal Pradesh and Assam percentage of cereal intake of poor is less than that of state level. At state level percentage of cereal consumption in rural areas varies from 32.45 per cent (Mizoram) to 75.92 per cent (Assam). As percentage of cereal consumption is higher in North-Easten states, so both poor and non poor get the highest percentage of protein from cereals rather than other sources like pulses, milk and milk products, eggs, fish and meat in rural areas. This is also applicable for rural India. But percentage of protein from other sources at state level are more than poor both in North-Eastern and India as a whole. In rural areas of Manipur highest protein at state level comes from pulses (37.39 per cent) and milk (10.56 per cent) which are significantly higher than all India (10.91 per cent and 9.19 per cent) percentages. At state level percentage of protein intake from fat is maximum in rural Nagaland (19.41 per cent) which is more than that of rural India (4.04 per cent).

Concluding Observations

During recent decades the concept of human well-being has been shifted from solely economic to economic and non-economic aspects of life. From this point of view, we tried to assess the condition of the poor in te North-Eastern region, considering economic and non-economic aspects of human lives, as are permitted by the existing database.

We initiated the study with a mindset that incidence of poverty is very high in this region. But our estimation of poor clearly depicts a low incidence of poverty in all the states in this region, especially in urban sector, except in Assam, compared to the incidence of poverty in the country as a whole. Analysing the factors responsible for such a low poverty rates, needs an in-depth study, which is beyond the scope of this study. What can we say only, is that a marked feature of these states is to fall under a special category where 90 per cent of assistance is received from central government as grant; the per capita devolution of central Plan and Non-Plan funds is amongst the highest in the country, as are evident from different reports of Centre for Policy Research. Still, Assam has high HCR which may be due to insurgency, terrorism and corruption (Singh, 1999) on the one side, and abnormal growth of population, especially due to continuous influx of migrants in the state (Mali, 1993). Thus, the actual problem to show high poverty rates in the region probably is due to that, we always think of the region as a homogeneous entity, and ascribe all characteristics of Assam to the whole region.

Coming to the magnitudes of the selected indicators, considered so far, the level of consumption of the poor in urban sector does not differ widely than their counterpart in the rural but the level of consumption is far low compared to the state or all-India levels. In respect to literacy rate, the performance of the poor, especially in urban North-East, out performs the poor of the nation as a whole and they are not left behind the state level average also. But the situation is not so hopeful when primary, middle or secondary level of education is considered. It also demands in-depth study. The overall low incidence of poverty is well matched with the adequacy of food in the region. Since poverty line was calculated from the minimum calorie requirement PCPD, so low poverty rate should co-exist with moderately adequate food among the people in these states.

The chapter suffers from paucity of data for drawing valid conclusion concerning the well being and extent of deprivation of the poor in the region. The first deficiency is due to unavailability of consumer price indices, so that separate poverty lines could not be estimated for each state for their rural and urban sectors. Secondly, NSSO did not provide data on some important aspects, like availability of safe drinking water, sanitation facilities, mortality level etc. by expenditure classes of the population for the present survey, so that we were bound to consider few selected indicators. Selection of few indicators may give a narrow picture. However, NSSO covered three broad aspects of human lives, viz., economic condition, educational status, and health status, which is partially reflected in food adequacy and nutritional intake.

REFERENCE

1. Dubey, A. and Gangopdhyaya, S. (1998): Counting the Poor. Where are the Poor in India, *Sarvekshana, Analytical Report,* Number 1, Department of Statistics, Govt. of India
2. Gopalan, C., Sastri, R.B.V., Balasubramania, S.C. (1987): *Nutritive Value of Indian Foods,* Indian Council of Medical Research.
3. Indian Experience on Household Food and Nutrition Security: Nutritional Requirements in India, www. fao. org/ DOCREPx0172e/x0172e/0172e2.htm
4. Mali, D.D. (1993): *Economic Problems and Planning in Assam,* Omsons Publication, Revised Edition.
5. NSSO (2001): *Level and Pattern of Consumer Expenditure in India,* 1999-2000, Ministry of Statistics and Programme Implementation, Govt. of India.
6. ....(2001): *Literacy and Levels of Education in India, 1999-2000,* Ministry of Statistics and Programme Implementation, Govt. of India.
7. ....(2001): *Nutritional Intake in India, 1999-2000,* Ministry of Statistics and Programme Implementation, Govt. of India
8. Planning Commission (1979): *Report of the Task Force on Projection of Minimum Needs and Effective Consumption Demand,* Govt. of India.
9. Planning Commission (2002): *National Human Development Report 2001,* Govt. of India.
10. Registrar General of India (2001: *Provisional Population Tables,* Census of India.
11. Sen, A.K (1985): *Commodities and Capabilities, Cambridge* University Press, New York.
12. ....(1987): *The Standard of Living,* Cambridge University Press, New York.,
13. Singh, B.P. (1999): North-Easterly Wind: Sun Over the Brahmaputra, Times of India, January 6.

12

Roots of Urban Poverty: A Note on Transformation of Entitlement Relationship

Gorky Chakraborty

Introduction

Poverty is multi-dimensional. Conceptually one might be poor if s/he doesn't earn 'enough' income or doesn't have command over 'enough' resources in *lieu* of which s/he can earn livelihood or has not bequeathed 'enough' wealth for sustenance. Under such situation of being an income— poor and/or resource poor, the person concerned will also be 'poor' in terms of education, health, sanitation and related facilities as s/he will not be in a position to avial them. A vicious cycle thus sets in operation.

Various theories have interpreted and analysed poverty within their respective theoretical frameworks. The Biological Approach[1] has been one of the earliest theories on poverty which states that a man is poor if his/her total earnings are insufficient to maintain minimum necessities. Critics have argued against this theory on the grounds of variation concerning working habits, nutritional requirements, physical features of persons concerned and their minimum requirements and estimations. The Inequality Approach[2] deals with poverty in terms of stratification in society and pleads for transfer of resources from the rich to the poor. Critics argue that this theory although throws enough light on inequality but in the process confuse inequality with poverty. The Theory of Relative Deprivation[3] deals with poverty by ascertaining how poorer sections of a society are deprived of basic necessities of life. Critics are of the view that the feeling of deprivation vary from one population group to another and thus cannot be generalised. The Theory of Value Judgement[4] relates poverty with value judgement and takes an idealistic stand regarding its interpretation, estimation and process of amelioration. Critics are of the opinion that relating moral with poverty is not only unscientific but misleading too as it varies between various population groups around the world. Of late, The Theory of Entitlement[5] in terms of poverty analysis has gained momentum which argues that poverty is related with loss of 'endowment' which transforms entitlement relationship ultimately affecting the economic status of the person concerned. In order to minimise poverty the poor should be endowed in such a way that it enriches their entitlements. Critics argue that there are often ambiguities in specification of entitlements that might lead to different set of conclusions.

II. The Entitlement Approach

Sen has applied 'entitlement approach' to analyse the causes leading to starvation and famines. In the process he has highlighted upon the 'ability' of the affected population group to command food through the legal means available in a society. According to this theory a person starves because s/he ceases to posses the ability to command food. This situation arises as there is either loss or depletion of endowment pattern of the person or the population group concerned which affects their exchange entitlements ultimately adversely affecting their 'ability' to command food. This leads to starvation.

In this paper the concept of entitlement has been applied to trace the roots of urban poverty. An attempt is being made to understand as to how a change or depletion in endowment pattern of individual households brings about a transformation in their entitlement relationships and thereby in poverty relations. 22 Househols of Bechimari char village of Beki river located at Rupsi Block of Barpeta district of Assam has been surveyed. Data analysis reveals that in case of all the households there has been either a total loss or major depletion in endowment pattern (e.g. agricultural land in case of these households) due to flood and land erosion, which has compelled them to migrate to nearby urban centres. In the process there has been a simultaneous transformation of their entitlement relationship from production-based entitlement to own labour-based entitlement relation. The change in their poverty relations due to a transformation of entitlement relationship has been studied over a period of 25 years (March 1980 to March 2004).

III. Production-Based Entitlement

There are mainly four entitlement based relations[6] in a private ownership market economy, namely, (i) trade-based, (ii) production-based, (ii) own labour-based and (iv) inheritance or transfer entitlements. Production based entitlement has been defined as that which one is 'entitled to own what one gets by arranging production using one's own resources, or resources hired from willing parties meeting the agreed conditions of trade.'

Here production based entitlement is agriculture (crops produced) whereas endowment for this entitlement relationship is land. All the households in our sample own land and are/were solely dependent upon agriculture at Bechimari char village. Various issues related with their production-based entitlement are analysed below.

(1) Land ownership: All the households in the sample owned land during March 1980, exactly 25 years prior to this survey, 27.27 per cent of the total households owned land between 1 to 3 *bighas,* 36.36 per cent of the households owned between 3 to 6 *bighas,* 13.64 per cent owned between 6 to 9 *bighas* and 4.54 per cent owned land between 9 to 12 *bighas.* There were 18.18 percent households who owned land in excess of 12 *bighas* and between them 2 households owned land in excess of 35 bighas (See Table 12.1). In all there were not a single landless household in our samples 25 years ago.

Table 12.1
Ownership of Agricultural Land, 1980

Land (in *Bigha*)	<1	1 to 3	>3 to 6	>6 to 9	>9 to 12	12 and above
Number of Household	-	6 (27.27(	8 (36.36)	3 (13.64)	1 (4.54)	4 (18.18)

Source : Field Survey

Table 12.2 Ownership of Agricultural Land, 2004

Land (in *Bigha*)	<1	1 to 3	>3 to 6	>6 to 9	>9 to 12	12 and above
Number of Household	1 (4.54)	3 (13.64)		1 (4.54)		

Source : Field Survey

(2) Agricultural Production: Crop production and productivity varies largely in *char* areas. Those *char* villages which are often affected by flood, erosion and large scale silt deposition, both crop variety and productivity are less.

In Bechimari char village, *Aush* paddy has been the principal crop. *Sali* and Boro variety of paddy were also grown but at limited scale. Among other foodgrains wheat and *matimah* production were common among the cultivators. Among cash crops, jute was cultivated in large scale. other than jute, brinjal, tomato, chillies and *dhania* were common.

Crops variety largely depended upon the amount of land cultivated. More land under the ploguh meant more diversified crop production. Usually a cultivator owning 3 *bighas* of agricultural land would cultivate 2 *bighas* of *aush* paddy and 1 *bigha* of jute during summer while during winter pulses, vegetables and wheat followed suit.

(3) Other Activities: Among the sample households 41 per cent employed themselves as part time agricultural daily wage labourers. They undertook wage activities either in between two agricultural seasons or when there was requirement for immediate cash. It was evident that those cultivators who owned less than 3 to 4 *bighas* of land resorted to part time daily wage activities. However, neither they left their families nor their fileds while undertaking daily wage activities.

IV. The Transformation

The transformation from production based entitlement to own labour based entitlement happens due to the loss and depletion of endowment pattern. The havoc writ large by natural forces particularly flood and accompanying land erosion destroys the endowment (agricultural land) of the *char* villagers which affects life, livelihood and ownership pattern. This force them to migrate to new areas. Many among the *char* dwellers who suffer due to land erosion move to adjoining *char* villages while others flock to urban centres with the hope of turning fortune in their favour.

(1) Cause for transformation

In the sample households of Bechimari *char* village every household has been affected by land erosion. It is an annual phenomenon which wrecks havoc in *chars* of Beki and *Brahmaputra* rivers thereby affecting the endowment pattern of *char* villages. In our sample 47.83 per cent of the households were victims of erosion during the decade of 80s; 39.14 per cent during 90's, whereas 13.05 per cent of the households have been affected since 2000. It has been evident during the course of survey that there has not been a single household who have not changed their homestead at least once during their lifetime due to erosion.

(2) Land lost due to Erosion

Over the last 25 years (1980-2004) there has been a sea change in the endowment pattern of the *char* villagers. It has changed from bad to worse. If we compare the land ownership pattern during 1980 and 2004 (See Fig. 12.1), it is evident that whereas there were no landless households during 1980s, presently 77.27 per cent of the households have become landless. These cultivators have lost land that have changed their endowment pattern and subsequently transformed their entitlement relations.

Figure 12.1
Bar diagram showing land ownership and landlessness during 1980 and 2004

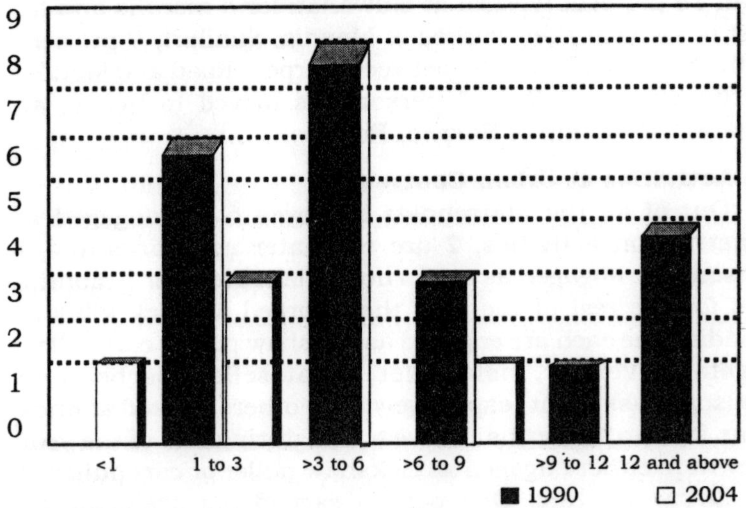

NOTE:

(1) During 1980 all the 22 households possessed land but by 2004, 77.27 percent of these households have become landless due to land erosion.

(2) Total cultivable land lost during 1980-2004 is 183.25 *bighas* or 93.97 percent of total land has been lost during this period.

Total agricultural land during 1980 has been 195 *bighas* that has diminished to 11.75 bighas only during 2004. In other words, 183.25 bighas or 93.97 per cent of total land has been lost due to erosion over a span of 25 years.

V. Own Labour Based Entitlement

When the households loose their endowment they cease to be entitled with production-based entitlement. On being landless they are left with no other option but to sale their own labour in order to sustain themselves and their families. They therefore migrate to urban and *mofussil* areas to earn a livelihood in exchange of their own labour based entitlements. In our sample at least one member of each household have migrated to urban centres.

(1) Place of Migration

To earn livelihood these people from Bechimari *char*

village has moved to number of urban and *mofussil* centres. More than 45 per cent have migrated to Guwahati whereas nearly 23 per cent have migrated to Barpeta Road. More than 18 per cent worked at Guwahati for 6 months and for rest of the year they worked at Mondia. Similarly 9 per cent of the households shifted between Barpeta Road and Mondia during the year. Only 1 person has moved to Howly, an adjacent township of Barpeta Road.

(2) Activities at Urban Centres

Out of all the households surveyed 6 are engaged in construction activities, 2 are carpenter assistants and 4 persons are engaged as construction labourers for 7 months and for the rest of the year they worked at brick kilns at Mondia. One each are engaged as rickshaw puller, cart puller, vegetable vendor, fish seller, meat seller, barber and goldsmith assistant respectively. Two others worked at brick kilns for 3 to 4 months in a year and during rest of the year they were either engaged as rickshaw puller or cart puller at the urban centres. One person earned his livelihood by begging. During his childhood he bas been seriously injured in a flood, which has de-capacitated him. As a result of which he earned his livelihood by begging in the streets of Guwahati.

Table 12.3 Activities at Urban Centres

Occupation		No. of households involved
1.	Barber	1
2.	Beggar	1
3.	Cart Puller	1
4.	Carpenter Assistant	2
5.	Construction Labourer	6
6.	Construction Labour and Brick Kiln Labour	4
7.	Fish Vendor	1
8.	Goldsmith Assistant	1
9.	Meat Vendor	1
10.	Rickshaw Puller	1
11.	Rickshaw/Cart Puller & Brick kiln Labour	2
12.	Vegetable Vendor	1
	Total	22

Source: Field Survey

All the construction workers, carpenter assistants and rickshaw puller were stationed at Guwahati while those working as vegetable, fish and meat vendors as well as barber and cart puller were stationed at Barpeta Road. On the other, when the brick kilns were in operation these labourers moved to Mondia, where the kilns were located. The goldsmith assistant worked in a jewellery shop at Howly (See Table 12.3).

(3) Housing Status

There were 10 households, who migrated to Guwahati for livelihood and among them 7 stayed with their respective families. All these families were located in three different settlements namely, Hatigaon, Dhiren Para and Birubari. In these settlements there are cluster of huts situated around a well and a place for defecation. The rent of these houses varied between Rs. 200 to Rs. 450 depending upon the locality and of course the size of the hut rented.

Those residing in Barpeta Road paid a rent in between Rs. 200 to Rs. 250 for their dwellings. All the 5 households who earned their livelihood at Barpeta Road stayed alone and frequently visited their families at Bechimari *char* due to the locational proximity between these two areas. Sanitation and drinking water facilities were equally worse both in Barpeta Road and Guwahati, the only difference is that a tube well at Barpeta Road replaces the well.

(4) Economic Status

The shift from the cultivable land to the harsh realities of urban life has never been easy for any household in the sample. When erosion uproots them from their land, they remain in wilderness for a while. Thereafter when they move to urban centres both their skills (for whatever job they undertake) and 'identity' is viewed with suspicion, which results in they being paid lower wages. This makes their urban livelihood more difficult.

There were not large fluctuations in per day wages/ income of the households engaged in different activities in the urban centres. Yet each earning member managed to send some amount of remittances to their respective families in the *char* village. The rickshaw puller at Guwahati earned in between Rs. 90 to Rs. 100 per day whereas the construction daily wager earned around Rs. 70 to Rs. 80 per day. Carpenter assistance earned Rs. 70. The vegetable and fish vendors of Barpeta Road earned Rs. 50 to Rs. 100 per day depending upon sale, while the *thela* puller earned Rs. 50 to Rs. 60 at the same urban centre. The meat seller quoted an income of Rs. 125 to Rs. 150 per day, which has been certainly the highest among the lot. Even the beggar at Guwahati earned between Rs. 40 to Rs. 45 per day. The barber earned Rs. 50 to Rs. 60 per day while the brick kiln labourers of Mondia earned Rs. 50 per day.

The remittances of course varied along with their income and it ranged between Rs. 500 to Rs. 1,000 per month depending upon the nature of their jobs. These figures related to wages have been quoted by the concerned persons which evidently portrays that they are surely hovering around the poverty line with minor fluctuations on a day to day or seasonal basis.

(5) Related Hazards

During the course of survey when the respondents were asked to categorize the problems of their urban existence, they among scores of other problems mentioned about two common hazards (i) related with housing, health, sanitation and (ii) related with their 'identity' and low wages. These two problems were common to all households.

Each and every household narrated about their deplorable housing status. These little houses are all stuffed together within a minimum space. During the rainy season, water logging is a common problem both within the house and the area surrounding these settlements. Moreover unhealthy drinking water and unhygienic sanitary conditions were a constant threat in these settlements. The settlers now have been used to these condition as neither the land/ house owners nor the local administration seemd to be concerned about these problems.

Unhygienic living conditions and their poor economic status make them prone to several diseases namely malaria, tuberculosis, diarrhoea, several stomach related ailments to name a few. But the income-poor status often force them to curtail health related expenditures which leads to serious consequences. This is very much evident in case of children. Infant mortality among these households throws some light into this aspect. Nearly 55 per cent of the households reported infant deaths in between the age group of 1 month to 5 years. In all 23 children have died in recent past, including 9 girls and 14 boys due to various ailments including diarrhoea, fever, measles, hydrophobia, fire burns and tetanus.

Another related hazard is concerned with their 'identity.' People in urban areas often (due to their self-created myth and propaganda) term these hapless *char* dwellers as illegal infiltrators. Without any understanding about the ground reality the urban middle class label these daily wagers as 'Bangladeshis'. This has a tremendous negative psychological impact upon these poor people. They suffer from an unknown fear. Moreover their skills are never considered good enough to earn the stipulated daily wages. Their 'suspicious identity' reduces their bargaining power and they are therefore too often paid less.

VI. Suggested Measures

Anti-poverty programmes in India have been largely government based. Of late there has been participation from other sources particularly voluntary organizations and NGOs. But all the programmes are more or less relief oriented and piecemeal in their orientation, which therefore have a limited dent on poverty. Poverty alleviation measures should be multidimensional since poverty is multifaceted in nature. Programmes related with livelihood skills, income generation, awareness regarding sanitation, health and housing along with affordable education should operate in tandem so that the poor can participate and earn sustainable benefits from them.

Poverty alleviation programmes in the *char* areas of Assam are limited if not non-existent. The *char* dwellers are one of the most backward and neglected population groups in Assam. More than 69 per cent of the *char* dwellers live below poverty line and nearly 79 per cent of them are illiterate. Under these circumstances, loss of endowment (e.g. agricultural land) spells doom and they flock to the urban centres in search of livelihood.[7] But they enter the urban scenario at a disadvantageous position. Their loss of endowment leaves them with only one option i.e. to sell their own labour in order to earn a livelihood. Life in urban centres is no less precarious. They reside in unhealthy shelters under unhygienic conditions and are exploited by their employers due to lack of bargaining power. Moreover the threat of being harassed under the pretext of being an illegal infiltrator always looms large over their head. Under these circumstances until and unless certain policy measures are undertaken immediately to improve the plight of these people, the situation may become worse.

(i) Public expenditure on the provision of public good particularly health care, sanitation, education and drinking water should be increased in the urban settlements where the poor reside.

(ii) Scope for employment opportunities particularly wage employment should be increased. Simultaneously emphasis should be laid upon generation of sustainable livelihood skills through training and market linkage so that the scope for their labour-based entitlements is enriched.

(iii) Efforts should also be undertaken to utilize the skill and potential of the women folk of these *char* dwellers who migrate to urban centres. The concept of self-help groups can also be initiated no matter how meagre their saving potentials are.

(iv) Efforts should be undertaken to sensities the population regarding childcare so as to minimize the high rate of infant mortality. Health awareness programmes should be undertaken frequently with the help of voluntary organisations.

(v) Immediate steps should be undertaken to minimise land erosion and the damages caused due to it through proper soil conservation techniques. It will surely reduce the rate of soil erosion and therefore endowment depletion which will certainly retard the flow of *char* dwellers to urban areas.

(vi) Steps should be undertaken to prevent 'communalisation' of poverty. Urban residents should be sensitised regarding the origin and cause for migration of these *char* dwellers. Media can certainly play a positive role in this direction.

REFERENCES

1. Rowntrees, S., *Poverty: A Study of Town Life* (London: Macmillan, 1901).
2. Miller, S.M. and Roby, P., 'Poverty: Changing Social Stratification', in Townsend, Peter, *The Concept of Poverty* (London: Heineman, 1971).
3. Runciman, W.G., *Relative Deprivation and Social Justice* (London: Routledge & Kegan Paul, 1966).
4. Orhansky, M., 'How Poverty is Measured', *Monthly Labour Review*, 1969.
5. Sen, A.K., *Poverty and Famines* (Oxford: Clarendon, 1981) and *Hunger and Entitlements* (Helsinki: WIDER, 1987).
6. Sen mentions about four entitlement relationship
   - (i) Trade-based entitlement: one is entitled to own what one obtains by trading something one owns with a trading party.
   - (ii) Production-based entitlement—mentioned in the text;
   - (iii) Own-labour entitlement—also mentioned in the text, and;
   - (vi) Inheritance and transfer entitlement: one is entitled to own what is willingly given to one by another who legitimately own it. For further details see (Sen: 1981).
7. Loss of endowment is the major cause of poverty and subsequent migration from rural to urban areas in case of Bechimari *char* village as highlighted in this paper. But if one considers the macro-scenario, it is evident that during the last ten years growth rates of employment in general has been dismal and that of rural employment has been pathetic. Under such situation without any state support, migration from rural to urban areas and subsequent increase in poverty is natural.

Growth rates of employment
Annual compound rates (%)

	Rural	Urban
1987-88 to 1993-94	2.03	3.39
1993-94 to 1999-2000	0.67	1.34

** I am extremely grateful to Mr. Khandakar Abdul Gaffur, Sr. Lecturer and Head of the Department, Political Science, Nabajyoti College, Kalgachia, Assam for introducing me to the *char* villages of Beki river.

13

Elimination of Urban Poverty in North-East—A Reachable Goal

H.K. Mazhari

Introduction

Much has been discussed on urban poverty in the past few decades both within and outside the country. International Agencies have also supported the initiatives of member countries in reduction of poverty. The millennium goals to which India is a signatory promises to reduce the poverty level to half by 2010. There have been efforts in reducing the urban poverty since the time the country embarked on planned development when existence of slum manifested urban poverty. Hence the resolve of the central government to eradicate them completely was given priority in the first few five year plans. This did not work due to resource constraint and other difficulties faced in the implementation. Planning commission came up with program varying from complete eradication of slums to improving the existing slums with upgraded urban infrastructure in seventies to Nehru Rojgar Yojana in late eighties and finally Swarn Rojgar Yojana in late nineties. The Program has mixed results, only a few states could utilize the earmarked fund, most of the states found it difficult to do so. Nevertheless it did make some difference in the urban poverty scenario, there has also been recognition of the fact that merely shelter and urban infrastructure, calorie intake cannot be taken as the only factors for identifying the poor and defining poverty.

What is Poverty and who are poor?

A poor is one who is not having

* A job and not able to earn
* Food intake of at least 2100 calories per day.
* Access to health care and medical facilities.
* Access to school, remaining illiterate and deprived of the capacity to read and write.
* Access to clean water and safe sanitation.
* Shelter
* Empowerment, feeling of helplessness and deprivation.

However urban poverty in the official documents of planning commission is based on calorie intake of 2100, according to which urban poverty has shown a downward trend and in 2000 it came down to nearly 24 per cent, it is estimated to be now`21 per cent.

What is the extent of urban poverty in the North-East?

As per the National Human development report, poverty in the country has reduced from 49 per cent during 1973-74 to 23.62 per cent during 1999-2000 during the same period urban poverty in the north-east reduced from 21.7 per cent to 7.5 per cent. It may be interesting to note that during 1983-94 to 1993-94, urban poverty reduced by 8.5 per cent and 8.7 per cent during 1993-94 to 1999-2000 at the national level. The data for the North-East for the same period is 14 per cent and 0.2 per cent. In other words urban poverty levels were much less than the national level being nearly half two decades back and is now nearly one-third of national figure despite the fact that reduction in the poverty level during the last decade has been very small. As per the data collected by Lea Associate on the urban poverty in connection with the study sponsored by ADB in the North East for the capital towns, urban poverty varies from 8 per cent to 31 per cent.

Table 13.1

Urban Poverty in State capital cities in North-East

Project City	Based on Indian Poverty Line		Based on Millennium Development Goals	
	BPL	APL	Below Us $ 1/Capita /Day	Above Us $ 1/Capita/ Day
Agartala	24.8	75.2	76.5	23.5
Aizawl	16.0	84.0	74.3	25.7
Gangtok	17.6	82.4	57.7	42.3
Guwahati	31.1	68.9	77.6	22.4
Imphal	26.7	73.3	65.1	34.9
Itanagar	8.2	91.8	44.2	55.8
Kohima	14.5	85.5	56.0	44.0
Shillong	14.3	85.7	53.6	46.4

Source: Report on North Eastern Region Urban Sector Profile Project 2003.

How do we explain the vast difference in the data on level of urban poverty at national level with that of the North-East? The plausible explanation lies in the following.

* North-East had higher percentage of population above the poverty level two decades back
* Though many advanced states have been able to alleviate urban poverty and have performed well, many backward states affected the data at the national level on reduction of poverty.
* Many new States in the North-East were created during the above period when investment in governance and infrastructure were made leading to creation of jobs mostly in the government sector. This happened in the decade 1973-74 to 1983-84.
* Reduction due to the focused program on urban poverty alleviation in late eighties and early nineties
* Drying up of government jobs in the nineties after the reforms were initiated resulted in slowing down of reduction of poverty.

* Poverty line for North-east is based on Rs. 386 per capita per month while it is Rs. 454.11 per capita per month for the country as whole.

North-East may be much better of in terms of poverty ratio if we strictly go by the income criteria and calorie intake but other associate factors brings out a complete different picture of poverty; the 54th NSS round reflects that urban services are poor. As per the report on project profile of urban areas in the North-East sponsored by ADB, urban services available are given in table 13.2.

As seen in table 13.2 North eastern Region has the low poverty levels in urban areas and there is every possibility of poverty being eliminated within the next decade provided the Government of the day avoids the following which has been their main strategy so far and these are:

* Not much efforts to create wealth
* Priority on reservation of government jobs which do not exist or at best are only in small numbers, losing the woods for the trees.
* Most of the time energy of the Government machinery is wasted in ensuring that the local population gets their quota of jobs as well as the contracts is settled in favour of the local contractors often not on merit.
* Heavy investment in infrastructure is not encouraged for fear of influx from outside of investors and labor. That is the efforts to increase the size of the cake is not given the priority it deserves. However the number of those wanting a share in the cake is increasing leading to reduced share of the cake per person and creating social tension.
* The political leadership is focusing on smaller issues than on major investment decisions in the region which would make big impact on alleviation of urban property.
* Political considerations are paramount even while taking important decisions on socio-economic matters.
* Politician play the politics of exclusiveness and always have some emotive issues like the pot of influx from

Table 13.2

Proportion of Vulnerable Population (%)

S. No.	Indicators	Agartala				Aizawl				Gangtok				Guwahati			
		1	2	3	4	1	2	3	4	1	2	3	4	1	2	3	4
1	Access to Basic Services :																
a	Water Supply : HH Dependent on Stand posts	7.9	0.0	0.0	0.0	8.7	0.0	6.8	2.7	44.0	18.8	9.8	0.0	7.5	2.3	4.8	3.3
	HH Dependent on Tankers	0.0	0.0	0.0	0.0	8.7	17.5	9.1	5.4	8.0	6.3	2.4	0.0	0.0	0.0	0.4	0.0
b	Sanitation HH with no Toilets	21.1	20.0	0.0	0.0	34.8	30.0	16.3	2.7	20.0	15.0	12.0	10.0	25.0	20.0	15.0	12.0
2	Financial Situation : % Unemployed (Head of HH)	5.9	4.2	2.4	8.3	0.0	1.8	0.0	0.0	10.0	0.0	0.0	2.3	1.5	0.7	0.0	0.0

S. No.	Indicators	Imphal				Itanagar				Kohima				Shillong			
		1	2	3	4	1	2	3	4	1	2	3	4	1	2	3	4
1	Access to Basic Services :																
a	Water Supply : HH Dependent on Stand posts	22.9	6.7	21.1	9.8	8.3	13.3	8.7	1.2	4.5	0.0	0.0	2.9	65.0	36.4	30.3	11.9
	HH Dependent on Tankers	2.9	0.0	13.2	9.8	0.0	3.3	8.7	0.0	0.0	3.3	0.0	1.4	0.0	0.0	3.0	0.0
b	Sanitation HH with no Toilets	59.0	68.8	42.5	1.9	25.0	17.2	28.6	13.6	34.8	16.1	16.2	17.4	83.3	40.9	54.5	27.7
2	Financial Situation : % Unemployed (Head of HH)	0.0	0.0	0.0	0.0	0.0	0.0	0.0	0.0	0.0	0.0	0.0	0.0	0.0	0.0	0.0	2.6

(Condt.)

		1	2	3	4	1	2	3	4	1	2	3	4	1	2	3	4	1	2	3	4	1	2	3	4	1	2	3	4	1	2	3	4
3	Heath :																																
	% Reporting Illness Due to Environemtnal Sevices	12.9	18.5	12.5	14.3	50.0	50.0	47.4	42.4	45.0	23.1	48.5	23.6	49.4	49.2	43.3	51.3	54.5	66.7	50.0	53.2	55.6	55.6	68.4	59.7	23.8	37.0	43.8	36.4	62.5	46.7	37.5	32.7
	% Reporting Alcohol/Drug Use	0.0	0.0	0.0	3.4	23.1	4.5	14.3	0.0	5.3	0.0	3.2	4.0	21.6	19.7	15.6	12.5	11.1	16.7	3.6	8.3	100.0	50.0	100.0	88.9	15.0	0.0	3.8	5.4	12.5	30.8	18.2	2.1
4	Gender :																																
	% HH Women Headed	5.3	12.3	2.2	15.4	30.4	57.4	51.1	16.7	20.0	29.4	22.0	16.0	16.8	16.0	7.9	0.0	17.9	9.3	13.2	9.1	58.3	20.0	28.6	25.0	13.0	17.2	10.2	18.2	70.0	27.3	25.0	11.9
	Female Literacy	74.5				78.2				67.1				64.4				63				50.6				65.3				66.6			
	Work Participation Rate	12.4				25.8				21.0				8.7				15.5				15.1				14.5				16.9			
5.	Education :																																
	% Graduate and above	65.6	41.9	71.7	75.0	19.0	5.4	34.9	52.8	0.0	7.7	29.7	37.3	48.6	67.4	68.7	78.3	30.6	31.3	60.0	81.3	10.0	33.3	52.2	56.4	22.2	50.0	57.1	77.1	16.7	28.6	40.0	60.9
6	Housing :																																
	%HH Kutcha Houses	P	12.9	25.0	21.3	13.6	15.0	7.3	5.7	12.0	6.7	2.7	0.0	11.8	1.1	4.4	2.0	65.7	33.3	23.7	12.0	0.0	13.8	4.8	6.1	47.6	24.1	8.8	7.2	0.0	0.0	3.1	4.9

Notes: 1 Population Below Poverty Line (INR 386/Capita, Month); 2: Populaion below 0.5 US$/Capita/day i.e., INR 683/Capita/Month; 3. Population below Us 1$/Capita/Day or INR 1367/Capita/Month 4: Population above Poverty Line (Above 1367/Capita/month).

Source: Sample Socio-Economic Survey, LASA, 2003.

outside boiling and in this endeavour of theirs, they are given a helping hand by the NGOs and welfare organization.

These lead to the following:

* Low level of investment
* Low wealth generation
* Low creation of jobs
* Low level of employment
* Low rate of poverty reduction
* Low level of consumption and demand for goods and services
* Low infrastructure development

If the objectve is to eliminate poverty completely, perhaps the following course of action is to be adopted

Heavy investment in infrastructure

* Physical infrastructure like roads power, water, sanitation, housing, commercial complexes, communication
* Social infrastructure like education, health care, human resource development including skill upgradation
* Heavy investment in city infrastructure will create jobs in construction industries. Skill upgradation in construction will enable people to get jobs as well as create good quality infrastructure
* Generate income and demand for goods and services
* Investment on urban infrastructure in the capital cities in the North-East to the extent of $300 million is expected to be sanctioned by ADB for augmenting the urban infrastructure and tackling urban poverty issues in the region. The technical assistance includes $40 million for capacity building and $260 million for urban infrastructure. State Governments can also access fund from Department for Development of North-Eastern Region (DONER) and other ministries. The State Governments cannot take the plea that lack or inadequacy of fund comes in the way of taking up massive

infrastructure development program. In fact the state governments are yet to give the due priority to urban development sector in their investment schedules.

Encourage investment both from within and outside the state and the country for creation of world class infrastructure.

To facilitate investment what all is required to be done apart from improving urban and rural infrastructure:

* Improve Governance; make the official machinery transparent and accountable.
* Ensure secruity and let people have the feeling of being safe and secured. Let there be no self imposed curfew after sunset and let the evening in the urban centers in the North-East be pleasant as enjoyable as in the past.
* Initiate reforms; pricing of urban services and levy of user charges and creating conducive environment for investment in urban infrastructure, strengthening of urban local bodies and empowerment of Resident Associations to be the focus of such reforms.
* Improve the functioning of the institutions and set up institutions of excellence and encourage professionals to move in and contribute in making of institutions. Such institutions may preferably be set up in the private sector.
* Improve the management of health care centres through tie-ups with medical centres and hospitals of repute and cover the urban poor by appropriate medical insurance scheme with subsidy from the government
* Create wealth by focusing on travel, tourism and hospitality services.
* Organic agriculture and horticulture, their processing and marketing can also create wealth and jobs both in rural and urban area.
* Mineral based industries can be leading industrial activity in the region and may create skilled jobs.
* Bring in the latest technology and expertise from outside the region/country. This would need a strong politicial will and determined action on the part of the state governments in the region.

* Make the functioning of government participatory and transparent.
* Ensure compliance of law and rules and even playing field for all.

It must be understood that politics of exclusiveness has failed to bring peace, security and prosperity for the people. The 21st century is for inclusiveness, plurality, fair competition and equal opportunities for all. If we do not change our mind set, policies and strategies we are likely to be left behind. The leaders will have then to blame themselves for the plight of the people and nobody else.

14

Urban Poverty : Issues and Challenges

D.R. Das

Introduction

Poverty ratio in India has been on the decline from 1977-78 to 1999-2000, both urban and rural poverty rates have declined by almost the same margin. However, absolute figures tell another story. It seems that the number of urban poor has actually risen, even when the number of rural poor has declined.

The total number of rural poor stands at 193 million, down by 71 million from 264 million in 1977-78. On the other hand, the number of urban poor has risen from 65 million in 1977-78 to 67 million during 1999-2000. The rural poverty ratio from 1977-78 to 1999-2000 has declined from 53 per cent to 27 per cent. The urban poverty ratio has declined from 45 percent to 24 per cent.

Study from 1993-94 to 1999-2000 shows that during this period there has been a 19 per cent decline in the total number of the poor. Most of this decline has been brought about by a decline in the total number of rural poor. Rural poor accounts for about 75 per cent of the people below poverty line while the urban poor contributes only 25 per cent of the total population below poverty line but they have contributed only 15 per cent to a decline in the total number of poor. The absolute number of urban poor stands at 67 million down from 76.3 million in 1993-94.

The period from 1983 to 1993-94, show that both urban and rural poverty ratios have consistently declined over the period. In comparison absolute figures for urban poverty have risen over these years. Rural figures over the period shows a rise in absolute terms during only one period from 1987-88 to 1993-94.

From 1993-94 to 1999-2000, both urban and rural poor in absolute terms has actually declined. It is interesting to note that even over the 1993-94 period, when the number of urban poor has been declining, the decline in rural poor makes a proportionately larger contribution.

Urban Poverty Scenario in Meghalaya

The National Tenth Plan document prepared by the Planning Commission indicates that as compared to the national percentage of population below poverty line which declined from 54.88 in 1973-74 to 26.7 in 1993-2000 and is expected further to decline to 19.34 by 2006-07, the position in respect of the state of Meghalaya is somewhat dismal in the sense that the percentage of population below poverty line which was 50.40 in 1973-74 i.e. lower than the national percentage could decline only upto 33.87 in 1999-2000 and is expected further to decline upto 31.14 by 2006-07.

Table: 14.1
Percentage of Population below Poverty line in India and Meghalaya

Year	1993-94	1999-2000	2006-07 (Projected)
National Percentage	54.88%	26.7%	19.34%
Meghalaya	50.20%	33.87%	31.14%

The urban poor consists mainly of poor people living below poverty line in metropolition cities, towns, commercial hubs, urban centres who do not enjoy the basic amenities of the urbanisation and yet form the integral part of the urban life. The city rickshaw pullers, cart pullers, daily laboures, etc. constitute the urban poor. Those urban poor are generally confornted with the following constraints:

* inaccessibility and marginalisation
* increasing population
* underdevelopment
* environment degradation
* poverty
* despair

All these factors consist of a vicious cycle and the urban poor is caught in between this vicious cycle.

Urban poor is caught in vicious circle

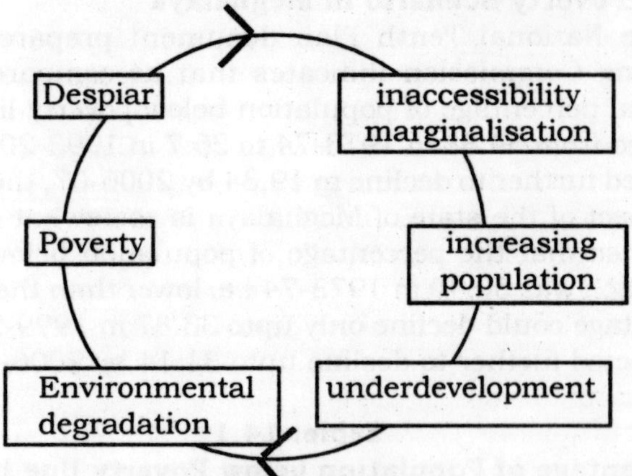

Figure 14.1

The Socio-economic indicators of the states of the North-East relating to urban poverty is summarised in table 14.2.

Table 14.2

Socio Econimic Indicators

Sl. No.	Items	Reference Year	Meghalaya	Assam	Arunachal	Manipur	Mizoram	Nagaland	Tripura
1.	Area sq. kms	2001	22,429	78,438	83,743	22,327	21.081	16,579	10,486
2.	Population density per sq. km	2001	103	340	13	107	42	120	304
3.	Literacy Rate	2001	63.31	64.28	54.74	68.87	88.49	67.11	73.66
4.	Birth Rate (per 000)	1999	28.57	27.0	22.3	18.6	17.0	11.8	17.00
5.	Death Rate (per 000)	1999	9.20	9.70	6.00	5.4	5.5	2.3	5.7
6.	Infant Mortality Rate	1999	58.0	76.0	43.0	25.0	19.0	—	42.0

Source: Annual Plan 2004-05, Govternment of Meghalaya.

Conclusion

The Ministry of Urban Development and Poverty Alleviation along with the Ministry of Social Justice and Empowerment, Govternment of India, focus on urban poor in conflict with social evils and social injustice. The need of the hour is to evolve an integrated approach to provide empowerment to the urban poor and focus on to provide equal opportunity to the urban poor in difficult circumstances. All efforts to be made to sensitize agencies such as police, hospitals, municipal corporations/civic bodies towards the betterment of their living conditions. What is required is the establishment of an Apex Agency to identify, provide support and monitor efficient service delivery of various agencies in these urban centres. The Apex Agency is to provide a platform for networking amongst various organisations and to strengthen the support efforts of the government agencies and the various NGOs working for the urban poverty alleviation. Among the urban poor, the living conditions of the women and the children living in slums of the urban centres, metropolis, cities, etc. are very much deplorable, which in fact is the breeding place of urban crimes and evils. The Association for Social Health in India (ASHI), an organisation set up under the 'swadhar' scheme of the Department of women and child development of the Ministry of Human Resources Development (HRD), Govternment of India, has been providing counselling as well as shelter to distressed women and girls. Assam state branch of ASHI has been functional since Feburary, 2003 and has been playing a vital role in providing shelter and repatriation to the urban distress women and children of the state. Formation of more and more such organisations is the need of the hour and this will go a long way for complete poverty alleviation in the country.

15

Poverty Alleviation Approach to HIV/AIDS Control: A Study of the Urban Slums of Assam

Shabeena Yasmin Saikia

Poverty is considered as curse and urban poverty is even more degrading than the rural poverty. Both illiteracy and health hazards prevail upon the poor urban dwellers effortlessly and in course of time paralyse the society they live. in. It is said that urban poverty lives mainly in slums and there is truth in it. The common fact about the urban slums is that these are spontaneous creation of the migrant poor families who come to these destinations with a hope to find a source of livelihood and finally had to live there year after year till they meet their death.

Slums are usually the growth in the darker part of the towns—people consider it as the obscene part of the city and try to maintain a distance as far as possible. To a common man in the city, a slum is a dirty, chaotic, lawless and dangerous space, where most of the inhabitants are criminal (UN Habitat, 2001). Such type of impression emerges due to lack of knowledge about the slums. Slums are not always like this. It is due to the continuing social negligence and social exclusion and indifference from the part of government that the social risk factors like poor habitat, poor quality of preventive health measures and health promotion measures, job scarcity, inadequate promotion and protection of local human resources, unsafe local conditions, gender-related risks, crisis in the family structure, poor access to communication, poor public administration, institutional chaos and inadequate social safety net etc. all remain active among the urban slum dwellers (Goldfinger, 1998).

Due to extreme poverty and unhygienic living conditions the slum dwellers are prone to different types of diseases. In absence of strong social organizations, social control mechanism is almost absent in slum societies. As a result, such settlements have become the den of various anti-social activities. Poverty and illiteracy induce some of these persons to take up jobs, which improve health hazards. In many slum areas women join the flesh trade in order to supplement family income.

Due to such unorganised activities, slums have been considered as the potential threat for infection of HIV/AIDS virus. It is a known fact how HIV/AIDS viruses take shelter in the human body. AIDS and HIV although are common words, yet very few people care to know the basic details about these two. It would, therefore, be not out of place to give a brief informative account of these two. So far, the acquired knowledge about HIV suggests that this virus cannot infect the animal bodies and as such there is no chance of getting infected from animals. How do we get infected is an important question: In HIV, H stands for human, becuase this virus is only capable of infecting human beings. The presence of this virus creates a deficiency within the body's immune system as a result of which people fail to work properly that is why the I stands for Imuno deficiency. And as it is a virus, it is not capable of reproducing by itself. It reproduces by taking over the machinery of the human cell. The difference between HIV and AIDS is that HIV is the virus that is responsible for causing AIDS. It takes six to twelve weeks from implantation of HIV virus to the formation of antibodies against the virus.

Various types of complaints are reported on being infected by HIV virus. Some complain flue like symptom, which remains for few days, which may also accompany fevers, chills, night sweat and rashes. Few others may have mild symptom that usually goes unnoticed. However, in case of AIDS, there are no common symptoms. It has been observed frequently that people infected with HIV takes 7-10 years to diagnose as AIDS. This time length however varies from person to person depending on the health status and behaviour of a person. AIDS is transmitted from one person to another through blood, semen, vaginal discharge, breast milk while blood is the most active source. In India, till December 2002, as many as 42947 cases have been reported of which Tamil Nadu is accounted for 45 per cent i.e 18276 AIDS patients. Depending on the prevalence rates, the Indian states have been classified into three groups viz., (i) high prevalence states where prevalence of HIV among the antenatal women is more than one per cent. Tamilnadu, Andhra Pradesh, Karnataka, Maharastra, Manipur and Nagaland (ii) medium prevalence states are those in which prevalence among high-risk population is more than 5 per cent and prevalence among antenatal women is less than one per cent. The state of Gujarat, Goa, and Pandicheery fall in this category. The third category is the low prevalence states where prevalence of HIV among the high-risk population is less than 5 per cent. Assam is one among these states.

It has been observed from the study of the above reported cases that although the transmission efficiency through sexual route is low, yet it accounts for highest number of AIDS cases. Usually the risk factors for HIV infection include multiple homosexual or heterosexual partners; contaminated blood transfusion, injection with contaminated needles and syringes and infected mother to foetus/infant. The efficiency of transmission of HIV is determined by the amount of virus in a body fluid and the extent of contact. The most efficient vehicle of transmission is blood. However, the risk of infection through blood transfusion today is extremely low due to strict HIV screening of donated blood. Today the most common route of transmission is unprotected, penetrative sexual contact. Table 15.1 shows the details.

Table: 15.1
Transmission Route of HIV/AIDS

Sl. No.	Transmission Route	Number of cases	Percent
1	Sexual	36201	84.29
2	Perinatal transmission	1119	2.61
3	Blood and blood products	1282	2.99
4	Injectable drug users	1232	2.87
5	History not available	3113	7.25
6	Total	42947	100.00

Today there are various types of medical treatments that enhance the ability of the human immune system to withstand the HIV/AIDS attack and in the process slow down the rate at which the virus attacks the immune system. There are also treatments targeted to cure the illness associated with AIDS.

In India, the National AIDS Control Organisation (NACO) carries out the country's National AIDS Programme, which includes formulation of policy and implementation of prevention and control programmes. It was established in the year 1993 and is now running the second phase of the National AIDS Control Project (NACP-II). Similarly, at the State level, under the advice of Ministry of Health and Family Welfare, the State AIDS Control Societies were formed for the implementation and management of HIV/AIDS programmes in states. These registered societies are under the chairmanship of the Secretary Health. The society is broad-based with members representing various ministries like Social Welfare, Education, Industry, Transport and Finance and NGOs for implementation of the National AIDS Control Programme. It was in the same tune that the Assam State AIDS Control Society was formed.

The first phase (NACP-I) as organised by NACO had ended in March 1999. The duration of NACP-II is from December 1999 to March 2004. The National AIDS control project was the only project in India at national level for prevention and control of AIDS, which started in 1992 and continued for 7 years period till 1999. The basic objective of the project was to slow down the spread of HIV, to reduce future morbidity, mortality and the impact of AIDS by preventing HIV transmission. To realise these objectives, the project identified the following components to be impacted upon; (i) strengthening the awareness and community support for AIDS prevention with the primary attention on sexual transmission, behavioural change and condom promotion through television and radio stations, private advertising agencies, NGOs and the health system; (ii) improve blood safety from 30 per cent to 90 per cent screening of the blood supply, enhancing the rational use of blood and the share of voluntary donations, (iii) building surveillance and clinical management capacity to monitor the spread of the epidemic and to strengthen the skills of health staff and social workers in managing and counselling persons with HIV/AIDS and (iv) controlling sexually transmitted diseases by improving clinical services and case management in the country's STD clinics and in private practice in metropolitan areas.

As per the NACO report, the overall outcome of the project was satisfactory as it achieved specific objectives after overcoming the initial challenges faced by the Union and State Governments. The project had succeeded in the nationwide capacity buidling in managerial and technical aspects of the programme in all 32 States and Union Territories.

Thereafter the National AIDS Control Programme Phase-II had started since 1999 and it is still continuing. It shifted the focus from raising awareness to changing behaviour through interventions, particularly for groups at high risk of contracting and spreading HIV. There are also various other objectives but here we are mainly concerned with the Targeted Intervention programme.

The targeted interventions are a set of activities and approaches aimed at reducing the risk of HIV infection among people who practice high-risk behaviour. Empirical evidences in many countries have shown that one of the ways of controlling the disease from further spread is to carry out direct intervention programme among the most vulnerable and marginalised population. The main aim of targeted interventions is to reduce the transmission of HIV infections from sub populations with high prevalence to sub populations with low prevalence. One of the core principles of targeted intervention is the community participation. It suggests that the target community should be involved from the planning till the end of the project. It also involves creating and sustaining shared vision and encouraging a re-examination of values relating to risk behaviour and risk sub-population requires organisational time structures and priority. A successful intervention policy aims at changing the behaviour at individual level, which occurs at the social level and in an enabling environment. An environment which is not criminalizing, non judgemental upholds dignity and self worth, reduces constraints on making appropriate decisions and increases options that lead to growth and development of the persons.

It has been worked out that the risk of getting infection and spreading infection is high among certain subgroups of population who are really poverty ridden and indulge in certain high-risk activities. By targeting them to modify their risk behaviour through behaviour change communication, counselling, providing healthcare support, treatment of STDs and creating an enabling environment the spread of their infection could be controlled.

The high risk groups that have been identified and concerns this study are (1) commerical sex workers, 2) truckers, 3) street children and 4) slum population. Evidently in the context of Guwahati, the home of the first three categories are in slums. As such, slum population in Guwahati is a threat to the environment itself.

The ORG Centre for Social Research, a Kolkata based organisation while conducting a survey under the State Aids Control Society Assam found that there are at least 39 probable sites in Kamrup district where the High Risk population can be found. Although no scientific methodology was adopted during this study, yet this is the first extensive study made in this context in the State. The study had taken i). female sex workers, ii) injecting drug users (IDU), iii) male and female labourers, iv) truckers, v) bus drivers and vi) street children as target group. The study report indicated the need for further operations/intervention research to discover what strategies would work best to improve the sexual and reproductive knowledge, and health of young people living in these very poor slum communities. These include activities targeting policy makers as well as working with parents and young people (ORG Centre, 2002). The following findings of the study need mention:

(i) Majority of the female sex workers studied have heard about HIV/AIDS and sexually transmitted diseases either from friends, family members etc. Only in 25 per cent cases, NGOs are involved while government doctors were involved in 29 per cent cases.

(ii) Similar is the case with the truckers. 96 per cent of the truckers studied by the ORG had heard about HIV/AIDS and STDs mainly from friends, relatives etc.

Taking the ORG findings as the base line data, this researcher has taken up to study the impact of poverty on various social aspects, the resultant health hazards and the nature of government intervention in reducing HIV/AIDS infection in eight slum segments in Guwahati city. All the eight slum localities were identified as the potential sites by the ORG study group. In this chapter, we will concentrate only on the findings related to the areas of poverty and its association with HIV/AIDS. The study was conducted on a person-to-person interview basis: A total of 652 persons were interviewed of which 52 per cent were males. The respondents were later classified into two basic age groups namely 14-30 and 31-50. The major findings of the study are stated below.

The findings of the study are quite astounding considering the fact that despite remaining so nearer to the educational centres of the town, 95 per cent of the population in these slum localities are found illiterate. It revealed that about 84 per cent of the young people living in these slums are out-of-school, and many of those who are still in school (16%) indulge in various types of economic activities to generate income for their school needs (such as examination fee, pencils, exercise books, etc. and also to supplement family earning. Poverty is rife in these localities. The localities also house mainly female sex workers, injecting drug users, street children and in smaller proportion, the truckers. More than 70 per cent of the young people are sexually active. In 8 per cent cases multiple sexual partnership was found to be very common. The State Aids Control Society, a Chapter of National Aids Control Organization has regularly been making HIV awareness campaigns through various NGOs in the areas under study but these campaigns appear to be quite ineffective, as both young and old respondents' knowledge about STIs/HIV/AIDS remains poor.

Awareness towards STIs/HIV/AIDS appeared to be quite high (99%), but knowledge of sources of infection, signs and symptoms are low. The slum dwellers discolsed that their major sources of information about STIs/HIV/AIDS are radio and T.V. The male folks rarely attend the awareness programme by the NGOs. Percentage of male attendance was 19 while among the females 31 per cent. The usual reaction towards such programme was indifferent. They all know that HIV/AIDs are very bad diseases and therefore one should not go to the house of the prostitutes. But there is no harm in meeting them elsewhere.

While examining the respondents' knowledge about condom and their use, it was found that their attitudes about condoms is negative, and knowledge regarding codoms and condom use is extremely low. The youths in the age group 14-30 poorly fared in the test. Almost 80 per cent of the youth group does not know the use of condoms. Thus, despite the recognition of condoms as effective preventive measures, there are other social, cultural environmental and economic barriers to their use. But the persons in the age group 31-50 years were found to have fair idea about condoms and their use. They gather the knowledge from their experience. The slum dwellers discolsed that their major sources of information about STIs/HIV/AIDS are radio and TV. They indicated that the best strategy to increase young peoples' knowledge is through health education. The influence of peer group in their case is not significant.

The health condition of all the informants was found alarming. 68 per cent of the respondents had very severe types of ailments with specific focus on abdominal pain, chest pain and asthma; dysentery in various forms is very common. 12 per cent of the informants had common ailments like coughing, cold and headache. They do not have any knowledge about the ailments from which they are suffering. The common scene is that despite acute fever and pain, they attend their duties as most of them work on daily paid jobs. Unable to see a doctor in times of need due either to financial hardship or their immobile status, many of them embrace death without having the barest minimum treatment. In 13 per cent cases, it was found that the respondents have been suffering from cough and cold for as long as 3 to 4 years with fever rising occasionally. But they were never examined for any serious type of diseases. Due to acute poverty and lack of knowledge, in times of need, the slum dwellers mainly depend on low cost traditional healers, herbalists etc. Youth friendly services are not in place in any of the localities studied.

Out of the 13 female sex workers interviewed, all street based and nearest to the slum localities under study, 11 took up the job due to acute poverty. For them, it is income generating and they accept money in exchange of the sexual service offered to their customers. They are not very much concerned about HIV/AIDS but they revelaed that their customers take protection. Extent of poverty is such that they have no desire to extend the length of life. In fact they have lost the desire to live. Several voluntary organisations are working on several Targeted Intervention (TI) projects in these slum areas under the banner of Assam State Aids Control Society. But most of these are oriented towards truckers only while only few truckers are found in the area. So far no slum-oriented projects have been taken up in the area.

Urban poverty alleviation programmes as designed by the Government of India have not reached any of the localities surveyed. There are no facilities for pure drinking water or sanitation. Poverty is the main reason why some women take up jobs like commerical sex workers. Unless poverty alleviation programmes are remodelled focussing on this aspect of potential threat of HIV/AIDS infection, the programmes will not succeed. Neither the slum dwellers nor the district authority are aware of any authority that implements the urban poverty alleviation progammes. While the NGOs working under the AIDS Preventions Societies do not know anything about the poverty alleviation programmes of government. It is at this point that an integrated approach is necessary. An authority who should be entrusted with this job of implementing poverty alleviation for the urban poor.

Assessment

The weaker the educational and socio-economic structure of a society the greater is the chance or vulnerability of the population towards HIV/AID. The relationship between the poverty and HIV is complex and several complicated casual and consequential factors are involved in the process. The above discussion has clearly shown the actual nature of poverty. Lack of human and financial resources (low levels of education and low levels of literacy), weak marketable skills and the consequential low labour producitivity, poor health condition are all related cyclically to poverty. Due to poverty and absence of sustainable livelihood, the poor labourer migrate from rural areas leaving their traditional cultural network behind and in the new situation due to the absence of any social control mechanisms indulge in risky sexual behaviours which may generate HIV infection. We have also seen how the poor women are involved in commercial sexual trading as their survival strategy for themselves and their families and in the process got exposed to HIV related infection. Due to absence of financial resources, they are unable to meet the cost of health care such as cost of drugs, physicians fee, transport cost to health centres etc. and hygiene which lead them to various types of infections and finally to death. An attempt to meet these costs means withdrawal of precious labour time in favour of attending patients, sometimes loss of employment through illness, or death and sale of any productive assets. This does not end here; the death again opens the way to funeral costs and costs of other rituals. The psycho-social and economic consequences of illness inflict tremendous pressure on the capacity of families and sometimes in the process many families experience great distress and often disintegrate as social and economic units.

Another fundamental point is their social and political exclusion, which make it difficult to reach them in times of need. Again such situations are also responsible for generating various types of behaviours that are inconsistent with the messages of the targeted intervention programmes or any HIV specific programmes (Rekodi, 2000). In fact, as we have seen, such messages hardly reach the poor and even when it reaches, becomes irrelevant or in exercisable for them. It was observed that in most cases they have understood what they are expected to do, but they do not have the incentive or resources to adopt the recommened behaviours.

Thus, the urgent necessity at this hour is to formulate policies that could intervene their existing pattern of living and able to change it; otherwise they will continue with their behaviours that expose them to HIV infection. Some poverty alleviation programmes directed towards stimulating reproductive health intervention are the urgent necessity in these area. Parents and adults need to be empowered to contribute positively to the reproductive and sexual health needs of their children and wards. Sexual and reproductive health programs need to be targeted if they are to impact on the health of young people.

REFERENCES

1. Goldfinger S. et al., 1998, HIV, Homelessness, and Serious Mental Illness: Implications for Policy and Practice. Prepared for the National Resource Center on Homelessness and Mental Illness.
2. Executive Director of UN-HABITAT, 2001, Habitat statement to the special session of the General Assembly on HIV/AIDS, New York.
3. Mosar, Carolin, 1998. The Asset Vulnerability Framework: Reassessing Urban Poverty Reduction Strategies, World Development, Vol. 26, No. 1, pp. 1-19.
4. ORG Centre for Social Research, 2002, Final Report of Assam Maping Study, Assam State AIDS Control Society.
5. Rakodi, Carole, 2001, *Urban Poverty: Issues and Interventions,* University of Cardiff
6. *Urban Poverty Alleviation Initiatives in Inda: A General Assessment and a Particular Perspective* (2002), a publication of the Ramanathan Foundation.

16

A Sociological Study of Urban Poverty in Shillong

Surojit Sen Gupta

Urbanization is the movement of population from rural to urban areas and the resulting increasing proportion of a population that resides in urabn rather than rural places. Thompson Warren (Encyclopedia of Social Sciences) has defined it as "the movement of people from communities concerned chiefly or solely with agriculture to other communities, generally larger whose activities are primarily centered in government, trade, manufacutre, or allied interests." According to Anderson (1953), urbanization is not a one-way process but it is a two-way process. It involves not only movement from villages to cities and change from agricultural occupation to business, trade, service and profession, but it also involves change in the migrants' attitudes, beliefs, values and behaviour patterns.

Urbanization is a continuous and complex process. It is continuous in the sense that , it involves becoming urban, moving to towns, cities and metroplitan centres shifting from agriculture to other non-farm economic pursuits common to urban centres and corresponding change in behavioural pattern. It is complex process in the sense that it is related to the transformation of society, including some drastic social, economic and geographical changes. However, the features of urbanization and its effect vary from economy to economy.

The behavioral concept of urbanization is well known

and usually related to Louis Wirth's paper "Urbanism as way of life." In which he defines an urban centre as a relatively large, dense and permanent settlement of socially hetrogeneous individuals. While accepting the size as criterion, Wirth added other factors which appear more to be dependent on size than to be pre-condition for urban development. Wirth formulated a theory of urbanism based on existing knowledge of soical groups. The size of the aggregate population will effect relations between membrs, increasing the process of differentiation which ultimately leads to segregation. Density also adds to diversification and gives rise to urban contrasts of wealth and poverty.

Thus understood, urbanization may be viewed as the process of population concentration in which the ratio of urban people to the total population in a territory increases. From this point of view, an increase in both the size of individual urban concentrations and the number of points of urban concentration may occur without an increase in urbanization of a territory, although these changes usually are accompained by a rising proportion of population living in cities.

The recent rapid rate of urbanization visible in developing countries, does not speak of corresponding growth of industries. Thus, the demand of the labour in the urban centres specially in developing countries is now decreasing. Consequently, these migrants can only get employment in activities with very low productivity or swell the rank of unemployment. Hence urbanization is now a shift of people from low productive agricultural employment to another section of employment marked by low productivity as handicraft production, retail trading, domestic services in urban areas.

Urban Poverty

Urban poverty is a complex and multifaceted problem. High urban population growth and rapid urbanization have accelerated to decline in essential urban basic services and infrastructure and distribution of basic services like drinking water, sanitation, transport, housing and health care etc. Inadequacy of drinking water supply and lack of sanitary facilities have led to increased number of diseases which severely affect the children and the urban poor sections and lead to increased Infant Mortality Rate (IMR) and Morbidity rate. The impact of illiteracy affects the low income families and particularly their health and hygiene. The urban poor is defined (by planning commission, 1990-91) as those below, the per capita (adult) daily intake nutrition level of 2,100 calories. Urban poverty in India is considered by many to be a reflection of rural poverty in the sense that the poor from the villages flock to the cities in search of a living and make civic condition in the city worse. The long term solution of the problem of urban poor lies therefore in the upliftment of the poor everywhere and not merely in the cities. But urban poverty is not only very visible to the urban elite, but it also badly affects the life of the latter in the way the urban poor stretches civic amentities. Consequently action plans for relief of the urban poor, particularly of the segment which live in slums or on city pavements always attract the sympathy and support of the local authorities and international aid agencies.

Thus accentuating urbanization and growth of urban population has led to the increase of urban poverty, that is, population living below the poverty line, characterized by both the transformation of rural poverty to that of urban poverty growing through rural to urban migration as well as the unemployment and marginalization of the urban poor.

Urban poverty is more visible in the Slums and depressed areas where public utilities like health and sanitation services, water supply etc are utterly inadequate. So on the health front also an urban poor faces hazards which affect his efficiency. Urban poverty is not always a by-product of rural poverty. Those urban dwellers who fail to cope with the struggle for development may also fall into poverty trap. In the areas where urbanization is more due to administrative expansion (as in North-East India) than industrialization, many households which cannot win the race for development may have to join those below the poverty line. Hence the urbanization process itself may generate poverty. As for instance, the NSSO reports reveal that incidence of urban poverty in the North-Eastern region is low. On the other hand, it is acknowledged even at the national level that the region is economically poor. So, low incidence of urban poverty as found by the NSSO in a hilly, tribal dominated, under-industrialised North-East India is paradoxical.

Urban Poor

With higher intensity of economic activities, cities attract mostly poor people particularly from the adjacent rural areas. Most of these population have particularly no resources for living and are instrumental in establishing slums. In addition to providing the labour equity to the industrial base, a large percentage of such urban poor in Indian cities provide services to the other segment of population, i.e. vending and provision services; sanitation, plumbing and solid waste disposal services, domestic and transport services etc.

Past experience indicates that no amount of legal and regulatory mechanism could stop this process because of the economic reality of bargaining for the cheapest labour, goods and services by the city consumers and readiness of this migrant poor population, or the so called informal sector, to provide the same. In order to earn the maximum income with least possible cost for living and commuting while providing the above goods and services, the urban poor frequently invades open land if these are optimally located. Even if these areas are not fit for human habitation, such as low lying areas, slope of drainage channels etc.

Cities act as the engines for growth in terms of production and market/service centre for their hinterland, leading to overall economic development of the regions. As there is industrial and commercial expansion in cities, people migrate from nearby and far-off areas to such cities in search of jobs. The vast bulk of such migrant belong to the weaker sections of society. The city, upto a point, is able to absorb them as cheap labour, but is not built to accommodate them. Such migrants contribution to the city's economy and other services is of paramount importance, but in the process they are relegated to sub-human conditions of living.

Thus, the urban poor differ qualitatively from the rural poor, while earning opportunity and basic survival remains essential to rural poverty, the urban poor have to confront the additional problems of housing, appalling sanitational problems high mortality and morbidity of women and children.

Sociologically speaking, the poor are caught up in vicious circles. Being poor means living in poor neighbourhood, which means being unable to send children to schools, which means not only the poor themselves but their children too will have low-paying jobs or no jobs at all, which means being doomed to remain poor for ever. Also, being poor means eating poor food, which means having poor health, which in turn means being handicapped or too weak to handle the heavy manual work, which also means accepting low paid work, which leads to remaining poor for ever. Thus, each circle begins and ends with being poor.

The City of Shillong

During the Pre-British period, Shillong existed in the form of a few cluster of scattered hamlets under the jurisdiction of the Syiem of Mylliem. However in 1863, the British Administration shifted the headquarter of united Khasi and Jaintia Hills District from Cherrapunjee to Shillong and consequently upon the separation of Assam from Bengal in 1874, Shillong became the provincial headquarter of Assam. The newly assigned function to the tiny settlement resulted in rapid growth of population from 1363 persons in 1872 to around 4000 persons in 1875. Further due to its favourable climate a Sanatorium was setup by the Britishers and later on, a Cantonment was also established. With the expansion of offices and establishments commerical activities expanded considerably to serve the growing population. During this period the missionaries also established various educational institutions and the town became an educational centre of the eastern region of India.

The post independent period marked an accelerated growth due to influx of migrants from the neighbouring states as well as from other parts of the country in pursuit of employment opportunities. Being a border state, the defence establishments also increased to a great extent.

However, in 1972 Meghalaya attained its full statehood and Shillong became the Capital of the State. This gave a further boost to the growth as various regional institutions of Central Government which was set up in Shillong. Hence over a century this tiny settlement has overgrown to a flourishing city and functionally undergone a radical change from a hill resort to a multifunctional unit and acts not only as an administrative centre but also as a regional commercial centre for the entire North-Eastern India.

Urbanization, Poverty and Growth of Slum—Shillong Situation.

The process of economic development and that of urbanization are in many respects interrelated. The urbanites generally have greater access to modern amenities of life, education, health and other civic services then the ruralities. Employment opportunities are also much more diversified and numerous than the villages. But urbanization may also give rise to a host of problems like over-crowding and scarcities in housing, water supply, and educational and training facilities, lack of proper sanitations and health services and unemployment and city of Shillong is no exception to this.

The urbanization process is very rapid in Shillong as it provides certain unique characteristics due to its typical socio-cultural and environmental settings. It is a typical case of urbanization mushrooming even with low level of development, harsh life of the surrounding rural areas and the vicious cycle of poverty and under-development. The inevitable consequences of this pseudo-urbanization is the emergence of more slum areas in the city. The poverty scenario in the city of Shillong is relatively different from cities in other areas as it is relative deprivation which appears to be more significant because in most slum areas of Shillong the harrowing existence of life with widespread hunger and malnutrition is far lower compared to slum dwellers of other cities.

Slums constitutes the most important and persistent problem of urban life. Slums are the court, alley or street of dirty crowded houses having highest density and lowest standard of living with the city. These residential areas are the sore spots of the city landscape. Slum development is the general character of all the cities of the world. The city of Shillong is also suffering from the same problem. In Shillong, Urbanization is taking place at a very rapid pace today. The growth and development of transport and communication system is adding a new dimension to the present pattern of urbanization. As a result, of this, not only the city is growing in both population and area, but the economic imbalances also have grown side by side. These outward symptoms are poor housing and inadequate community services, choked up city traffic, filth and squalor and diseases. These conditions mostly affect an ever growing number of population, especially the ones who under various circumstances are reduced to the state of slum dwellers. Due to rapid increase in population and uncontrolled and unplanned use of residential area Shillong is becoming over crowded leading to the formation of more slum areas.

Slums are more than the aggregate of the physical surroundings. They are partly a way of life of certain class of people. The private servants, milkmen, washer men and host of others often lead life that ultimately causes slums. In Shillong, even in a newly developed areas a petty shopkeeper (e.g. betel leaf seller) find a small space or room which he uses as his dwelling, his kitchen, godown, shop and for all that is meant for his economic and physical need. There is no proper latrine, urinal or bathroom which he can use.

The emergence of slums in Shillong are mainly due to accelerated high growth rate and unplanned physical development. The pace and magnitude of intra-State migration capitulated with an influx from out side the state has left the authorities concerned, lagging behind in providing the resources to meet the basic amenities and thereby the number of slum dwellers are increasing over the years. There ae 23 slum pockets identified within the Shillong Master Plan Area with an estimated 76,730 dwellers, which can be seen in Table 16.1.

All slums can not be construed under same category as each of them has its own character. Hence, it is appropriate to have understanding on characteristic features of slums in Shillong are less bleak because of its societal structures, topograhic advantage and low level of industrialization. Further, the slum dwellers in Shillong are not pushed to or compelled to occupy unfit or undesired marginal land but are occupying the land as a common city dwellers.

Since the land is owned by private individual except 3.02 sq. mt. within the Municipal area, most of the slums are developed in private land. Only in Jhalupara within Cantonment area and Sweeper Lane (at present the land is under possession of the Municipal Board) slums have developed. In the absence of the proper development control or regulation, indiscriminate plot subdivision and disposal for development devoid of proper provisions for access, services and disposal system leading to the growth of slum, degrading living environment. In area like Lumparing, Demseiniong, Malki, Madan Laban, Riat Laban, Lower Mawprem, Wahingdoh, Wahthabru etc. most of slum dwellers are having their own land and houses. In Barapathar, Qualapatti and Pynthorumkhrah etc. the maximum slum dwellers are in private rented houses.

Often the slums are termed as poorman's settlement, which don't hold good in case of Shillong due to the non-existence of caste system and class barrier in Meghalaya. The co-ordinal co-existence of people as neighbour irrespective of economic status is an unique distinctive of the slums in Shillong. Recent survey in some of the slum areas indicates that urban poor in the slum areas comprise 20 per cent ot 30 per cent of the total population. The main problems of slums in Shillong are (i) lack of basic civic amenities such as approach lane and water supply, drainage, lighting and sanitary facilities, (ii) over crowding, both interms of speace density and occupied residential unit, (iii) unliveable housing units, (iv) unemployment and underemployment accompained by (v) deprivation of educational facilities and health contingencies.

Table 16.1
List of Identified Slums in Shillong

Sl. No.	Localities	Population	Household
1.	Naspatighari	1747	349
2.	Qualapatti	2153	431
3.	Laitumkhrah (Harijan Colony)	817	163
4.	Polo Bazar	3358	672
5.	Par of jail Road	2955	591
6.	Sweepre lane (S.E. Mawkhar)	1250	164
7.	Part of Laitumkhrah	3124	520
8.	Demseiniong	500	77
9.	Malki	9826	1638
10.	Madan Laban	5838	1167
11.	Riat Laban	4323	720
12.	Lumparing	7645	1390
13.	Lower Mawprem	7375	1229
14.	Upper Mawprem	3113	518
15.	Wahingdoh	3221	644
16.	Barapathar	3145	629
17.	Wahthabru	1300	236
18.	Laban	7062	1405
19.	Part of Lamavila	250	45
20.	Part of Riatsamthiah	450	90
21.	Part of Umsohsun	500	111
22.	Jhalupara (Cantonment)	3028	505
23.	Pynthorumkhrah (Outside Municipal Area)	3750	750
Total		**76730**	**14044**

Source: Shillong Master Plan-1991-2011.

In the Slums of Shillong, one can find two distinct

patterns of migration; total family migration and part migration. In the first case, the migrants come to the city along with all the members of their family and they maintain either very weak or no linkages (social or economic) with their place of origin. The second group of migrants consists of mostly the working male members (the children, aged and female members are left at their place of origin). These two groups of slum dwellers come to Shillong with altogether different perspective which ultimately shape their life and their relationship with the dominant.

In Shillong slum, it was also found that people are not pursuing their traditional occupations, but here people are pre-dominantly engaged in non-traditional informal sector occupations like petty traders, maid servants, construction workers and so on. The settlement pattern of slums in Shillong is not either in mothertounge or religion or place of origin or kinship ties but however it is socially heterogenous. On the process of class formation, migration reinforces natural population growth. Persons migrating into this city from the rural hinterlands or the adjoining states are helped by a relative or community members of the same native place who has already settled in the city. Generally at the time of leaving their native place, the prospective migrants have some appriori idea as to where they would go to settle down in the city which are in most cases the slums of their kinsmen.

In the slum areas in Shillong, one can notice the close community life which the slum dwellers adhere to. The slum people know each other very well, their children play together, there is a relationship of mutual help which often crosses the religious boundary, they take part in many collective activities such as in social and religious functions and so on. The exchange of social visits among the neighbours is also very frequent. It can also be observed that the social groups and institutions such as family, marriage, kinship and religion are as functional as in any cross-section of Indian population. In terms of languages, dress pattern, the structure of beliefs and superstitions and in thought pattern, one can notice some degree of continuity of rural modes.

In the slum communities in Shillong, one can hardly fail

to notice the primary group—like face to face relationships. This is unfolded when we notice that people speak in their regional dialect, they migrate with the help of their kinsmen and fellow villagers and settle down in the slum, besides they uphold many of the values, beliefs and rationals of their village life while living in the city. When the Slum dwellers in Shillong tend to do so in general their traditional cultural forms are reproduced. Having been drawn from plural cultural backgrounds the slum dwellers live a community life and are successful in thwarting the unifying pressure from the dominant urban society. Thus, the cultural plurality of the Indian society is maintained and reproduced in the slums in Shillong as well. Therefore, rurality or at least some degree of it becomes a part of urbanity.

One can also see that in the Slum areas of Shillong, there is an acute lack of not only water supply and other basic sanitary facilities but also approach lanes, electrification and housing facilities. As these areas are inhabited by the economically deprived sections of the society, these areas suffers from inadequate educational and health facilities. They are usually the pockets of unemployment and underemployment. Thus, poverty drives these sections of the society into participating in criminal activities.

Moreover, with the ever increasing migration of the surrounding rural population into the urban centre of Shillong, the slums are growing larger in size. These recent migrants usually prefer to be in these depressed areas before they can eke out a better standard of living and usually in this competitive world, these migrants can never realise their aspirations and therefore, ultimately resort to anit-social activities to support themselves and their families. The slums in Shillong are thus overcrowded and in the absence of proper civic amenities, these areas are usually highly populated and become detrimental to the society at large. The slum environment in Shillong is also responsible for the degradation of mental outlook of residents, especially, its effect on growing children is most remarkable. Children daily witness scenes of violence, drunkenness, crimes etc, which encourage them to do the same. Because of the poverty and unhygienic conditions of the slums there is all-round deterioration in the environment with overcrowding full of all possible social and economic crimes.

It can be concluded that there is a need to investigate the emerging phenomenon of the development of Slums and the rising tide of urban poor in this beautifull Hill City. The experience and expertise of specialist departments in relations to their particular areas of activity; the large reservoir of talent and commitment available with professionals and voluntary organizations/NGOs and the great, existential wisdom of the Slum dwellers; will surely lay foundation for urban poverty alleviation and help to ushers in a brighter future of the urban poor in the City of Shillong.

REFERENCE

1. Anderson N. (1960): *The Urban Community,* New York.
2. Clinard, M.B. (1966): *Slums and Community Development,* New York: The Free Press.
3. Dube, K.K. and Singh, Alok Kumar. (1988): *Urban Environment in India, problems and prospects,* Inter-India Publishing, New Delhi.
4. Dandekar, V.M. and Nilakantha, Rath. (1971): "Poverty in India.", *Economic and Political Weekly,* Vol. VI (No.1).
5. Dutta Roy. B. (ed.), (2000): *Population Poverty and Environment in North-East India,* Concept Publication, New Delhil.
6. Ganguly, J.B. (1995): *Urbanization and Development in North-East India,* Deep & Deep Publications, New Delhi.
7. Master Plan of Shillong 1991-2011: Directorate of Urban Affairs, Meghalaya, Shillong.
8. Majumdar, T.K. (1983): *Urbanising Poor.* Lancers Publication, New Delhi.
9. Purkayastha, S. (2000): In Dutta Roy, B. (ed.), Ibid.
10. Roy, Prodipto. (ed) (1995): *Urbanization and Slums,* Har-Anand Publications, New Delhi.
11. Sinha, Satish. (1985): *Slum Eradication and Urban Renewal,* Inter-India Publication, New Delhi.

12. Singh, J.P. (1980): *Urban Land-use Planning in Hill Areas: A Case Study of Shillong, Inter India*, New Delhi.

13. Sarin, Geeta (2000): in Dutta Roy, B. (ed.), *Ibdi.*

14. Sen Gupta, Surojit, (2003): Urban Social Stracture : A Study of Urbanization in Shillong. Ph.D. Dissertation, Department of Sociology, NEHU, Shillong.

15. Wirth, L. (1938): 'Urbanism as a way of life', *American Journal of Sociology*, XLIV.

17

The Impact of Poverty on Social Institutions of Slum Dwellers in Guwahati

Upala Barua

The significant fact about the urban poor is that majority of them are slum dwellers. Slum, which we define as an area having no basic infrastructure and services, has been the heaven for this category of people in almost all the cities of India. These areas are usually overcrowded and the people sheltering here are habituated in living in such areas year after year. In fact, they are forced to live in such settlements, as due to their poor economic status they are unable to enter into the formal land and housing markets. These are the areas located generally along the railway track, unseen part of a riverbank, steep hilly slopes or near the garbage dumps and are generally reserved government lands, which have no scope for improvement. They are prone to all natural and man-made disaster, which very often dislocate their continuity of life. Due to the illegal status of their land, they do not get even the basic amenities (drinking water, electricity, kerosene, etc.), which they procure from informal markets at high costs resulting in further deterioration of their financial condition (Hurle, 1998: 2). Thus, they constantly live in unhygienic condition, degraded environment, which result in their poor health and early demise leaving the family in extreme distress.

The slum dwellers live in a pathetic condition and there is hardly any social control in the true sense of the term in the slum society. Social organisations hardly exist and this makes the basic difference between the mainstream society and slum society. The people living here are mainly destitute immigrants who come to the city from different locations for survival or in hopes of bettering their economic conditions. Due to this, they remain aloof from the mainstream society. This social exclusion adds further to the problematic life in the slum.

The present paper aims at studying at micro level the impact of urban poverty on the social system of slum dwellers in Guwahati city. Because majority of the urban poor are slum dwellers and it is poverty that pushes the impoverished rural migrants into city areas of substandard living i.e. slums. Only slums are considered here because other impoverished families living in formal residential areas live in more or less stable atmosphere and are not so much prone to various forms of hazards like health, ecodegradation, familial, personal and marital to which the slum dwellers are exposed to.

This study was taken up focussing on the impact of poverty on the functioning of the social and community life of slum dwellers in 11 slum localities of Guwahati. Altogether 185 families have been covered. They all belong to heterogeneous socio cultural background and live mostly in nuclear and sub nuclear families. Social system as usual refers to the orderly arrangement of parts or institutions of a society and are expressed in human interaction. Unlike slums in other industrial cities, slum dwellers of Guwahati are not industrial workers. The study reveals that heterogeneity in terms of ethinic background, occupations, working time schedule are major reasons why community feeling have not grown amongst them. They remain aloof from the mainstream society. And the wider society also does not try to integrate them into the wider social fabric—economy and polity.

The main features of slum life are also self-sustenance and struggle. Two main mechanisms that safeguard any social system from getting out of control—these two are mechanisms for socialisation and social control. The study reveals that on both the points the social system shows marked signs of disorganisation.

The results of this survey were shocking. The highest educational attainment of boys was registered as class six standard only; while for the girls, education was almost nil. Among the girls, only 10 per cent were found going to special schools occasionally. The school drop out cases are normal phenomenon for both boys and girls. People laugh at the children when they begin their schooling and wait for their final come back. Imparting education to the children is still a non-issue for them. They want their children to be their followers in their path for struggle and earn their bread. Unlike the slums in the industrialised cities where majority of dwellers are industrial wage labourers, these slums however have no specific character in regard to the occupation of the dwellers. Due to absence of any industrial units, the inhabitants of the slums mainly depend on the jobs like day labourers, assistants in different shops and establishments, garages; wine sellers, grocery vendors, truck driver, handymen, sweepers, rag pickers, etc. Due to such heterogeneous nature of works they have heterogeneous time schedule for works, which come on their way of getting united, and think about the development of their settlements.

The inhabitants are mostly north Indian. A small segment is constituted by the persons coming from Andhra Pradesh who identify themselves as the lower castes of the State and engaged in jobs like sweepers, garbage dumper, etc. All the inhabitants can speak Hindi and they understand and speak Assamese well. They could not provide enough information about their original family structure. But the information gathered from them sufficiently hint at their closeness towards joint family system. They also expressed their joy of living in a joint family—especially when it is the question of upbringing of children. 83 per cent of the respondents interviewed have come from rural settings, while the rest have come from small urban localities of Bihar, Orissa and other States of India.

The Family Structure

The family structures here are basically nuclear (38 families) but in some cases there are sub nuclear families, as described by Kolenda (2000: 305) i.e. the fragment of a formerly complete family such as a widow with her unmarried children or two unmarried siblings living together (ibid: 306) (8 families). In seven cases extended families were found where members were related lineally or afinally with simultaneous presence of nuclear relatives in the unit. There were 11 single member families. From the vulnerability point of view, Goldsmith (1971: 6) opines that nuclear family made up of two parents and their children is unstable. Thus, if one parent dies, the remaining one is incapable of fulfilling all the necessary functions required to bring up the children. This appears to be hold good in respect of the slum families studied.

Marriage

The institution of marriage has no specific shape. But marriage as usual is taken very seriously and heavy drinking and feast always mark marriage celebration. The usual Hindu or Muslim marriage system as the case may be, with some deviation here and there is prevalent among the slum dwellers. The rules regarding the marriages i.e. whether it is clan exogamy or endogamy, as prevalent in the parent societies are followed as far as possible. But unlike their parent societies, both intra and inter community marriages are prevalent and frequent here. Instances are there when a family goes to their village of origin for getting their sons or daughters married as per their traditional norms. In the intra community marriage—a discussion between the parents of both the parties sometimes takes place but that is not a set rule. While in inter community marriages usually no such discussion takes place; the consent or agreement between the bride and groom is taken as sufficient. In marriages, the role of parents is limited only in arranging the celebration.

They usually follow the system of patrilocal residence and one brings his wife to live with his family. But unlike the other patrilocal households, the father here is not under full control of the household resources or to direct the labour of all household members. This has been elaborately discussed in the context of resource division. There are instances when the married couple after few days of staying in the husband's natal family move out and establish their new residence thus forming the core of an independent nuclear family.

They trace their descent patrilineally, from father to sons. However, there is hardly anything they actually inherit. In 78 per cent cases the sons get separated before their father dies. Such separation only means economic freedom. Only in rare cases, the sons look after their parents at old age. Neither they have any means to do so nor do they have any such family tie that generates any feelings for their parents. In fact, separation from parents is the prevailing rule and only in rare cases the family remains united till the death of the parents.

Family Function

Apart from the sexual and reproductive functions that include the nurture and basic enculturation of the young in an atmosphere of intimacy, the families of the slum dwellers perform the economic and educational functions only partially. They do not have the complementary division of labour between the spouses and offspring.

Kinship

The slum societies under study are not kin oriented societies. Marriage for them is only institutionalisation of mating and channelling of sexual outlets. It does not establish any strong kinship tie in the resultant family. The inhabitants before reaching this destination had travelled thousands of miles leaving their villages and kin. During their lifetime they rarely go to their kith and kin. This is one reason why the strong kinship tie once existed in their family of origin gets weakened (Roy, 2000, 26). Kin knowledge among them varies according to the age and class. Among the children and youths of the age group 14-25, kin knowledge is significantly low. They can hardly identify 15 significant kin and could tell only about 5 living relatives. Persons of older generation however found to have fair knowledge of kin having identified as many as 35 kin and 18 living kin. Despite the fact that the older generation is continuing their tie with their long distance kin, had to live in complete isolation from their society of origin; however, this makes no impact on their way of living. Kinship relation is hardly accountable in their society. The society in that sense is individualistic. Firth (1956: 1970) rightly observed that kinship is less effective as the basis of urban social organisation, social sanctions here cannot be easily invoked in relation to the breach of kinship expectations.

Dissolution of Marriage

The phrase dissolution of marriage has been used as no further action takes place after a marriage is dissolved. Divorce or separation is practically unknown terms and they do not pay much attention to this. After dissolution they do not pass through the phases of separation to obtain divorce as required under law; for them once the family is separated the conjugal relation ends there. Dissolution of marriage has been a common feature and so also the remarriage of the males. In very rare cases, the deserted females got married. As many as 18 cases of dissolution were recorded in respect of the last three years (2000-2003) period, of which in 11 cases the males got married again but in only one case a female divorcee got married. But the life of deserted female is miserable. She neither is taken back in her natal family nor she had any place to take shelter. The working women in such a situation sometimes take shelter in the workplace or employer's place. But that is a rare case. Out of the 18 cases of dissolution of marriages, in eight cases the residences were belonged to the wives and as such the husbands had to get out of the residence. In 3 cases the women took shelter in the adjacent footpaths, in two cases the women are traceless, and in 2 cases the women took shelter in a nearby brothel. The distribution of these cases in the nine slum segments where the study was conducted is shown in Table 17.1

Table 17.1

Status of Males and Females after Dissolution

Sl. No.	Sites	No of Separated Families	Status of Females after Separation	Status of Males after Separation
1	Site-I	3	All remained unmarried	1 got married
2	Site-II	2	All remained unmarried	—
3	Site-III	1	Remained unmarried	got married
4	Site-IV	Nil	Nil	Nil
5	Site-V	4	2 traceless, rest remained unmarried	3 got married
6	Site-VI	3	Got married	2 got married
7	Site-VII	3	All remained unmarried	All got married
8	Site-VIII	1	Remained unmarried	Got married
9	Site-IX	1	Remained unmarried	Remained unmarried
	Total	18	1 got married, 2 traceless, others remained unmarried	11 got married, others remained unmarried

Source: Field Survey.

The main reasons behind the dissolution were stated as below:

(1) Superstition: Incidence of deserting a woman considering her, as omen is a common happening. Such ideas are sometimes pushed into the head of the person purposefully to get rid of the women he married.

(2) Barrenness

(3) Continual dying of offspring

(4) No male offspring

(5) Permanent sexual disability

(6) Unwillingness to perform the sexual act

(7) Neglect in time of sickness; "failure to cherish"
(8) Extra marital relationship
(9) Excessive drinking, drug abuse
(10) Failure to provide protection

The Society

Apparently in all the above cases the main reason behind the dissolution of marriage is poverty. The varieties of situations generated by the poverty in the long run leads to family disintegration in many cases. The study while attempting to enquire into the aspects confronted with unfavourable situation. The poverty was so acute that in two cases the wife was forced to go to another person in exchange of money for a night. In both the cases the marriage was dissolved immediately and police cases were registered. There were also instances when the wife willingly took such steps for earning money and in course of time becomes a prostitute. It was commonly observed that women in the society takes lead in preserving and realising the goal of the families and far more active than the males in the family and in 30 per cent cases were the principal bread earner for the family. This is a significant fact. The men-folk spend most part of their income in consuming liquor and gambling. The indifferent attitude of the males towards the females indirectly exerts tremendous pressure on the women in the family and this results in collapse of health in many cases. Women in such circumstances were also found going to work. The death of the women in the family is another factor that lead to a single parent family. Such death comes as a curse on the girl child in the family.

Having discussed the nature of the slums under study, it is now our turn to have a look at the development perspective of these slums. Evidently, slum society as discussed above has all the characteristics of a typical slum. The census of India has defined slum as "a compact area of at least 300 population or about 60-70 households of poorly built congested tenements, in unhygienic environment usually with inadequate infrastructure and lacking in proper sanitary and drinking water facilities" (Census, 1991). This definition fits well the area under study. Urban development although is a

State subject, so far the State Government have not been able to provide the minimum basic amentities to the slum population. The Ministry of Urban Development and Poverty alleviation, Government of India, is entrusted with the responsibility of policy making and planning of different facets of urban development. It has certain poverty alleviation programmes through which it assists the States by providing fund on sharing basis. Under the National Slum Development Programme (NSDP), Additional Central Assistance (ACA) is released to the States/UTs for the development of urban slums. The objective of this programme is upgradation of urban slums by providing physical amenities like water supply, storm water drains, community bath, community latriens, etc. Besides, the funds under NSDP can be used for provision of community infrastructure and social amenities like pre school education, non-formal education, adult education, maternity, child health and primary health care including immunization etc. The programme also has a component of shelter upgradation or construction of new houses.

Under the programme, between 1996 and 2003, an amount of Rs. 2022 lakhs was sanctioned to the State of Assam by the Central Government out of which only Rs 1043 lakhs was actually released. The State Government could utilise only Rs. 587 lakhs during the stated period. Incidentally, no development works under the scheme was taken up in the study areas. Another important scheme in this line is the Swarna Jayanti Shahari Rozgar Yojana (SJSRY), which is a composite scheme, but hardly beneficial for the urban poor in reality. Because the only component applicable in case of these slums is the urban self-employment scheme which only literate persons can apply. The Urban Self Employment Programme (USEP) is applicable to all urban towns in India, the programme is being implemented on a whole town basis with special emphasis on urban poor clusters. The benefit of even this scheme has not reached the people under study.

For implementation of the schemes of development of poor urban women and children, a minimum of 10 women is necessary to form a group. The social system of the slum is such that it is not possible to mobilise even three women at a time. Thus for effective implementation of the scheme, the design of the scheme needs to be changed suitably. Community participation is the cardinal principle for successful implementation of any programme. The community is to be involved right from the planning stage of the schemes to their operation and maintenace. Involvement of non-government organisations (NGOs) and private agencies was to be explored and given due importance by the State Governments and Urban Local Bodies.

Empowerment of the poor women needs to be fixed as a basic goal. It was commonly observed that women in the slums take lead in maintaining the family and also realising the goal of the families and in the process become far more active than the males—not only within their own families but also in the community life too. In their community life, women play two roles (i) they had either to fight for their share of community resources such as water or share of their own resources in whatever small quantity may be, like fuel, kerosene, with the neighbours to meet the temporary needs. In the process they initiate a sense of social control mechanisms within their community. So one key solution is women and their empowerment.

The root cause of poverty is the lack of assets (land). The slums studied are located along the railway track unseen part of a riverbank, steep hilly slopes or near garbage dumps. These lands are generally reserved government land having no scope getting settlement or even for temporary improvement. The dwellers here live in fear of being evicted at any time. Several such operations have already been carried out by the railway authority in collaboration with the district administration. Now the only way out of this cycle seem to lie in the government by giving temporary settlement in the names of these families wherever possible as per rules and situation. This will give them a sense of stability and security and they can also avail different government schemes. Once they are stable at an area, the social system can at least avail the funds for poverty alleviation schemes. Effort should be made to bring them within the urban system and should be given an opportunity to participate in the social system. Concept of urban agriculture may also be experimented as is done in many South East Asian countries. Any scheme to improve the slums would not work in its existing location unless they are given the security to hold their plot of land.

REFERENCES

1. Goldsmith, Edward, 1971, The Underlying Causes of Social Breakdown, *The Ecologist*, Vol.1 No. 13, July 1971.
2. Goode, William, J. 1989, *The Family*, Prenticehall of India Pvt. Ltd., New Delhi.
3. Hurle, Michael, 1998, *Public Housing and Urban Renewal Programmes in South-East Asia*. An Essay. University of Hull, May 1998.
4. Kolenda, P.M. 2000, *Family Structure in Village Lonikand, in the Indian Family, Change and Persistence*, P.K. Roy (ed.), Gyan Publishing House, New Delhil.
5. Mosar, Carolin, 1998, The Asset Vulnerability Framework: Re-assessing Urban Poverty Reduction Strategies *World Development*, Vol. 26, No.1, pp. 1-19, 1998.
6. Supriti, Sharon, M. Barnhardt and Ramesh Ramanathan. "Urban Poverty Alleviation in India: A General Assessment and a Particular Perspective" (2002), Ramanathan Foundation, Bangalore 560094.
7. World Bank, World Development Report 2000/20001.

18

Urban Poverty: An Appraisal of Slums in Shillong

P.K. Ryngnga

Introduction

The phenomenon of slum has come to be regarded as a major problem of urbanization. While no Indian city is free from slums, the problem appears to be more acute in metropolitan cities. Slums are known by different terms in different regions: *katras, gallis, juggi-jhopdi* (in Delhi); *chawls* (in Bombay); *ahatas* (in kanpur); *bustees* (in Kolkatta); *cheris* (in Chennai); *keris* (in Bangalore); *petas* (in Andhra Pradesh).[1]

It is only in recent year that the problem of urban slums has attracted the attention of some sociologists and social anthropologists in India. Different studies have been taken up on slums in Mumbai (Desai and Pillai, 1972[2], Ramachandran, 1972[3]), Kolkatta (Calcutta Metropolitan Development Authority), Delhi (Singh, 1978[4]), Chandigarh (D'Souza, 1968[5]), Vijayawada in Andhra Pradesh (K. Ranga Rao and MSA Rao, 1984[6]).

A major problem in the study of slums relates to the conditions under which slums emerge particularly in hilly area, and these are varied. Broadly, we may identify two sets of situations for the growth of slums. *First,* a slum develops as a result of squatting of poor migrants in which a majority of migrants coming to cities are unskilled workers who are too poor to rent a house and pay for urban infrastructure facilities. So, they are forced to squat on vacant public land in which the city administration considers such settlement as illegal and does not provide any municipal services.

The *second* set of conditions under which a slum develops is the deterioration of a group of buildings in the old part of city. The area gets congested and overcrowded and in the absence of adequate municipal services[7], slum conditions increase.

Methodolgy

In order to understand the general pattern and types of slums and their growth in Shillong, basic data available with the Directorate of Urban Affairs, Municipality and the so-called Non-Governmenal Organization henceforth called World Vision were collected and analyzed. The history of each slum and the characteristics of its population were gathered through interviews with knowledgeable persons from the above-mentioned departments, also from within, and without the slum localities.

It was felt that an appropriate strategy for analyzing slum conditions and their economic improvement through World Vision was to study the slums intensively. After making a general study of slums in Shillong three particular slum areas (Mawprem, Nongmynsog and Jingthangbriew—between Jaiaw and Mawlai) which have come under the purview of World Vision were selected for intensive study. Two procedures were adopted for collection of data. At one level, information was gathered on social, economic, political, and cultural life in the slums in general from the government departments. At another level, socio-economic survey of the three mentioned slum areas was made through interviews and observations.

Emergence of Slums in Shillong

The emergence of slums in Shillong is mainly due to high growth and unplanned development of Shillong urban area which has been one of the oldest, largest and fastest growing hill area in the country. Initially developed to sustain a few thousand population has accommodated nearly two lakhs of people today. This high growth is mainly attributed to the migration of poor sections of the rural population in search of better economic opportunities[8]. The pace and magnitude of intra-State migration capitulated with an influx from outside the State has left the authorities concerned, lagging behind in providing the resources to meet the basic amenities[9] and thereby the number of slum dwellers are increasing over the years. There are 23 slum pockets with an estimation of 76,730 dwellers during 1991 (Table 18.1).

The population of slums in Shillong in 1991 was 76,730 persons and 14,044 households.

Table 18.1
Identified Slums in Shillong in 1991

Sl No	Localities	Population	Percentage	Household of Population	Percentage of Household
1	Malki	9826	12.80	1638	11.66
2	Laban	7062	9.20	1405	10.00
3	Lumparing	7645	9.96	1390	9.89
4	Lower Mawprem	7375	9.61	1229	8.75
5	Madan Laban	5838	7.60	1167	8.30
6	Pynthorumkhrah	3750	4.88	750	5.34
7	Riat Laban	4323	5.63	720	5.12
8	Polo Bazar	3358	4.37	672	4.78
9	Wahingdoh	3221	4.19	644	4.58
10	Barapathar	3145	4.10	629	4.47
11	Part of Jail Road	2955	3.85	591	4.20
12	Part of Laitumkhrah	3124	4.07	520	3.70
13	Upper Mawprem	3113	4.05	518	3.68
14	Jhalupara (Cantonment)	3028	3.94	505	3.59
15	Qualapatty	2153	2.80	431	3.06
16	Naspatighari	1747	2.27	349	2.48
17	Wahthapbhru	1300	1.69	236	1.68
18	Sweeper Lane (SE Mawkhar)	1250	1.62	164	1.16
19	Laitumkhrah (Harijan Colony)	817	1.06	163	1.16
20	Part of Umsohsun	500	0.65	111	0.79
21	Part of Riatsamthiah	450	0.58	90	0.64
22	Demseiniong	500	0.65	77	0.54
23	Part of Lamavilla	250	0.32	45	0.32
Total		**76,730**	**100**	**14044**	**100**

Source: Department of Urban Affairs; Master Plan of Shillong 1991-2011. (Figures in percentages are calculated by the author)

From the Table 18.1 it can be seen that Malki has the highest slum dwellers with 9826 population accounting to 12.80 per cent and 1638 households followed by Laban with 7062 population accounting to 9.20 per cent and 10 per cent households. Lumparing has 9.96 per cent of slum dwellers with 9.89 per cent of households whereas Lower Mawprem has 9.61 per cent of slum dwellers with 8.75 per cent of households. The localities having least population of slum dwellers are part of Umsohsun, Part of Riatsamthiah, Demseiniong and Part of Lamavilla, but when compared with Table 18.2 it can be seen that Pynthorumkhrah (Slum 1and 2) has 16.89 per cent of slum population followed by Raid Laban with 10.88 per cent. The estimated slum population in 2000 shows that Part of Riatsamthiah, Part of Umsohsun, and Part of Lamavilla are been eliminated although the total population still revealed an increase of 1302 people.

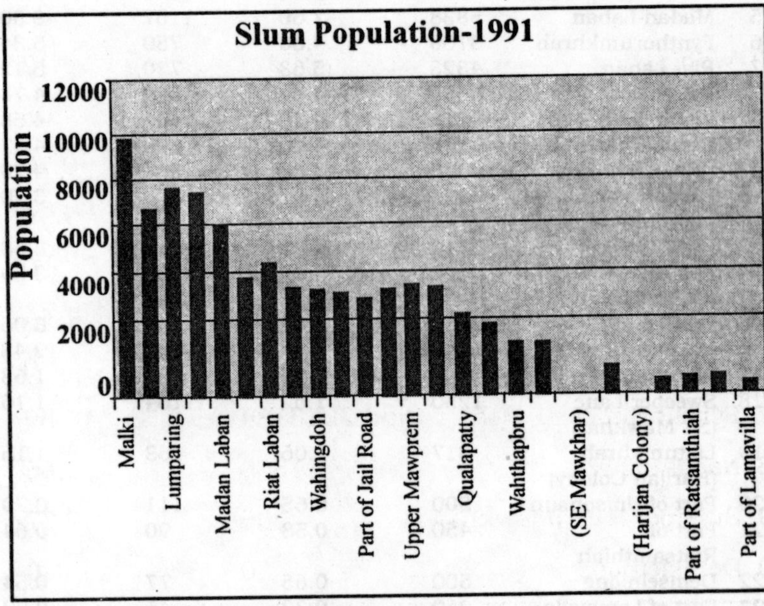

Fig: 18.1

Table 18.2

Identified Slums in Shillong in 2000

Sl. No	Localities	Population	Percentage
1	Qualapatty	1603	2.05
2	Lumparing	5782	7.40
3	Malki	7314	9.37
4	Laitumkhrah	6715	8.60
5	Upper Mawprem	3085	3.95
6	Lower Mawprem	6238	7.99
7	Madan Laban	6238	7.99
8	Raid Laban	8492	10.88
9	Jhalupara	3145	4.03
10	Wahingdoh	3221	4.12
11	Barapathar	3145	4.03
12	Wahthapbru	599	0.76
13	Laban	6238	7.99
14	Garoline (Laitumkhrah)	0	0
15	Harijan Colony	1127	1.44
16	Dymmiew (Lower Mawprem)	0	0
17	Pynthorumkhrah (slum 1and 2)	13184	16.89
18	Naspatighari	1300	1.66
19	Sweeper lane (Mawkhar)	606	0.77
20	Demsieniong	0	0
Total		**78,032**	**100**

Source: Department of Urban Affairs.

(Figures in percentages are calulated by the author).

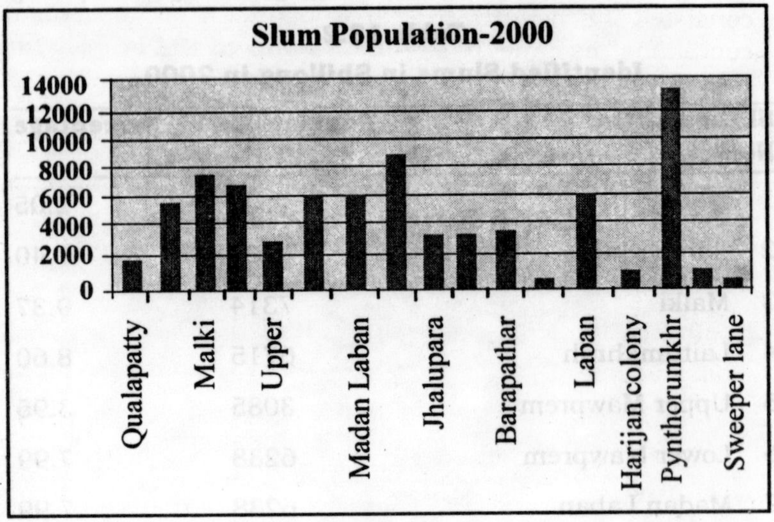

Fig: 18.2

Problem of Slums Area

The main problems of slums in Shillong are:

(i) Lack of basic civic amenities such as water supply, drainage, lighting and sanitary facilities

(ii) Overcrowding, both in terms of space density and occupied residential unit

(iii) Unliveable housing units

(iv) Unemployment and under employment accompanied by deprivation of educational facilities and health care[10]

Slum Characteristics

Over a period of 10-15 years, the location of slums has acquired area specific characteristics that vary from one area to the other. Shillong, being a hilly area, slum areas may be located at hilltops, on hill slopes or in low-lying areas. The socio-economic characteristics of these slum areas differ from those of other slum areas in the country. For instance, in a particular slum a mixed composition of slum population comprising both the Mixed-Income group and the Lower-Income group. Though a majority of the slum population consisted of Scheduled tribe population, the socio-economic conditions may vary from one section to the other. Ours being a casteless society, a slum area represents an amalgamation of all income groups.

Nevertheless, the slums of Shillong are less depressing because of its societal structure, topograhic advantage and low level of industrialization. Furthermore, the slum dwellers are not compelled to occupy unfit or undesired marginal land but are occupying the land as common city dwellers.

Socio-Economic Conditions of Slums in Shillong

Housing pattern

Almost the entire slum consists of Assam type of housing with tin roofing and only a small section in the slum area of Garoline Laitumkhrah, RCC building is found. There is a difference in the pattern of construction of houses built by the tribal slum dwellers and other non-tribal slum dwellers. In the case of the former, generally three to four households together construct a long structure and partition the same among themselves with one portion for each household. In the case of others, each household builds its own separate house. The houses, however, looked rectangular or long square-like type. The houses are constructed without any plan. With the result, there is no straight passage or road anywhere except a narrow road is found only from one side or two sides around the slum areas.

Drainage facilities

The entire area gets slushy during rainy season. For want of drainage facilities even in other seasons, sullage water-logging takes place at various places. The Municipality takes no interest in removing the waste or rubbish thrown on the streets. Normally each household tries to clean the surroundings and footpath in front of its own house. Except for a new households, others have no lavatories. Both men and women usually go out to nearby jungles or even to the open drain early in the morning for their toilet purposes. A majority of the houses do not have any bathrooms. Only a few of them enclose small areas behind or by the side of their house and use the same for bathrooms.

Water supply

Since the slum areas are located within the municipal limits, usually the Municipal Board supply water but for slum areas, falling outside Municipal limits the Public Health Engineering (PHE) supply water through Rural Water Supply Scheme. For other slum areas who do not benefit from the two, usually go to the nearby small streams to collect water for cooling, drinking and washing.

Power supply

Slums falling within Manicipal limits somewhat exhibit a slight improvement in this area, since they are connected with proper lighting except that power supply is low (low megahertz) which can only be used for basic domestic requirements. However, the community pays for the power used. But for slums outside the Municipal limits gets one-to two point temporary connection from some middle income group or lower income groups household in which they have to pay monthly.

General Slum Improvement

* The Urban Affairs Department started the slum improvement works back in 1974-75 and continuing doing so under environmental improvement of urban slum scheme by way of providing physical amenities.
* To facilitate the aspect of physical amenities the Urban Affairs Department has introduced the Urban Basic Services Scheme as well as Nehru Rozgar Yojana in these slum area.
* **Physical**—Drain, Footpath, Streetlight, Sanitation
* These scheme takes care of both social input such as health care and health facilities for the vulnerable section i.e., the children and woman nutrition,
    1. Pre-school learning,
    2. Adult literacy,
    3. Up gradation of housing units
    4. Supplementing nutrition

* Economic upliftment by way of
   1. Providing job opportunities through wage employment,
   2. Enhance and impart skill and
   3. Facilitate finance for entrepreneur which will augment family income
* For the last four years work was done only in Pynthorumkhrah.
* Usually assets are been created and handed to the Municipal Board for maintenance
* In 1997-98 new scheme known as National Slum Development Programme was implemented.

Table 18.3
Schemes Under Environmental Improvement of Urban Slums (ELUS) Implemented by the Directorate of Urban Affaris

Localities	Started	Completed	Type of work
Demsieniong	1986-87	1997-98	Footpath, Drain,
Laban	1986-87	1989-90	Retaining wall
Wahthapbru	1991-92	1991-92	Toilet Blocks
Upper. Mawprem	1990-91	1990-91	
Pynthorumkhrah	1991	Still continuing	

Source: Directorate of Urban Affairs.

Intensive Case study of Mawprem, Nongmynsong and Jingthangbriew—(between Jaiaw and Mawlai) under the purview of World Vision.

Characteristics

Mawprem Slum Area: It was in early 1990's when Municipal Board demolished houses in Polo area. Those people had to vacate the land and were forced to occupy the empty houses of Small Pox Dispensary in Lower Mawprem. These people claimed themselves as refugees since they are not counted as Mawprem residents. It is poignant to point out that in this area, nearly five to six families occupied one long structure and partitioned the same for two rooms each among themselves with no proper toilet, electricity, water. The size of one family is 12 to 14 numbers. The earning per monthly is Rs. 300-400 and their labour is been charged for Rs. 20-25 per/day. The health condition of those people is found to be pathetic where malnourishment and Tuberculosis is common.

Nongmynsong

This slum area consists of a mixed community that comprises of low occupational group of people and broken families. The housing pattern in this slum area is that the houses are scattered from one another and the condition is worse but still these people had to pay rent of Rs. 150-300 per month.

Jingthangbriew

This particular slum area is not so large when compared with the above two. The vivid standpoint of this slum area is that the standard of living is quite an improved one and the housing condition is also better in comparison with the other two. Only about 35-40 households are found to reside in this location. The size of the family is also comparatively smaller with only 6-7 family members.

Improvement of these three slum through World Vision

Since 1996, World Vision started working among the Mawprem slum people but the slum dwellers vehemently opposed to this initiative. It was until 1999 the persistent sacrifice of World Vision witnessed changes in the slum area of Mawprem, which find the way even in their moral values, and code of conduct etc.

The World Vision took the initiative to have a talk with the Dorbar Shnong and the Local headman so that the same will accept their existence in the locality and to check poverty. It was in the occasion of World Environment day in 1999, the organization introduced community involvement in planting trees in which most of these slum dwellers of Mawprem took a great interest, which is also an icebreaker for their interaction.

With the opening up of the slum dwellers, the World

Vision tried to convey the people to be self reliant in which economic upliftment of the slum areas was their target. So in this connection, the World Vision formed a society called "*Iatyllilang Credit Society*" that grants a sum of Rs. 75,000 to deserving slum residents in order to establish their self-support-business through Mobile Catering Centres.[11] At least twenty families from these three different slum areas have been benefited. The World Vision also arranged a six months free training on catering in Monsoon hotel, Police Bazar, Shillong after which only they hand over to them the mobile vehicle. However, in future every maintenance for this vehicle is to be taken care of by these people themselves. The most constructive initiative made by World vision in this relation was that they helped them open Savings Account in the bank so that whatever they collect from this small incentive they can deposit in the bank. Alternatively, these twenty families income have increased from the usual Rs. 250 per month to Rs. 2000-3000 per month in which they also shift their residents to a better rented house.

As present the World Vision has set up two mobile catering centres in town one in Laitumkhrah (for slum dwellers from Mawprem), and the other one in Polo (for slum dwellers from Jingthangbriew and Mawprem). Apart from this, sewing machine is also been distributed to some households so that they can earn their living

The World Vision also focuses on health care and health facilities for vulnerable section i.e.; the children—nutrition, schooling, women—adultliteracy etc. so as to improve the quality of life of these people.

Nevertheless, other facilities have been provided by the Government on a large scale are drains, footpaths, approach road and retaining walls.

Conclusions

Slum is a problem of poverty that is evident in each and every society but every society is a dynamic organism, which is inhabited by the rich and the poor, so, realization of the importance of people under Below Poverty Line in also essential since they form an important segment in the society. Their existence and services is also important to make the socio-economic service cycle complete. It is also imperative that slum dwellers should be involved in maintaining the civics amenities of the urban area as a whole.

Since, slums are neglected parts of cities where housing and living conditions are appallingly lacking which do not have basic municipal services—water, sanitation, waste collection, storm drainage, street lighting, paved footpaths, roads for emergency access to schools and clinics within reach, safe areas for children to play, places for the community to meet and socialize.

Slums are worsening: as the average age of people in cities in increasing, the average age of slum dwellers is decreasing, so the youth suffer most from unhealthful conditions. There is also a visible disparity between slums and better-off neighborhoods, which increases the social tensions in poorer areas. Therefore, care should be taken by Government authorities, Non-Profit Organizations, Philanthropists in general to formulate plans, schemes etc. that would reach them and make a difference in the slum areas. However, planning and scheming is not an end in itself but sincere concerted efforts should be adopted in deploying the schemes.

In addition to the above, the need of the hour is the emergence of well meaning apex agencies comprising of Professionals, Administrators, Public Servants, and Academicians who has proper defined knowledge of slums and its characteristics with respect to slums in the hilly topography so that suitable plans will benefit them in a proper way.

Thus, in conclusion it is strongly recommended that here should have an exchange of views and opinions before planning and implementation of schemes for the betterment of poor people in the society.

REFERENCES

1. K. Ranga Rao and MSA Rao, *"Cities and Slums—A Study of Squatters". Settlement in the city of Vijawada*, Concept Publishing Company, New Delhi, 1984.

2. Desai, A.R. and Pillai, S.D. (ed.), (1972 : *A profile of an Indian Slum,* Bombay: University of Bombay.
3. Ramachandran, P (1972): *Pavement Dwellers in Bombay City,* Bomaby: Tata Institute of Social Sciences.
4. Singh, A.M. and A.de Souza (1978): *The Urban Poor,* Delhi, Manohar
5 B. Datta Ray and S.K. Agnihotri, Dynamics of a Tribal Society, 1993, ed. 117.
6. Government of Meghalaya: Master Plan of Shillong 1991-2011.
7. B.B. Goswami, 1979, (ed.), *Cultural Profile of Shillong,* Anthropological Survey of India.
8. B. Pakem, 1984, (ed.), *Shillong 1971-1981,* Research India Publications, Calcutta.

19

Slums and "Culture of Poverty": A Case Study of Jayashree Harizan Colony of Guwahati City

Ujjal Kumar Sarma and Indrani Barpujari

Slum a Physical and Social Fact

Various theories have been propounded by different authorities on slums and life in the slums. Early writers in the West started by viewing the slum only in terms of its physical aspects. Patridge (1958) provides us with the ancestry of the term itself which in his view came from the word slumber since slums were originally "to the majority—unknown, back streets or alleys, wrongly presumed to be sleepy and quiet". One of the first monumental studies on slums in the city of New York by James Ford (1936) did not go futhrer than such a view when he said: "Any area of old, neglected and deteriorated housing or of new markedly substandard housing is a slum as soon as it becomes unsanitary or otherwise injurious to its occupants..." Numerous other studies on slums also concentrated on the physical aspects of the slum.

It was Michael Harrington who first preferred to venture beyond such an idea of slum when he said, "A slum is not merely an area of decrepit buidlings, it is a social fact..." (1962, p. 140). While defining a slum in physical terms cannot be avoided, a serious limitation of this approach however, is that it conditions most planners and policy-makers to think of a slum problem merely in terms of 'housing standards' or 'real estate' or 'finance.' It also turns their attention away from the complexity of the various forces in the society that produce poverty, slums and the related social evils. By 1960s, as researcher after researcher explored this theme deeper, new and subtle characteristics of slums and slum life not realized earlier began to surface. Hunter, the author of a authoriative volume on slums, does justice to these complex characteristics and their interplay by using the phrase the 'feel' of a slum. He elaborates: "This refers to the feel when a non-resident is in a slum, or the feel of things when one lives in a slum. The attitude of the slum dwellers toward the slum itself, toward the city, toward the system. This is the element which as much as anything else will determine whether or not it is possible to do something about slums."

The theory of the "culture of poverty" is one celebrated theory famous for its treatment of slum as a human problem. It is argued that wherever there are cities there will be slums and they are associated with poverty and a specific culture. Oscar Lewis (1966), who proposed the theory of "culture of poverty" insists: "The culture of poverty is not just a matter of deprivation or disorganization, a term signifying the absence of something. It is a culture in the traditional anthropological sense in that it provides human beings with a design for living, with a ready-made set of solutions for human problems, and so served a significant adaptive function." He developed this in the context of his investigations of urban Latin America and New York. He showed how the "culture of poverty" was manifest in urban slums as a sub-culture.

The menace of slums has come to be regarded as a major problem of urbanization in India with no Indian city being free from slums. According to the 1988 UNI report, between one-fourth and half of the urban population in India's largest cities lives in makeshift shelters and slums. With the country's slum population of 1991 standing at nearly 40 million, slum dwellers form 44 per cent of population in Delhi, 45 per cent in Mumbai, 42 per cent in Kolkata and 39 per cent in Chennai. The situation is no better in eight other metropolises of Bangalore, Hyderabad, Ahmedabad, Kanpur,

Pune, Nagpur, Lucknow and Jaipur. Slum population, governmental efforts notwithstanding, is expected to show a sizeable increase by 2010 aggravating the existing housing problem and squalor conditions. The city of Guwahati is no exception with 21 slum pockets having been identified in the city by the District Office, Town and Country Planning, Guwahati.

In the present chapter, a humble attempt has been made by the authors to examine the Jayashree Harizan Colony of Guwahati city, Assam, in the context of its emergence as a slum area, the main parameters on the basis of which it may be identified as a slum area and also to test the validity of popular theories on slums like that of "culture of poverty." It is based on fieldwork conducted for a period of 21 days from 7.2.2000 to 27.2.2000 followed up with another short field work conducted for 2 days in May, 2004, thus, affording a perspective on the issue of urban poverty based on actual ground realities. It is hoped that this study would facilitate a better understanding of the problems of slums and urban poverty in the context of the entire North-East India, which has witnessed a rampant increase in the growth of urban centers, and slums as a natural corollary in recent times. It aims at throwing an insight on factors contributing to the growth of a slum, physical and social attributes of a slum, the nature of the community organization and linkages between the economic conditions of the slum dwellers with the overall process of growth and development of the city.

Methodology and Universe of the study

The universe of the study is the Jayashree Harizan Colony of Guwahati city, a homogenous colony inhabited exclusively by members of the Bansphor caste, with a population of about 2805 individuals in 418 households. The large size of the population makes the prospect of collecting demographic data on the entire population a formidable task as such 12 per cent sample has been drawn from the universe of the study confined to 50 households, males numbering 202 and females 200.

The primary tools employed in collecting data in the field are observation, interview, and case study and survey schedule.

Genesis and Growth of Jayashree Harizan Colony

Assam, in the late nineteenth century and early twentieth century, was a favourite destination for immigrants. The rise of new townships with their newly constituted. Municipal Boards, responsible for maintaining sanitary conditions in the towns, created a huge demand for sweepers and scavengers. Absence of indigenous sweeper castes in Assamese society (the Haris who performed the jobs of scavenging and bone removing during the Ahom rule having abandoned this occupation) provided impetus to government encouraged immigation of Scheduled Castes from outside Assam (Dev and Lahiri, 1984, p. 38). It was during this period that large-scale migration of the Bansphors from different parts of Bihar and Uttar Pradesh into Assam took place, most of whom found employment as sweepers and scavengers in the Municipal Boards.

The Jayashree Harizan Colony of Guwahati city constitutes the oldest Bansphor settlement in Assam, established in 1933 by the Guwahati Municipal Board (which later became the Guwahati Municipal Corporation) to house its sweeper employees. In the year 1933, the Board constructed 16 Assam type homes in the Solapar area of Guwahati to house the sweepers and their families. This settlement was then known as the Marakhali Harizan Colony, 'Marakhali' meaning cremation ground. This area was chosen for the establishment of the sweepers colony by the G.M.B. due to the fact that it had dug a huge trenching ground in this deserted area for disposal of night soil and other refuse collected from all over Guwahati city and it was convenient to house the sweepers, employed in the removal of night soil and refuse, nearby.

The G.M.B. from time to time carried out extension works to accommodate the increasing number of Bansphor sweepers employed by it. The Guwahati Municipal Corporation undertook the last extension work in 1970 when three two- storyed R.C.C. buildings were constructed. At present, there are 78 official quarters. But over the years, the population has increased manifold resulting in the mushrooming of small hutments and shanties all over the colony, constructed by the people themselves as the offical quarters fail to accommodate the burgeoning population.

Emergence as a Slum

The District office, Town and Country Planning under the Assam Slum Areas (Improvement and Clearance) Act, 1959, has identified the Jayashree Harizan Colony as one of the 21 slum pockets of Guwahati city.

The Act follows the following procedure in the declaration of slum areas: "Where the State Government upon report from the Authority or other information in its possession, is satisfied in respect of any area that the buildings in that area

(a) are in any respect unfit for human habitation or

(b) are by reason of dilapidation, over-crowding, faulty arrangement and design of such buildings, narrowness or faulty arrangement of streets, lack of ventilation, light or sanitation facilities, or any combination of some or all of these factors, are detrimental to safety, health or morals of the people of the area; it may, by notification in the Official Gazette, declare such area to be a slum area. In determining whether a building is unfit for human habitation for the purpose of this Act, regard shall be had to its condition in respect of the following matters, that is to say—(a) repair (b) stability (c) freedom from damp (d) natural light and air (e) water supply (f) drainage and sanitary conveniences (g) facilities for storage, preparation and cooking of food and for the disposal of waste, water and the building shall be deemed to be unfit as aforesaid if it is so defective that it is not reasonably suitable for occupation in that condtion" (The Assam Slum Areas Act, 1959, Chapter 11, pp. 7,8).

Ranga Rao and Rao (1984, pp. 3,4) identify three sets of situation in the growth of slums : "First a slum develops as a result of squatting of poor migrants on vacant public land near the places of work. Again, as the city expands, it sucks in the colonies of fishermen, herdsmen and the like, and villages situated on the periphery. Since the rent and cost of living would be low in this area many poor unskilled workers come to live here. The area gets overcrowded and in the absence of adequate municipal services, slum conditions increase. Ranga Rao and Rao believe that a variation of the process is the segregated Harizan Colonies in the city which mainly consist of sweepers as salaried employees of municipalities and hospitals, and coollies and cobblers. Such areas become overcrowded and unsanitary conditions prevail in the absence of adequate civic amenities. The Jayashree Harizan Colony, on the basis of a careful perusal of ground realities, may be placed in this category of slum.

The main parameters on the basis of which the Jayashree Harizan Colony may be identified as a slum area are as follows:

(1) Housing conditions

The houses of the colony may be divided into two categories, the living quarters provided by the Guwahati Municipality to its sweeper employees and the one-roomed shanties constructed by the people themselves. The former appear to be in a state of utter disrepair and dilapidation due to lack of maintenance and timely repairs. The walls and roofs of the buildings are seen to be broken at places and according to inhabitants of these houses, due to roof leakages, rainwater enters the houses and during the monsoon season, their plight knows no bounds. Moreover, the pipes connected to the septic tanks of the R.C.C. buildings suffer from leakages and are even disjointed at place as a result of which filthy water drips from above continuously creating a most unhygienic conditions. Dinanath Basfor, the pradhan (chief) of the colony apprehends that if the buildings are not repaired immediately and reconstruction works initiated, a major catastrophe may take place in the near future due to house collapse.

The shanties constructed mostly of bamboo and thatch and occasionally with tin roofs afford bare shelter. These are dark and damp with no windows and are liable to easy destruction due to fire and heavy rain. Built in very close proximity to one another and the housing materials being of combustible nature, they present a serious fire hazard. In fact, in December 1984, a fire from a stove in one of these shanties engulfed the whole colony reducing many houses to ashes and many received serious burn injuries while a couple of the inhabitants succumbed to their injuries.

(2) Overcrowding

The lack of adequate space and a huge growing population created conditions of overcrowding and congestion in the Jayashree Harizan Colony. The magnitude of the problem can be gauged best from table 19.1, obtained through sample survey of fifty households:

Table 19.1

Size of Household in Relation to Size of House

Type of House	Total Number of Household	Size of Household (Number of Persons)			
		1-3	4-8	7-9	10
One Roomed	35	1	18	15	1
Two Roomed	15	-	2	10	3
Total	50	1	20	25	4

Source: Field Survey.

From Table 19.1, it is seen that 70 per cent of the sample population or 35 households live in one-roomed houses while only a mere 15 households (30%) have two rooms at their disposal. From the above figures it can be gleaned that quite a large number of persons have to share a single, small room with the average size of the room being ten feet by eight feet, thus not affording basic comfort and privacy.

(3) Lack of basic amenities

Lack of a proper drainage system constitutes a major problem afflicting the colony, which is situated in a low-lying area. The drains existing at present are inadequate as a result of which there is accumulation of stagnant dirty water at various places in the colony and during the rainy reason, the situation worsens. The existing open drains are in a state of utter neglect and clogged with all kinds of filth, become a source of insanitation.

Another major problem faced by the colony dwellers is acute water shortage with the main sources of water supply being municipal water taps and a community well. The water supplied by the Guwahati Municipality, two times a day at 7 a.m. in the morning and 4 p.m. in the evening, is woefully inadequate.

The Guwahati Municipality takes no interest in removing the waste or garbage generated in the colony. There is no dustbin in the colony leading to the accumulation of filth and squalor all over the colony.

Except for the government quarters, the other houses do not have individual latrines of their own. There are only ten community latrines in the whole colony, which are in broken down condition and the flushes do not work. The inhabitants are forced to ease themselves in the vicinity of the latrines, street corners, lanes and open spaces thus making the entrie locality foul.

(4) Health

The unhygienic, unsanitary conditions prevailing in the Jayashree Harizan Colony have a serious bearing on the health of the inhabitants. The stagnant ground water all round make a good breeding ground for mosquitoes leading to malaria. A large number of inhabitants suffer from tuberculosis, estimated at around thirty per cent. Diarrhea, dysentery and enteric diseases are the most common ailments suffered by children and adults alike. One positive aspect observed in the fifty household surveys was that all the fifty households have had their children immunized. This could be attributed to the fact that the Ulubari Urban Health Centre is situated in close proximity to the colony and also agencies like the Red Cross Society take active initiative in this respect.

(5) Education

Low level of literacy and education are predominant in the colony. Out of the sample population of 402 individuals, about 55.5 per cent are illiterate (illiterate referring to a person who does not know how to read and wirte). In the literate group, highest number of people is to be found to have studied up to the primary level (13.7 per cent) while the number of matriculates (2.2 per cent), those who have passed their Higher Secondary (0.9 per cent) and graduates (0.5 per cent) are very less.

(6) Economy

Another parameter, which is widely used to identify a slum, is poor economy and widespread poverty. A caste traditionally associated with sweeping, scavenging and the manufacture of fans, the Bansphors of the colony profess these traditional pursuits. The primary economic base is the profession of sweeping and scavenging with about 77 per cent of the total working population being employed as 'Safai Karmacharis' with the Guwahati Municipal Corporation. Majority of the households have a regular source of income with about 50 per cent of the total number of households having a monthly income in the range of Rs. 3,000-4,000. Inspite of regular monthly earnings, as a result of large size of households, addiction of males to drinking and gambling on a daily basis, absence of good saving habits, huge expenses incurred in holding feasts, rituals and marriages—all contribute to a poor economy. The standard of living is low and the nutritional, educational, health and other basic requirements of the individuals cannot be adequately met. Immovable property in the form of land is owned by very few households (only 4 households) though most households possess consumer items like television, radio with a few households also having refrigerator, motorcycle etc.

Culture of Poverty in Jayashree Harizan Colony

An attempt has been made here to find out whether a "culture of poverty" or a specific characteristic of an urban slum can be discerned in the colony. This has been accomplished by investigating the presence of certain distinctive traits identified by Oscar Lewis, the exponent of this theory. These traits may be described in four dimensions of the system : the relationship of the sub-culture and the larger society, the nature of the slum community, the nature of the family and the attitudes, values and character structure of the individual.

According to Lewis, "the disengagement, the nonintegration of the poor with respect to the major institutions of the society is a crucial element in the culture of poverty..." This does not hold true in the context of the colony and the residents display an active interest in the political affairs of the state and country. In fact, all of the 50 households have at least one of its male members enrolled in the Communist Party of India (Marxist). The people of the colony, with majority (77.66%) of the working population employed as sweepers, find their strength enhanced and rights safeguarded as members of various trade unions like the All Assam Harizan Mazdor Union, G.M.C. Harizan Mazdoor Union etc. The people of the colony also make effective use of post-office, banks, hospitals etc. In the sample population of fifty households, at least one member of every household had at one time or other maintained an account in the bank or post-office. Hospitals are used frequently.

People in a "culture of poverty" produce little wealth and receive little in return. Chronic unemployment and underemployment, low wages, lack of property, lack of savings, absence of food reserves in the home and chronic shortage of cash imprison the family and the individual in a vicious circle. The Jayashree Harizan Colony, unlike a typical slum, is not characterized by poor economic condition. Ironically, despite having a regular source of income, we find the presence of many traits generally associated with "culture of poverty" in the colony. There is a higher percentage of dependants as against the working population (35.57 per cent) constituting the working population. There is lack of savings and investments, squandering of money on drinks and gambling, high incidence of pawning and borrowing at high rates of interest. Also, the people are seen to exhibit almost a fatalistic approach to life in the sense that they spend lavishly without a thought for the future as soon as they receive the salary. The salary is almost exhausted in the first few days and the rest of the month is spent amidst much hardship. Food reserves in the home are virtually absent and almost daily purchases of small quantity of food are made.

Lewis maintains that among the urban poor, a free union

or consensual marriage is the order of the day and with the instability of consensual marriage, the family tends to be mother-centred and tied more closely to the mother's extended family. However, among the Bansphors of the colony, the marriage bond is strong and the incidence of divorce is very low (about 1%). The father always occupies the seat of authority in the family and the family shows a greater leaning towards the paternal kin.

"With its poor housing and overcrowding, the community is high in gregariousness, but it has minimum of organization beyond the nuclear and extended family" (Lewis). In sharp contrast, a very high level of community organization manifest in the form of kin networks, colony panchayat Mahila Samiti etc. is to be found among them. They also have a strong sense of belonging to a caste and kin group, which give them a sense of identity and at no point of their lives do they experience isolation or despair.

Conclusion

Thus, it has been found from the study that the colony exhibits all the essential features of a slum like overcrowding, dilapidated houses, lack of basic amenities, poor health conditions, low level of literacy etc. With respect to the economy, certain "culture of poverty" traits have been discerned.

But the presence of a distinct identity, strong solidarity and cohesion, efficient organization distinguishes it from a typical slum.

It may be suggested that one of the major problems afflicting the community is that of wide-spread illiteracy which in turn leads to many evils like an ever increasing population, low health and nutritional status and social vices. While majority of the people are poor and illiterate, there is a small elitist section who are educated and have political clout and this section as alleged by some residents, in cahoot with political leaders, divert all funds meant for the welfare of the community to fill up their personal pockets. Thus the urgent need of the hour is that the community should revitalize itself through a high level of awareness and motivation and mould its own destiny through its own initiative. To achieve this end, the educated section among the Bansphors should take the lead. The community should be mobilized to fight for its own rights and exert pressure on government agencies to fulfill its legitimate demands and redress grievances.

The government and the NGOs have a very crucial role to play in the upliftment of the community and amelioration of the problems of these slum dwellers. It is suggested that the work of the 'Safai Karmacharis' should be mechanized as far as possible and reduce the manual handling of filth. A massive campaign is called for to make the community realize the value of education and ensure that the younger generation is rendered eligible to pursue alternate forms of livelihood. Education would go a long way in eradicating the social vices. The government, through the National Slum Development Programmes (NSDP) for 1998-99, has targeted the colony for slum development measures. Shelter upgradation, toilet repairing and construction of new drains in the colony are aimed at. Sulabh International of Patna is also proposing to set up a biogas plant here in the near future.

Only time will tell how far these measures would be successful in bringing about improvement in this urban slum and in providing a minimum standard of living to its inhabitants.

REFERENCES

1. Desai, A.R. and S.D. Pillai (ed.), 1990. *Slums and Urbanisation,* 2nd edition. Bombay Popular Prakashan Private Ltd.
2. Dev, B.J. and D.K. Lahiri, 1984. *Cosmogony of Caste and Social Mobility in Assam,* Delhi: Mittal Publications.
3. Dutta Ray, B.,A.K. Neog and H.K. Mazhari (ed.), *Urban Development in North-East India: Potentiality and Problems,* New Delhi, Reliance House.
4. Ford, J., 1936. *Slums and Housing: History, Conditions, Policy,* Cambridge: Harvard University Press.
5. Gupta. S.C. anb B.G. Prasad, 1965. "A Note on the Living and Working Conditions of the Sweeper Community in Lucknow." *The Eastern Anthropologist.* Vol. 18, No. 3.
6. Harrington, M., 1962, *The Other American Poverty in the United States,* New York: The Macmillan Co.

7. Hunter, D.V., 1964. *The Slums: Challenge and Response*, London, The Free Press of Glencoe, Collier Macmillan Ltd.
8. Lewis, O., 1966. "The Culture of Poverty", *Scientific American*, Vol 215, No 4.
9. Ranga Rao and K. MSA Rao, 1984. *Cities and Slums—A Study of Squatters Settlement in City of Vijaywada*, New Delhi: Concept Publishing Company.
10. Singh, K. and F. Steinberg (ed.), 1996. *Urban India in Crisis*, New Delhi: New Age International.

20

Poverty Alleviation Programmes in Shillong: A Note

Sumana Paul

Poverty amid plenty is the tragic experience of the world. Poverty is the curelty of life. Poverty is what the poor encounter. It may be characterized as the phenomenal dearth of attaining even the basic necessities of life. Injudicious and inhuman deprivation from the rights to use the heavenly world—its resources, its ecstasies is poverty. It is poverty that makes the poeple unhappy and destitute. What poverty is can be better realized from the sparkling comments of a poor man of Kenya in an interview: "Don't ask me what poverty is because you have met it outside my house. Look at the house and count the number of holes. Look at my utensils and the cloths I am wearing. Look at everything and write what you see. What you see is poverty." (World Bank, 2000) Social justice and freedom are denied to the poor altogether. The meaning of democracy remains almost shrouded to them. It is the poor who bears the ultimate burden and undesirables of the society.

Urbanisation Trend

Indian census authorities have adopted a strict definition of what may be called 'urban.' Under this definition, fulfillment of the following criteria is necessary for a place to be designated as 'urban'.

1. All places with a municipality, corporation, cantonment, board or notified town area committee, etc,

2. All othese places which satisfy the following criteria:

(a) a minimum population of 5,000;

(b) at least 75 per cent of male working population engaged in non-agricultural pursuits;

(c) a density of population of at least 400 persons per square kilometer.

Besides, the directors of census operation in states/union territories were allowed to include in consultation with the concerned State government/Union territory administrators and the Census Commission of India, some places having distinct urban characteristics as urban even if such places did not strictly satisfy all the criteria mentioned under category (2) above. Such marginal cases include major project colonies, areas of important tourist centers etc.

In terms of the degree of urbanization measured by the percentage of population living in urban places, India is by no means a highly urbanized land. According to 1991 census, only about 25.7 per cent of the total Indian population reside in urban areas.

Regional Variation in Urbanisation

There is large variation among the states and union territories in the level of urbanisation. While explaining urban growth, one must consider at least three components, namely increase in population in urban areas, net migration to urban areas, and the impact of reclassification.

With reference to Shillong, the capital of Meghalaya it can be said that the total population of Shillong urban area has increased from, 2,23,366 in 1991 to 2,67,881 in 2001, where decadal growth becomes 19.93. The density of population per square km has increased from 8794 in 1991 to 10,546 in 2001, though sex ratio is almost balanced with 993 females per 1000 males.

At present, the Shillong urban agglomeration consisting of Shillong Municipality, Mawlai, Nonghtymmai, Madanrting, Shillong Cantonment, Pynthorumkhrah, and Nongmynsong has a total population of about 2,67,881, as per 2001 census. Of this total population more then 50 per cent is concentrated in Shillong Municipality, which is occupying about 10.36 sq km of the total Shillong urban agglomeration.

Urban Poverty

The most demanding of the urban challenges, unquestionably, is the challenge posed by poverty. This challenge is of reducing exploitation, relieving misery and creating more human condition for working, living and growth for those disadvantaged people who have already made the city their home, or are in the process of doing so. Not all of the urban poor live in slums and shanty towns and not all those who live in slums and shanty towns are poor. The poor can often be found distributed throughout a city; living in servant quarters, chawls, small squatter settlements and on pavements. Very often they are found in middle class and affluent areas where they perform needed services for well to do people as domestic servants, drivers, malis, sweepers, dhobis etc. Urban poverty manifests itself in may forms. The most visible of these are: (a) growth of slums, (b) growth of informal sector, (c) crushing pressure on civic amenities, and (d) growing sense of hopelessness.

(a) Growth of Slams

The poor cannot afford to pay the growing market prices of pucca shelter or buy land at the fabulous prices charged near their work places. They cannot afford the cost of transporting themselves or their stock in trade over long distances. They, therefore, settle on marginal lands near their work places, which are otherwise considered unfit for habitation by the non-poor classes. Their construction are of cheap scrap and salvaged material like gunny bags, tarpaulin, scrap tin sheets, wooden plants etc. The habitat is irregular as it is unplanned. Civic amenities, if available, are minimal. As a result public sanitation and personal hygiene break down.

(b) Growth of Informal Sector

When the capacity of urban areas to create jobs is exhausted, then the non formal sector starts growing at a faster rate. It includes waste collection and recycling, cart and lorry transport, low-cost catering services, repair and maintenance services and street vending.

(c) Crushing Pressure on Civic Amenities

The Civic authorities are finding themselves increasingly

incapable of providing civic amenities to the large influx of population within their boundaries. According to the report of the task force of the planning commission on financing of urban development, 31.2 per cent of urban population was not covered by sanitation services (Govternment of India, 1988-95). Analysis based on the NSS data shows that (Kundu, 1991) about 34 per cent of the population among the urban poor is not being covered by formal piped water supply.

(d) Growing Sense of Hopelessness

Most of the urban poor are frustrated. For coping with this frustration they consume liquor and hallucinatory drugs. This is giving rise to addiction which in turn is responsible for increasing rate of crime and group violence.

Review of Current Programmes for the Urban Poor with Special Reference to Shillong Urban area

Data show that approximately 30 per cent of the urban population lives below poverty line. But it is indeed a very difficult task to identify the BPL (Below Poverty Line) families. Government has decided an annual family income of less than Rs. 11,850 at the 1991-92 prices as one of the criteria to identify BPL families. Government is giving economic support to those families so that they can improve their living condition. In the context of Shillong it could be said that Department of Urban Employment and Poverty Alleviation has introduced two schemes in 1997-1998 for urban poverty alleviation. These are (i) Swarna Jayanti Sahari Rajgar Yojana (SJSRY); and (2) National Slum Development Programme (NSDP).

But NSDP has actually been implemented in the year 1999-2000. Department of Urban Employment and Poverty Alleviation is the monitoring agency for the implementation of these programmes and actual implementation is done by Urban Poverty Eradiction (UPE) cell of Shillong Municipal Board.

A Brief Outline of SJSRY

The Swarna Jayanti Sahario Rozgar Yojana (SJSRY) shall seek to provide gainful employment to the urban unemployed and underemployed poor through encouraging the setting up of self employment ventures or provision of wage employment. This programme will rely on creation of suitable community structures on the UBSP (Urban Basic Services for the Poor) pattern and implemented through the ULBs (Urban Local Bodies) and such community structures.

The SJSRY shall be funded on a 75:25 basis between the centre and the states.

The SJSRY consists of special schemes like

(1) The Uban self employment Programme (USEP)

(2) The Urban Wage Employment Programme (UWEP)

USEP: This programme has three distinct parts:

(a) Assistance to individual urban poor beneficiaries for setting up gainful self employment ventures.

(b) Training of beneficiaries, potential beneficiaries and other person associated with the urban employment programmes for upgradation and acquisition of vocational and entrepreneurial skills.

(c) Assistance to group of urban poor women for setting up gainful self-employment ventures

Self employment programmes encourage the underemployed and unemployed youths to setup small enterprises relating to servicing, petty business and manufacturing, for which there is a lot of potential in urban area. To avoid duplication with the ongoing Prime Minister's Rozgar Yojana (PMRY), this component of SJSRY is confined to below poverty line beneficiaries who have got educational qualification up to tenth standard and residing in the town for at least three years. The maximum unit cost will be Rs. 50,000 and the maximum allowable subsidy will be 15 percent of the project cost subject to a limit of Rs. 7500. The beneficiary is required to contribute 5 per cent of the project cost as margin money. 95 per cent of the project cost would be sanctioned as composite loan by bank at the rates of interest applicable to such priority sector loans fixed by Reserve Bank of India, from time to time. The loans would not require any collateral guarantee. Only assets created under the programme would by hypothecated/mortgaged to the bank advacing the loans. Repayment schedule ranges from 3 to 7 years after initial moratorium of 6 to 18 months as decided by bank.

Under USEP every year UPE Cell entertains 400 applications. Then they forward these applications to 28 Nationalised Banks and accordingly Banks and UPE cell jointly select the candidates.

The Community Development Society (CDS)/UPE cell will extend help to bank for ensuring repayment of loans as per rules. UPE cell of Shillong Municipality has a field officer who monitors the performance of beneficiaries under this scheme.

Table 20.1
Amount of Subsidy Given by UPE Cell of Shillong Municipality and the Number of Beneficiaries.

Phase	Subsidy amount	No of Beneficiaries
April-June 2000	1,87,611.00	40
July-Sept 2000	4,01, 362.00	68
Oct-Dec 2000	2,24,643.00	42
January-March 2001	4,24,191.00	67
April-June 2001	83,250.00	14
July-September 2001	1,91,400.00	31
October-December 2001	3,84,234.00	63
January-March 2002	3,49,477.00	53
April-June 2002	43,860.00	09
July-September 2002	2,55,992.00	42
October-December 2002	3,93,600.00	63
January-March 2003	1,08,000.00	17
April-June 2003	1,73,724.00	30
July-September 2003	3,34,447.00	48
October-December 2003	2,81,925.00	47
January-March 2004	4,20,585.00	49

Source: Shillong Municipality.

Table 20.1 shows that, from April 2000 to March 2001 total subsidy amounts Rs. 12,37, 807.00 involving 217 beneficiaries. April 2001 to March 2002 total subsidy amount was Rs. 10,08,361.00 involving 161 beneficiaries. April 2002 to March 2003 total subsidy amount was Rs. 8,01,452.00 involving 131 beneficiaries. April 2003 to March 2004 total subsidy amount was Rs. 12,10,681.00 involving 174 beneficiaries.

Skill development through appropriate training is another element of this programme. Training includes variety of service and manufacturing trades as well as in local skills and local crafts so that they can set up self-employment ventures to secure salaried employment with enhanced remuneration. Training is imparted in beautician course, plumbing, tailoring, electrician course, TV/radio/refrigerator mechanism, sales and marketing, travel and tourism, computer training and also in manufacturing low cost building materials based on improved local technology.

UPE cell of Shillong Municipality has negotiated with BDPS, APTECH, NIIM for imparting training in various trades.

The unit cost allowed for training is Rs. 2000 to 2500 per trainee, including material cost, trainer's fees, other miscellaneous expenses to be incurred by the training institution and the monthly stipend to be paid to the trainee, the total training period for skill up-gradation may vary from three to six months, subject to a minimum of 300 hours.

Table 20.2
Amount spend on Training and No. of Beneficiaries

Phase	Subsidy Amount	No. of Beneficiaries
April-June 2000	NIL	---
July-Sept 2000	NIL	---
Oct-Dec 2000	NIL	---
January-March 2001	91,150.00	92
April-June 2001	54,900.00	25
July-September 2001	2,07,750.00	74

(Condt.)

October-December 2001	37,500.00	15
January-March 2002	56,000.00	24
April-June 2002	NIL	---
July-September 2002	NIL	---
October-December 2002	2,00,800.00	137
January-March 2003	2,03,000.00	199
April-June 2003	30,000.00	25
July-September 2003	NIL	---
October-December 2003	NIL	--
January-March 2004	NIL	---

Source: Shillonng Municipality.

Table 20.2. shows that from, April 2000 to March 2001 amount spend on training was 91,150.00 involving 92 beneficiaries; April 2001 to March 2002 amount spend to training was. 3,56, 150.00 involving 138 beneficiares; April 2002 to March 2003 amount spend on training was 4,03,800.00 involving 336 beneficiaries; April 2003 to March 2004 amount spend on training was 30.000.00 involving 25 beneficiaries.

Development of Women and Children in Urban area (DWCUA) is distinguished by the special incentive extended to urban poor women who decided to setup self employment ventures.

Groups of urban poor shall take up an economic activity suited to their skill, training, aptitude and local conditions. Besides generation of income, this group strategy shall strive to empower the urban poor women by making them independent as also providing a facilitating atmosphere for self employment.

To be eligible for subsidy under this schme the DWCUA group should consist of atleast tem poor women. Before starting income generating activity the group members must get to know each other well, understand the group strategy, and also recognize the strength and potential of each member of the group. The group shall select an organizer from amongst the members. The group will also select its own activity. Care should be exercised in the selection of activity because the future of the group will rest wholly on an appropriate selection.

The DWCUA group shall be entitled to a subsidy of Rs. 1,25,000.00 or 50 per cent of the cost of project, whichever is less. It is mandatory on the part of the DWCUA group that each group should have one president and one secretary, where the DWCUA group sets itself up as a Thrift and Cedit Society, the group/thrift and credit society shall be entitled to a lump sum grant of Rs. 25,000.00 as revolving fund at the rate of 1000 maximum per member. UPE cell of Shillong municipality monitor these groups. The cell meet the group members once in a month.

The DWCUA group/Thrift and Credit Society shall be entitled for payment of revolving fund not earlier than one year after its formation.

Duing the period Oct-Dec 2003 first time, after the implementation of the scheme, Lumparing Thrift and Credit Society was formed with 20 members and a revolving fund of 20 thousand. During the period January-March 2004 there were four such groups. These are—

(1) Lumsohphoh Thrift and credit Society II with 17 members and revolving fund of 17 thousand.

(2) Lumsohphoh Self Help Group I with 18 members and 18 thousand as revolving fund.

(3) Riat Laban Kunjat Phutboll Thrift and Credit Society III with 20 members and 20 thousand as revolving fund.

(4) Riat Laban Kunjat Phutboll Thrift and Credit Society IV with 20 members and 20 thousand as revolving fund.

So during the phase January-March 2004 total expenditure incurred by UPE cell of Shillong Municipality was 75 thousand.

The Urban Wage Employment Programme (UWEP)

This programme seeks to provide wage employment to beneficiaries living below poverty line within the jurisdiction of urban local bodies by utilizing their labour for construction of socialy and economically useful public assets. The programme applies to urban local bodies the population of which is less than 5 lakhs as per the 1991 census. The nature of municipal works include low cost water supply, pour flush community latrines, drainage related earth works, community facilities. etc.

Community development societies (CDSs) survey and draw up a list of available basic minimum services in their areas. Missing basic minimum services shall be first identified.

The CDS is responsible for creating small community assets in low income area in consultation with town UPE cell and ULB.

The material labour ratio for works under this programme shall be maintained at 60:40. The prevailing minimum wage rate, as notified from time to time for each area shall be paid to beneficiaries under this programme.

For this (UWEP) Programme, the Govternment of Meghalaya gives the allocation, where as UPE cell proposes schemes and after getting propsals, Govternment of Meghalaya selects, and approve, the work and also sanctions money to implement the schemes.

Table 20.3

Total expenditure and Number of Mandays Under UWEP

Phase	Amount	Mandays
April-June 2000	4,66,227.00	9624
July-Sept 2000	2,77,897.00	5706.6
Oct-Dec 20007,98,	392.00	4978.48
January-March 2001	7,83,030.00	13430.57
April-June 2001	4,82,940.00	4542.85
July-September 2001	1,97,355.00	3035
October-December 2001	64,180.00	No advance payment
January-March 2002	NIL	
April-June 2002	45,000.00	No advance payment
July-September 2002	1,80,943.00	No advance payment

(Condt.)

October-December 2002	40,436.00	2853.71
January-March 2003	NIL	---
April-June 2003	5,98,376.00	1523.2
July-September 2003	4,11,465.00	No advance payment
October-December 2003	14,67,388.00	11704.3
January-March 2004	4,19,302.00	4306.49

Source: Shillong Municipality.

Table 20.3 shows that total expenditure incurred by UPE cell, during, April 2000 to March 2001 was Rs. 23, 25,546.00, April 2001 to March 2002 was Rs. 7,44,475.00 including advance payment, April 2002 to March 2003 was Rs. 2,66,379.00 including advance payment, April 2003 to March 2004 was Rs. 28,96,531.00 including advance payment.

National Slum Development Programme (NSDP)

As far as poverty alleviation is concerned, the Government of India has taken up a large number of programmes in urban and rural sector. The SJSRY was launched to cover the urban poor. This scheme replaces the NRY (Nehru Rojgar Yojana), UBSP (Urban Basic Services for the Poor), PMIUPEP (Prime Minister integrated Urban Proverty Eradication Programme). However as far as slum improvement and up-gradation are concerned the component of NSDP would include.

1. Provision of physical amenities like water supply, storm water drains, community bath, widening and paving of existing lanes, Swerage, community latrines, street lights etc.
2. Community infrastructure includes provision of community centres to be used for pre-school education, non-formal education, adult education, recreational activities etc.
3. Community Primary Health Care Centre can be provided with infrastructure facilities. After creation of infrastructure facilities the municipalty will seek the support of registered medical practitioners, Government doctors in the state.
4. Social amenities like pre-school education, non-formal education, adult education, maternity, child

health and primary health care including immunization etc.

The scheme should be implemented at the grass root level by neighborhood committees, and community development societies.

Table 20.4

Total Expenditure and Physical Achievement under NSDP

Phase	Total Expenditure	Physical Achievement
April-June 2000	14,50,513.00	Roads=0.203 km Construction/ Renovation) Sewarage =0.469 m.
July-Sept 2000	3,53,878.00	Roads=0,019 km, Sewarage=0.25. km 5 Community Hall, 9 Health centre
Oct-Dec 2000	17,40,720.00	Roads=0.274 km, sewerage=0.891 km, 5 Community Hall, 9 Health Centre
January-March 2001	13,00,724.00	Storm water drainage; 7 water tanks, 0.852 km installation of pipe lines
April-June 2001	4,41,650.00	Data not available
July-September 2001	4,91, 194.00	Data not available
October-December 2001	4,75,487.00	Water tap-1; Sanitation; 1; Roads=0.20 km, storm water drainage=0.063 km
January-March 2002	11,51,618.00	Water tap=1; Hand Pump=1, community bathroom 1

(Condt.)

April-June 2002	5,04,870.00	Sanitation=1, roads =0.123 km; storm water drainage=0.688 km
July-September 2002	5,39,886.00	Storm water drainage=0.094 km, water tap =1 community bathroom -1, sanitation =1
October-December 2002	26,69,600.00	Storm water drainage=1.264 km, water tap -1
January-March 2003	25,38,586.00	Storm water drainage=0 .785 km, Roads =0.696 km
April-June 2003	12,13,315.00	Roads =0.120 km; Storm water drainage =0.085 km
July-September 2003	11,91,805.00	Roads =0.364 km, Storm water drainage =0.204 km
October-December 2003	18,90,482.00	Raods =0.244 km; Storm water drainage =1.138 km
January-March 2004	NIL	---

Source: Shillong Municipality

Table 20.4 shows that under NSDP from April 2000 to March 2001, total expenditure incurred was 48,45,817.00 and physical achievements (construction, renovation/ installation) were roads, sewarages, community halls, health, centre, storm water drainage, water tanks and installation of pipe lines.

During April 2001-March, 2002 total expenditure was 25,59,949.00 and physical achievements wear water taps, sanitation, roads, storm water drainage, hand pump, community bathroom.

During April, 2002-March 2003, total expenditure was

62, 52, 942. 00 and physical achievements include sanitation, roads, storm water drainage, water tap, community bathroom.

During April 2003-March 2004 total expenditure was 42,95,603.00 and physical achievements include roads, and storm water drainage.

Community structure

One of the composite functionaries of SJSRY and NSDP is the community structure.

The community structure has the activities of health checkups and immunisation programme where it caters to the urban slum areas covering nine villages that is; (1) Demseiong, (2) Lower Lumpering, (3) Mynsian, (4) Lumsohphoh Lumparing, (5) Kynjat phutboll Lumparing, (6) Baraphater, (7) Upper Mawprem, (8) Lower Mawprem (Lumkshaid) and (9) Dymmiew.

The beneficiaries are the women and children. The health officer along with the nurses accompanied by the RCV (Residential Community Volunteers) of the villages carry out health check up to the beneficiaries, distribute contraceptives and medicines for common ailments and also give immunization. They also go for home visit from village to village as under the scheme.

Another activity of the community structure under the supervision of the C.O. i.e. Community Organizer with the R.C.Vs is that, food items are distributed to the nursing mothers, expected mothers and children up to 6 years of age under the supplementary nutrition Programme (SNP). The R.C. Vs receives a monthly stock of SNP items then does the daily distribution to the beneficiaries. The RCV also gets an honorarium of Rs. 150 per month for doing these works.

When other schemes related to the above beneficiaries are to be implemented the H.O. along with the team of nurses and RCVs coordinate together to achieve the goal.

Under the Scheme Balika samridhi (Girl Child) 33 girls child born on or after 15.8.1991, have received a grant of Rs. 500 each and they are to be followed up for free education; and this has been recorded for pursuance.

Table 20.5 shows the phase wise community structure programme.

Table 20.5
Community Structure Programme

Phase	Immunisation Pregnant mothers, infants	Health cheek up	UP to 6 year	S.N.P. Lactating mothers
April-June 2000	232	1,346	150	50
July-Sept. 2000	187	724	150	50
Oct-Dec. 2000	190	633	150	50
Jan-March 2001	120	204	150	50
April-June 2001	169	654	150	50
July-Sept. 2001	159	723	150	50
Oct-Dec 2001	412	648	150	50
Jan-March 2002	333	881	150	50
April-June 2002	218	1382	150	50
July-Sept. 2002	218	1232	150	50
Oct-Dec. 2002	179	874	150	50
Jan-March 2003	206	542	150	50
April-June 2003	172	784	150	50
July-Sept. 2003	135	1016	150	50
Oct-Dec. 2003	80	514	150	50
Jan-March 2004	123	631	150	50

Source: Shillong Municipality.

Table 20.5 shows that under community structure programme, regarding SNP the target is 150 for children up to 6 years of age and 50 for lactating mothers. From Table 20.5 it is clear that from April 2000 to March 2004, target was achieved. Where as for other programmes such as immunization and health check up there is no such target. All deserving people are covered under this scheme.

During April 2000-March 2001 there was 729 cases of Immunication and for health check up it was 1346. During April 2002-March 2002, there were 1073 cases of Immunization and 2906 for health check up; April 2002 to March 2003,821 for immunization and 4030 health check-up. During April 2003-March 2004, there were 510 cases for Immunization and 2946 for health check up.

Conclusion

Above analysis shows that the major components of poverty alleviation programmes include primary health care services, early childhood learning, facilities, economic programmes for women and youth, skill training programme, water supply, sanitation etc.

The principal aim of these programmes is to improve the quality of life of the urban poor by giving them economic support so that the growing sense of hopelessness may be reduced to a considerable extent.

The poor people and the destitutes are highly vulnerable to social evils and injustice. Illiteracy adds fuel to this and makes the matter worst beyond our imagination. It is often said that poverty and illiteracy are the two sides of a coin. A favorable and moderate social-economic condition of a particular area is highly conducive to alleviate poverty to a large extent.

While the government is making all-out efforts to improve the socio-economic condition of economically disadvantaged people by providing liberal financial assistance under various poverty alleviation schemes, it is felt that imparting basic minimum level of education to them by introducing various tailored educational programmes would make them feel and realize their rights and responsibilities as responsible citizens which in turn will remove the social injustice and bring harmony and social cohesion in the society for a better tomorrow.

Index

C

D

E